W9-DEG-432

The Multiple Facets
of
Therapeutic Transactions

The Multiple Facets
of
Therapeutic Transactions

Chaya H. Roth, Ph.D.
Steven D. Kulb, Psy.D.

International Universities Press, Inc.
Madison   Connecticut

Library of Congress Cataloging-in-Publication Data

Roth, Chaya H.
    The multiple facets of therapeutic transactions / Chaya H. Roth,
Steven D. Kulb.
        p.   cm.
    Includes bibliographical references and index.
    ISBN 0-8236-3487-6
    1. Psychotherapist and patient.   I. Kulb, Steven D.   II. Title.
RC480.8.R68   1996
616.89′14—dc20   96-43562
                                                                 CIP
                Manufactured in the United States of America

Contents

PREFACE

How clinicians approach their patients depends on the type of people the clinicians themselves are, on the scope of their thinking about what makes people function or malfunction psychologically, and on the breadth of their experience in understanding themselves and others. Then, when all is said and done, clinicians can turn to the universals of human psychological aims to understand what goes wrong internally as people are affected by the outside world, and to devise psychological interventions to help remedy their dysfunction. This book submits that if the assumptions, principles, aims, conservative tendencies, and domains of psychic functioning are universal in their overarching design, then the theory of therapeutic transaction must also be universal. The infant–parent unit is taken as the model for developing a universal theory of psychological functioning and therapeutic transaction. The infant and parent are understood within two perspectives: as individuals operating out of their own unique spheres of individuality, and as members of a basic dyad (and triad) operating according to the rules of the interpersonal system. In terms of the therapeutic process, patient and therapist are seen from the perspective of their unique individual characteristics and goals of functioning, as well as from the perspective of their transactional processes.

Much is made here of distinguishing between form and content. Indeed, a comparison is made between the universals of psychological functioning and therapeutic transactions and the grammar and vocabulary of a language. The technique of an intervention, namely its form, is like the grammar of a language which spells out the general guidelines, rules, and exceptions to the rules a language must follow. The vocabulary of a language, its content, with its specific words, pronunciations, and dialects which have multiple roots in culture, geography, and history can be compared to the symbolic and concrete themes manifested in the therapeutic dialogue, as modified by the participants' unique biogenetic, constitutional, and developmental givens, their family history, and personal experience and training. Both form and content are requisites in mastering a language. Similarly, both structure and meaning are necessary if we are to appreciate the complexity and cohesiveness of therapeutic transactions.

ACKNOWLEDGMENTS

The authors gratefully acknowledge the Irving B. Harris Foundation for its support in the early years of this work, and the Jean and Walden Shaw Foundation for its ongoing and ever expanding commitment to the Parent–Infant Development Service (PIDS) and its mushrooming offshoots. To Bennett L. Leventhal, M.D., Chairman (Interim) Department of Psychiatry and Director of the Child and Adolescent Section at the University of Chicago, we owe more than words can express, because his unfaltering help in establishing the PIDS and supporting its work from its inception until today has been and is ever present. We will always be grateful for the teachings of our friend and colleague, the late Zanvel E. Klein, Ph.D. To our patients and our trainees, we owe everything in this work. In particular, we would like to acknowledge the contributions of the following therapists: Carole Emerson, Ph.D., Tracy Karnatz, Ph.D., Denise Newman, Ph.D., Margie Morrison, L.C.S.W., who was our first colleague when we opened the PIDS, Tom Rizzo, Ph.D., David Smith, M.A., and Lauren Wakschlag, Ph.D., who in addition to having trained within our project, is now its current Clinical and Research Director. To the late Sol Atschul, M.D., Leo Sadow, M.D., and the late Merton Gill, M.D., our appreciation for their wise counsel from the inception of this work through its final stage. To Joseph Marcus, M.D., we are indebted for introducing us to the infancy work. Dr. Erika Fromm is an invaluable friend and mentor who encouraged us to pursue working on this book after having read the first chapter. She approached Dr. George Pollock with it and he took it the distance. To Dr. George Pollock we offer our deepest thanks for his longstanding receptivity to our work, his introductions to International Universities Press, Inc., its President Mr. Martin Azarian, and Dr. Margaret Emery, its Editor-in-Chief. To her we owe out heartful gratitude for her warmth and intellectual stamina. She supported us throughout the work on the manuscript toward the publication of this book, encouraging our working out the kinks and asking the pertinent questions to sharpen our presentation.

In addition, we would like to express our appreciation to Ms. Dawn Graziano, Betty Melton and Associates, Ms. Doris Mendes, and Ms. LaJune Whitney and to Meredith Martin for their caring expertise and technical assistance when we were overwhelmed by the requirements of the many changes in computers and software that this work required.

Last, but certainly not least, we dedicate our book to our loved ones, to Walter Roth and Judith Kulb. We are grateful to all our children for their trust in us and help in bringing us along on the road of parenthood, and for the many lessons they have taught us over the years: to Laura and Jennifer Kulb, to Ari and Kate, Judy and Steve, Miriam and Mark, and Isabel, Sophie, Jonah, Emma, and Miko. And at the very last, but really first, to our parents—for where would this book be without them?

Introduction

Psychological functioning is of such complexity that it has given rise to a multiplicity of theoretical perspectives, with each theory focusing on and emphasizing a particular aspect of the subject. That no single theory has proven comprehensive or acceptable to all clinicians or applicable to all clinical conditions is apparent in the ongoing refinements of extant theories, formulations of new theories, and more recent attempts to consider various theories as perspectives that can be employed alternately to obtain a more comprehensive understanding of clinical issues. But then, theory can never be entirely comprehensive, for psychotherapy is a personal matter for clinician as well as patient. How a clinician approaches therapeutic work depends on the scope of the clinician's views about what makes people "tick," views that reflect both the clinician's and the patient's mind which come alive in the therapeutic transactions.

We hope this book may serve to expand the scope of the clinician's views about psychological functioning and provide a means by which his or her nature and subjective biases might be brought to bear in understanding patients and in facilitating their growth. To that end, we have brought together a number of theoretical perspectives that are conceptualized as facets of psychological functioning and include the interpersonal, developmental, characterologic, and intrapsychic. The common assumptions, principles, and various aims of these perspectives or facets are specified and their transactional influences and synergistic dynamics described, with the further intent of examining how particular theoretical orientations prompt particular therapeutic transactions, and how the correlations between theoretical orientations and therapeutic transactions can be identified and classified in technical interventions. We call these therapeutic interventions *therapeutic bids*. We show which therapeutic bids are common to most theoretical perspectives and which tend to be specific to one or another perspective. The therapeutic bids themselves were identified in observations of parents' positive transactions with their children and those of clinicians with their patients. Because the therapeutic bids are natural, growth-promoting responses to patients' behavioral and cognitive communications and affective appeals, they also provide a measure of the clinician's subjectivity.

This body of work has evolved over the past 16 years from the experiences we gleaned through teaching and clinical work at the University of Chicago in our development in 1979 of the Parent–Infant Development Service (PIDS) in the Department of Psychiatry. In attempting to conceptualize a general framework for psychological functioning encompassing both the needs and processes of developing infants and the evolving identities of their parents, the parent–infant dyad became the model that guided and organized our selection and coalescing of the most essential of the multiple facets of psychological functioning. This was not accomplished as a single feat, but evolved over time as we became experienced in this work. Yet there was an intuitive naturalness to our approach that we believed to be the result of long years of clinical training and experience with a variety of clinical populations of diverse ages and with different clinical manifestations. It became apparent to us, however, that to a significant extent the "intuitive naturalness" of our approach grew from an understanding that therapeutic interventions are relatively limited in kind and number. We discovered that the *how* and the *which* of the therapeutic interventions we used may vary across the diverse populations and broad array of pathologies treated and the explanatory theories employed for understanding. All interventions were used in all treatments, however, from disturbances of early childhood and adolescence, to adult intrapsychic and personality problems, and lastly to infant–parent disturbances and disruptions in development. These interventions were specifiable and definable, and they were relatively few in actual number. We learned, then, that the various facets of psychological functioning and therapeutic transactions were of considerable complexity when one took into account their attendant assumptions, principles, and aims, but also discovered that the therapeutic bids revealed themselves as being familiar and common in that they constitute the everyday exchanges of well-attuned social interactions. As it turned out, the form and technique of the therapeutic bids were relatively easy to categorize, as others have done before us with their findings from psychotherapy research and clinical work.

It became increasingly apparent that relatively few bids were used to address the psychological facets of human behavior. Thus the challenges and complexities of therapeutic work resulted largely from being necessarily constrained in the use of what is most natural and efficient. But it became evident, too, that focus on the bids and their communication effects highlighted the significance and relevance of various facets of psychological functioning for any particular individual, dyad, or family in the course of diagnostic and treatment work. This, in turn, suggested to us a general theoretical framework composed of what seemed to be the most useful conceptual classifications of these psychological facets: interpersonal, developmental, characterologic, and intrapsychic. In short, we found that attention to the effects of the simple and basic aspects of communication illuminated the complexities of human interaction and individual psychological functioning. And the importance of attending to the effects of the simple and basic was further driven home by our experience in teaching clinicians. That a clinician's psychological understanding and therapeutic effectiveness can only proceed from a grasp of the most simple and basic elements would seem obvious to any student of developmental psychology. Clinicians, however, do not typically examine simplicity for the complexity it reveals. In our experience, students came to PIDS with varying levels of sophistication in their theoretical and empirical knowledge about psychological functioning. Very few of them had sufficiently clear ideas about therapeutic interventions and their implementation to be able to use their knowledge of psychological functioning in understanding patients and promoting their development during therapeutic interactions and transactions. For too many clinicians (inexperienced and experienced alike), psychological theory tends to remain entirely abstract and, at best, more interesting than actually useful. Again, we learned that attention to the process of therapy, with focus on the therapeutic bids, proved most useful in providing a means by which conceptualizations of individual treatment cases specifically, and psychological theory generally, could be abstracted from actual treatment experience.

In describing what is most simple (therapeutic bids) in psychotherapy and what is most difficult (conceptualization drawn from a theory of multifaceted psychological functioning), we believe that this book can be helpful both to relatively experienced and inexperienced clinicians alike. As such, it is intended both to facilitate the efforts of experienced clinicians who practice and teach psychotherapy, and to promote the professional development and clinical skills of therapists in training who seek a conceptual as well as practical framework in which to select, implement, and evaluate their therapeutic behavior and their understanding of patients. In our view, the tasks for clinicians engaged in the practice and teaching of psychotherapy are twofold. On the one hand, they must be able to maintain a sufficiently broad theoretical perspective to entertain the assumptions, principles, and aims involved in any of the psychotherapies currently practiced, from the briefest to the lengthiest, and regardless of type (behavioral, cognitive, interpersonal, psychoanalytic, or a combination or integration of them). This is necessary in order to do justice to the complexity of human behavior and the human psyche. On the other hand, they also must convey what particular facet of the patient's psyche the patient–therapist dyad is addressing on a moment-to-moment, session-to-session basis. Moreover, psychotherapy trainees often must be disabused of the idea that they are supposed to have all of the answers to a patient's troubles. A multifaceted theoretical view anchored in specifiable treatment interventions can help keep a clinician's focus on the therapy process. This serves to inform the clinician that the patient is sometimes better able than the therapist to express needs and difficulties. The clinician, through the kinds of therapeutic bids the patient elicits, reveals to the patient how the patient shows him- or herself to be and hence informs the patient about the diagnosis as well as the level of therapeutic engagement they both have reached.

A multifaceted theoretical view informed by the effects of specific therapeutic bids provides a means to identify and specify treatment needs and goals. Thus, short-term treatments may be viable options, even when lengthy treatments are indicated, provided the therapeutic dyad is clear about the level at which they are working, and the therapist can convey to the patient the psychological facets within which she or he understands the patient to function and the general goals toward which they aim. The therapist can even convey directly to the patient the therapeutic bids she or he uses in order to achieve specific gains and identified goals. Then, should the patient have to discontinue treatment for whatever reason, whether from lack of personal motivation, family or work considerations, or financial and insurance/managed care restrictions, therapist and patient can agree to interrupt the treatment in a manner that is comprehensible to both and mutually respectful. We have found that patients are most likely to resume treatment, whether after a brief hiatus or even lengthier breaks, if the therapist explains in a clear, direct, and respectful manner what can and cannot be achieved in relatively brief treatment as well as the kinds of difficulties that are likely to persist with the immediate interruption of treatment.

The aim of this book, then, is to document both the complexity and the relatively cohesive simplicity of working with human psychological functioning across the span of development, with different kinds and severity of psychopathology. While some of the ideas and clinical material may be more pertinent to those individuals who work with and teach about high-risk infants and their families, other material will be of interest to clinicians who work with children, adolescents, and adults who are more moderately dysfunctional, whether their primary sources of distress are intrapsychic, characterologic, developmental, interpersonal, or more likely, an intertwining of two or more of those facets.

In short, we believe that the clinical theories presented here form the underpinnings for the multiple diagnoses and treatments discussed and are essential for disciplined and consistent work by seasoned clinicians as well as for those in training. We maintain that the "anything goes as long as it works" attitude does not make for good teaching or practice. Rather, we have found that the search for a theoretical framework informed by definable therapeutic interventions and supported by an underlying philosophical base is what teachers and students find exciting in their thirst to deepen their appreciation of the art and practice of psychotherapy. Finally, we lay no claims for having invented anything in what we present. Essentially, our work aims toward clarification in our field, from the clarification of theory to that of therapeutic techniques.

The book is organized in two parts, the first addressing an integrated theory of psychological functioning and the second the theory and methods of therapeutic transactions. In part I, chapter 1 discusses the clinical foundations and philosophical underpinnings of our work and the resulting theoretical views. Chapter 2 provides a conceptual overview of our theoretical model. Chapter 3 describes the interpersonal theoretical facet of psychological functioning and its systems theory perspective. Chapter 4 covers the developmental facet, its developmental stage theory, and universalist perspective. Chapter 5 covers the characterologic facet, which has its anchor in the concept of self and its various processes, the I, I/Me, and Me/I and the ideal self, which we conceive of as developing from genetic, constitutional, and temperamental predispositions in transaction with the environment. Chapter 6 covers the intrapsychic facet, based on psychoanalytic theories but construed more narrowly here in that the characterologic and developmental perspectives that are also influenced by psychoanalytic theories are treated as separate but transacting facets. Chapter 7 focuses on a diagnostic scheme that categorizes the forms of disturbance into deficits, delays, arrests, and conflicts, with the understanding that these categories are not mutually exclusive, but overlap and operate to create and define one another. A clinical case illustration demonstrates the transactional influences of the deficits, delays, arrests, and conflicts. In part II, which pertains to the theory of therapeutic transactions, chapter 8 presents an integrated theory of therapeutic transactions. A clinical case illustration demonstrates the origins of the multifaceted approach to treatment. Chapter 9 defines and discusses the nature and functions of therapeutic as well as antitherapeutic bids, followed by illustrations of coded sessions. Chapter 10 describes and discusses the various forms of parent–infant/child interaction treatment, and is followed by three illustrations of coded interaction sessions.

PART I

The Facets of Psychological Functioning

PART I

The Facets of Psychological Homicide

1

Clinical Foundations and Philosophical Underpinnings

The conceptual framework of this work derives from 16 years of clinical experience with a population of infants, children, and their parents. The children have ranged from newborns to 5-year-olds, and the parents have included teenage mothers, teenage fathers, as well as adult single parents, couples, and grandparents. The clinic, the Parent–Infant Development Service (PIDS) of the University of Chicago's Medical Center, was founded in 1979 to provide clinical services for this population, which had not often been served in the traditional programs of psychiatric training centers, and to learn about the psychological functioning of this population. The demand for psychiatric treatment for this population soon became evident. Over five hundred families were seen over the first 10 years. We saw our task not only as one of devising appropriate modes of treatment for developmental, emotional, and psychosocial problems for infants and their families, but also, as developing a coherent system for diagnostic evaluation. From its inception, too, the project became an integral part of the training programs for psychiatry fellows, psychology and psychiatric social work interns, and psychology externs. It was necessary, therefore, to develop a theoretical and clinical framework that was teachable; this necessity was a blessing, for in teaching what

3

we were learning, the teaching itself significantly fostered and honed our learning.

When we first began in the fall of 1979, we joined the emerging clinical infant mental health efforts in the United States which were spearheaded then by Provence and Lipton (1962), Solnit (1970), Fraiberg (1971), Provence (1972), Mahler, Pine, and Bergman (1975), Greenspan, Lourie, and Nover (1979) to name but a few. These clinicians, in turn, had built on the works of Spitz (1945, 1946, 1959, 1965), Bowlby (1951, 1969, 1973), Escalona and Heider (1959), Sander (1962), and many others before them. Interventions with infants had burgeoned from the 1960s on, due, in part, to advances in medical technology that significantly altered infant mortality and morbidity. The advances were also due, in part, to the findings associated with the Headstart enrichment programs of that decade which showed the positive effects of intervening with children ages 4 to 5. But these programs also later revealed their pitfalls: they started too late and did not continue long enough into the children's lives; in many cases, the children needed intervention much earlier and for considerably longer periods of time (Zigler and Trickett, 1978; Zigler, 1989).

The conceptual framework with which we began was fairly simple and consistent with what was known at the time. It may be expressed as follows: *Infants develop in the context of a parental environment, bringing with them their inherent genetic, biological, and temperamental endowment. Parents develop as a result of their inherent endowment modified in the course of their development by their own experiences of being parented and by their subsequent experiences in parenting their own children, particularly the infant for whom they seek therapeutic help and guidance.*

Although this general perspective implied our awareness of a broader theoretical framework, several years of clinical work evolved before we could formulate the building blocks that would make up our conceptual underpinnings. Experience was our best teacher. We learned through our clinical work with the parents, children, and parent-infant dyads, especially through trying to observe and reflect upon how, why, when, and with what success we did what we did, to articulate diagnostic issues, and to intervene on a moment-to-moment basis in therapy sessions. We were concerned as well with understanding what kind of environmental supports were necessary to help our patients in their psychological treatment, such as providing home care, working with social agencies, extended family members, and foster families, and in school settings. In addition, special remedial interventions, such as occupational, physical, speech therapy, and sensorimotor integration treatments had to be put in place for many of our children. Our diagnostic and therapeutic initiatives relied heavily on what we learned from ongoing research, on what was known about the nature of pre- and postnatal development, life-cycle development, and on the evolving theories of therapeutic intervention. But no understanding is possible without a theoretical framework that can orient perception to grasp and organize clinical experience in some meaningful description. We found it necessary to employ a number of theoretical perspectives to provide a view sufficiently broad to account for the complexities of our subject matter. The model presented here reflects a clinically adapted integration of empirical findings and formal psychological theory from several quarters. The theoreticians, clinicians, and empiricists upon whose work we leaned to guide and to inform our work include psychoanalysts, such as Sigmund Freud, Anna Freud, Erikson, Fraiberg, Gedo and Goldberg, George Klein, Melanie Klein, Kohut, Loewald, Mahler, Modell, Ogden, Provence, Schlessinger and Robbins, Solnit, and Winnicott; developmental and psychoanalytic researchers, such as Emde, Greenspan, Sander, and Stern; developmentalists, such as Piaget, Sroufe, and Vygotsky; and systems and information theorists, such as Ashby, Miller, Sameroff, and von Bertalanffy. Many more, of course, influenced our thought and work and we shall refer to them specifically in the text.

Theory, however, is not simply a question of putting together ideas that best explain how things work. Theory derives from a mind-set made up of ideals, beliefs, and philosophical underpinnings that guide and shape the organization of ideas. The beliefs the clinician holds constitute a background, or stance, that frames

5

his or her approach to theory and treatment, an approach that necessarily involves the interaction of the clinician's personal desires, attitudes, often unconscious beliefs, his or her expectations, hopes, and reasons for gravitating toward specific theoretical issues. We were building from the ground up in developing approaches to diagnosis and treatment from observations informed by an array of existing theories, which, in turn, generated concepts applicable to the particulars of our clinical situation and mandates. It became necessary, in our view, to articulate the underlying beliefs and ideals that motivated our work and that subtly, but forcefully, influenced our perceiving (selection of data) and thinking (organizing the perceived phenomena into meaningful relationships). We have delineated three derivatives of these ideals that we believe to be most instrumental in orienting our clinical and research approach: accountability, equality, and transmission.

ACCOUNTABILITY

Accountability in the diagnostic process involves describing clinical manifestations as observed, and wondering together with the patient about their possible purposes, the underlying strengths they may impart, and difficulties they may present.

In the treatment situation, accountability means that the therapist attempts to put into words the reasons for his or her interventions which can foster the patient's development. In our experience, all too often, the more complex the clinician's perspective, the less she or he imparts to the patient. The purported justification of this stance is based on the notion that the less said, the better will the patient be able to display all the vagaries of his or her psychological functioning. In our experience, diagnostic observations are not addressed beyond the diagnostic period, and treatment processes remain unexplained before and during the treatment. The patient is left with a sense of discomfort and worry as to the nature of the "disease" he or she may be carrying, in the first instance, and the "murky" treatment situation he or she is involved in, in the second. Moreover, in the treatment situation, accountability, joint exploration, or even only an attempt at a hypothetical explanation along the way on the part of the therapist as to seeming shifts in treatment focus may alleviate anxiety and support a joint effort at exploration. The patient might say, for example, "I thought we'd be working on my difficulties with my little baby and suddenly I'm finding myself discussing the terrible difficulties I have at work with my boss," to which the therapist might reply, "That is an interesting observation, and I myself have no immediate explanation either. Possibly, this baby makes you feel as though you are being bossed around, and that is a situation you don't take to very well, not in relation to parenting your child, nor in the work force." These transference reactions from still earlier relationships in the patient's family of origin may come up in due time, depending on the range of the treatment goals. Moreover, these observations stem from the patient's discomfort with the clinician in the treatment process itself, and constitute a transference in the here-and-now and may be addressed in due time, as well. However, this will depend on the treatment goals and on the phase of treatment. For it must be stressed here that a transference interpretation in the here-and-now is a very potent intervention and should never be addressed at the outset of the therapeutic exchange lest it create a rift, a real tear so to speak, in the beginning of the therapeutic working alliance. In brief, lack of accountability fosters authoritarianism in the relationship and pathologizes the patient's condition. The presence of accountability, on the other hand, prompts the development of a similar attitude on the part of the patient, if not immediately, then at some point in the future, when trust and a feeling of acceptance have taken hold in the therapeutic working relationship.

EQUALITY

The nature of the diagnostic or therapeutic task confers an essential equality on therapist and patient alike, inasmuch as all participants engage in a process of inquiry and learning. For both

7

therapist and patient (including parents and infants), the tasks consist of becoming knowledgeable about their unique field of study, which engages the reciprocal and transactional influences of the relationship. The effort consists of tolerating one's own ignorance and remaining open to exploration and discovery. This task of allowing oneself to remain unsure is a potent leveler and equalizer, for it makes learners of both therapist and patient alike in relation to one another, and makes both vulnerable, as well as at times unwillingly blind, even as it provides each with the pleasures of a sense of well-deserved competence when the task has yielded significant and satisfying gains.

The equality refers, of course, to *function*, not to *content* of experience. When we gradually succeed in regarding ourselves and one another as equals in the function of our tasks, we achieve something that is unique and different from what is ordinarily experienced by most individuals in their daily lives. For society has a way of organizing us into hierarchically defined entities: here we are teachers, there we are parents, women and men, elsewhere we are students, professionals, working people and so on. In ordinary life, role definition provides us with ready-made guidelines for carrying on our daily transactions. And while these guidelines ease our task of communicating with one another, something of our full-fledged selves is lost when we treat one another only in terms of our functioning roles. For example, we tend to leave our personal and family selves to the side when at work. Similarly, we tend to leave our work selves to the side within the confines of our families. In the clinical transaction between therapist and patient, however, all aspects of the patient's person eventually come to the fore. But the relationship between patient and therapist can also be seen as two equals embarking on a joint journey of discovery. For regardless of the therapist's general expertise or experience, the particular patient she or he treats is initially unknown to the clinician. True, it is helpful when the clinician can convey a sense of security and confidence derived from his or her confidence in the therapeutic process itself, rather than from an a priori sense of therapeutic authority. The state of working together can be achieved only when there exists between therapist and patient (including infant) this sense that equals are engaged in a common task of discovering the patterns of adaptation and the sources of troubles. Thus, we hold that the therapeutic task is not facilitated or promoted by any claims of privileged perspectives or special knowledge, but, rather, by the conviction that the clinician needs the patient as much as the patient needs the therapist.

TRANSMISSION

In the clinical situation, the word *transmission* refers to the exchange of information between patient and therapist. Transmission of knowledge is no simple matter, because the content of what patient and therapist learn is quite different, representing the personal perspectives and modes of understanding unique to each of them.

Transmission, of course, is central to the transactions between infants, children, and their parents. Parents transmit to their children the very essence of their being, for better and for worse. Infants and children transmit to their parents an essence of their own, which not only represents their sense of themselves and others but also affects the parents' reflecting views on them. And so it is for patient and therapist, as well, for they transmit to the other their sense of themselves and also how they see the other.

Transmission is a powerful force in human relatedness: survival of the human species relies on it. What is at stake for the individual is the passing on to another individual something of one's self, something valued, and some inherent sense of raison d'être, so too with therapists and their patients. What therapists transmit is their commitment to their work and to their patients. What patients transmit is their commitment to their condition. Patients bring to treatment the effects and process of their adaptive and maladaptive functioning. Often, in the middle phase of the work, when both patient and therapist have gotten to know something about how they work and what irks or pleases them, it is not uncommon for a patient to say, "I am always surprised by how many details you remember and how much you care about me!" And the truth is that the clinician has taken the patient in and responds to the patient from within with his or her entire being, but responds to the patient only with those interventions that are necessary and appropriate at any given time.

These three tenets, then, accountability, equality, and transmission, constitute the foundation that orients our perceptions and derived assumptions and principles, and constitute the essential configuration of attitudes that frame our approach to the clinical situation.

2

Conceptual Overview

To man the world is twofold, in accordance with his twofold attitude. The attitude of man is twofold according to the two-fold nature of the primary words which he speaks. . . . [These primary words] . . . are not isolated words, but combined words. The one primary word is the combination *I-Thou*. The other primary word is the combination *I-It*; wherein, without a change in primary word *He* and *She* can replace *It*. Hence the I of man is also twofold, for the I of the primary word *I-Thou* is different from that of the *I-It* [p. 3].

The man who experiences has no part in the world. For it is "in him" and not between him and the world that the experience arises. The world has no part in the experience. It permits itself to be experienced, but has no concern over the matter [p. 5].

As experience, the world belongs to the primary word *I-It*. The primary word *I-Thou* establishes the world of relation [p. 6].

I do not experience the man to whom I say Thou. But I take my stand in relation to him. . . . Only when I step out of it do I experience him. . . . In the act of experience Thou is far away [p. 9].

I become [I] through my relation to the Thou; as I become I, I say Thou [Buber, 1958, p. 11].

Buber's words capture the essential dichotomy between experience and relatedness in the psychology of the human being. For

11

Buber, experience appears to be an "I" thing, whereas relation remains a paradoxical concept. When he says, "I do not experience the man to whom I say Thou, but take my stand in relation to him," and further expands, "I become I through my relation with Thou; as I become I, I say Thou" he emphasizes the essential dichotomy of oneness and otherness in human experience. Also, he refers to "Man's" nature as being twofold according to his primary *words*, thereby alerting us to the significance of language and its meaning in defining "Humankind."

In this book we are trying to engage and understand the psychological derivatives of the dialectical processes anchored in this essential dichotomy. We present a multifaceted model for thinking about the dichotomous and manifold nature of human psychological functioning and the corresponding therapeutic transaction. The model takes the infant–parent dialogue and its developmental transformations as the organizing paradigm for theory, and the infant–parent/ therapist relationship as the paradigm for understanding the multiple facets of therapeutic transactions.

Our theoretical formulations derive from interpersonal, developmental, characterologic, and intrapsychic conceptualizations. In attending to what appears to be a movement toward interdisciplinary reciprocity in the development of psychoanalytic theory and clinical practice (e.g., Emde, 1983, 1988a,b, 1990; Sander, 1983; Lichtenberg, 1983; Kafka, 1984; Stern, 1985; Grotstein, 1986; F. Levin, 1991; and Schwartz, 1992), we have organized the findings and methods of our clinical work with infants and their parents in light of the burgeoning data and formulations emerging from research on infancy, systems theory, developmental psychology, psychoanalytic theory, neuroscience, and cognitive science. Our contribution then derives from our clinical work and systematic observations, and engages the current efforts at integrating a theory of psychological functioning with a theory of psychological treatment.

No single body of theory exists to date that explains and accounts for the complexity of human psychological functioning, which is best understood when considering the human being's development from infancy on. Here we would like to outline our formulation of a complex of theoretical perspectives that includes the systems, developmental, character, and intrapsychic facets.

In coalescing a number of theoretical perspectives, one must consider the common underpinnings that make such cohabitation and integration possible. In our view, the four theoretical perspectives share two basic assumptions, the first of which is that human functioning is inherently motivated and goal directed, and the second that it is psychologically meaningful from birth. Moreover, motivation, goal-directedness, and psychological meaning are not static givens, but, rather, are subject to maturation and experience from birth throughout the course of life.

The issues of motivated versus fortuitously prompted functioning relates to the more general issue of predetermined versus random functioning. We hold that human functioning is not random. It observes certain laws that lead to certain ends. To be sure, elements of chance, randomness, exist even in a lawful system, otherwise there would be no possibility for perturbation that elicits self-correction and attendant change. Motivation and goal-directedness, however, are not synonymous. The assumption of motivation means that all functioning is prompted by inner signals. The assumption of goal-directedness means that functioning within certain frameworks is purposive.

We define psychological functioning as the mindful aspect of the totality of human functioning. Psychological functioning encompasses affects, urges, needs, sensations, perceptions, thoughts, fantasies, wishes, ideals, and aspirations, all operative in basic and elemental forms at birth.

Finally, human functioning is the outcome of the transaction between heredity, biology, environment, experience, and the unexpectable. And the unexpectable, on the one hand, is a function of our inability to predict or control happenings in the environment, and on the other, it is a function of the most intractable characteristic unique to the human experience, what Dobzhansky (1967), called the inventive nature of man. The apparent randomness in human affairs, then, reflects not only our inability to predict and control external events but also our inherent capacity for inventiveness and creativity.

The overarching principle of our model rests on the principle of transactionalism, which is defined, on the one hand, by the reciprocal influences between the person and the environment, or nature and nurture, and, on the other, by person to person interactions (Sameroff, 1975, 1982; Sameroff and Chandler, 1975). The model defines the reciprocal influences of therapeutic action and reaction in the context of theory and empirical clinical practice. A transactional view focuses on relationships and their reciprocal effects on one another. Our view also emphasizes how an individual both changes and remains the same over time. Relationships, especially the earliest relationships, forge an individual's patterns of behavior, and affective inclinations are internalized as aspects of relationships, and it is the internalized relationship patterns and styles that endure as influential throughout later development in constructing novel experience in familiar ways (Sroufe and Fleeson, 1985; Stern, 1985; Beebe and Lachmann, 1988; Emde, 1988a). But no relationship is exactly like any other, and, as Piaget (1952) suggests, accommodation is always an aspect of adaptation. Transactionalism implies reciprocity in the mutual accommodations of interacting individuals that generates a spiral of mutually accruing influences. It is by understanding relationships between self and other (interpersonal), between self and the world of things, and between the experiential self and observing aspects of the self (intrapersonal), identified with by encouraging or inhibiting others, that core issues such as identity, autonomy, and interdependence can be clarified.

The transactional perspective is now widely held as a guiding view in infant developmental theory and research. The essence of the concept of transactionalism, however, is not altogether new to psychoanalysis either. Relationships can be seen as templates of and modes for internalization, a view that has been expressed increasingly in the developmental–clinical theories of, for example, Loewald (1960, 1978), Kernberg (1976), and Kohut (1977), in their construction of psychoanalytic theory. Moreover, the increasing emphasis on transference–countertransference interplay between patient and therapist (e.g., Tower, 1956; Racker, 1968; Bollas, 1983; McLaughlin, 1981), and the recent attempts to describe and advance relational aspects (Greenberg and Mitchell, 1983), intersubjective (Stolorow and Atwood, 1979; Atwood and Stolorow, 1984), and particularly a social–constructivist view of the psychoanalytic situation (e.g., Hoffman, 1991), convey much of the essence of transactionalism at work in a psychoanalytic theory of therapy.

The principle of transactionalism is embedded in systems theory. At core, it goes beyond the nature–nurture controversy in the developmental theory of biopsychosocial functioning, giving primary importance to neither nature nor nurture, but, rather, encompasses the understanding that nature comes into being through nurture, and that nurture is stimulated and shaped by nature that elicits, in turn, a range of nurturing response tendencies. The wisdom of this view has been expressed, for example, in Winnicott's (1960) notion that there is no such thing as an infant but, rather, that infant and maternal care form a unit; as well as the common understanding that no two children have exactly the same mother. With regard to psychological theory and therapy, transactionalism makes apparent the need for a model of human functioning and psychotherapeutic treatment that can grasp and handle the multiple perspectives necessary to view and understand the multiple and reciprocal influences on psychological functioning.

A transactional perspective that focuses on relationships between and among phenomena is a perspective that employs modern structuralism (e.g., Piaget, 1970), and as such, emphasis is given to structural analysis of the underlying arrangement of elements to determine the lawful transformations of the phenomena observed in an open system. From a structuralist perspective, then, the contexts and facets might be viewed as operating in a manner similar to that conceptualized by Piaget (Flavell, 1963) in his notion of structures. Any structure exists and functions in reciprocal operations with other structures, and, hence, is structured while it structures. Whatever the aim of specific intervention, whether directed at intrapersonal or interpersonal contexts, or at any facets of psychological functioning, a therapeutic intervention can engage the patient's functioning, including the infant's and parent's functioning and the relations between them as they relate to one another. This takes place within both contexts and all facets, so that the influence exerted by the intervention toward any given point necessarily rebounds to all other points to greater or lesser degrees (Table 2.1 illustrates our entire theoretical model).

We view psychological functioning and therapeutic activity as operating transactionally within and across two contexts of psychological functioning, the interpersonal and the intrapersonal. As would be expected with the transactional perspective, the interpersonal and intrapersonal contexts operate as figure or ground for the other, depending on the focus of the observer and subject of the transaction. The inter- and intrapersonal contexts encompass a number of psychological facets. These facets in turn comprise different domains of functioning. Each facet is engaged by several operating principles toward the fulfillment of aims that are of interest to both contexts and to all the facets and domains.

The interpersonal context is conceptualized in terms of the interpersonal system, and the conceptualization draws upon systems theory; the intrapersonal context is conceptualized in terms of facets that include the developmental, characterologic, and intrapsychic, conceptualizations that draw upon developmental and psychoanalytic theories. These facets, in turn, involve different (but transacting) domains of functioning. For example, language acquisition is a domain of the developmental facet, and the superego (i.e., the functions attributed to the concept denoting a particular form of interiorized psychological influence) is a domain of the intrapsychic facet; similarly, the sense of self and the ideal self are key domains of the characterologic facet. Also, each facet is engaged by several operating principles toward the fulfillment of aims that are of interest not only to that facet but to all four facets within both contexts, the interpersonal and the intrapersonal. For example, the principles of the developmental facet include organization, regulation, adaptation, and integration, as defined by Louis Sander (1987). These principles serve aims that include the fulfillment of biopsychological requisites, social connectedness, and the exploration of novelty and pursuit of effectance[1] (White, 1959). These aims influence the aims of the other facets, just as the aims of the other facets influence the developmental aims.

One of our major premises in building an integrated model of psychological functioning and therapeutic transaction is that the separate perspectives are universal; that is, they pertain to all human beings regardless of age and psychopathology. Each perspective, however, takes into account the specific challenges, tasks, achievements, and disturbances within its own framework.

The conceptual framework espouses the view that the aims of the developmental facet are genetically preprogrammed, inherently motivating, and universal. We conceptualize the aims as threefold: (1) the fulfillment of biopsychological requisites (e.g., neurophysiologically based cravings, sleep, hunger, circulation and breathing rhythms, subcortically triggered affective responses, and sensorimotor–cognitive appetites); (2) social connectedness; and (3) the interrelated aims of novelty-seeking, exploration, and pursuit of effectance.

Our model also takes a fresh look at familiar phenomena and concepts to provide new perspectives on theoretical and clinical issues. A new perspective on character and self-psychological functioning is presented, wherein the self represents the central axis through which character is woven. The concept of character armor (Reich, 1949) is elaborated to describe the development of functions that provide an envelope that guards and informs character and self which interweave inextricably in development. Character is defined as the combination of genetic, constitutional, and maturational givens that contribute to a system of

---

[1]We use the term effectance rather than competence striving because our observations of the infant's earliest manipulation of objects in the environment appear to begin not as attempts to be competent but as attempts to do something with the objects before them, i.e., to have an effect. Effectance striving then leads to competence striving.

TABLE 2.1
The Multiple Facets of Psychological Functioning

Overarching Assumptions: Human functioning is motivated, goal-directed, psychologically meaningful from birth on, and subject to maturation and experience throughout the course of life.

Overarching Principle: Transactionalism within interpersonal and intrapersonal contexts.

	Interpersonal Facet	Developmental Facet	Character Facet	Intrapsychic Facet
Domains	Mutual:	Neuromotor	Self-Processes:	Ego
	Reciprocal	Cognitive	I	Superego
	Joint	Affective	I/Me	Ucs needs, wishes,
	Nonmutual:	Social	Me/I	fantasies, dreams,
	Asynchronous	Language, speech	Ideal-Self	imagery
	Parallel	Fantasy, play,	Regulation of	
	Unilateral	creativity	Temperament	
	Invasive		(Activity/Rhythmicity)	
	Avoidant			
	Clashing			
Principles	Feedback	Organization	Feedback	Compulsion to
	Disjoin	Adaptation	Disjoin	repeat
	Tension Regulation	Integration	Tension Regulation	Transference
	Equifinality		Equifinality	Construction and
				reconstruction of
				personal reality
				and meaning

TABLE 2.1 (*continued*)

The Multiple Facets of Psychological Functioning

	Interpersonal Facet	Developmental Facet	Character Facet	Intrapsychic Facet
Aims	Optimal balance between autonomy and interdependence	Social Connectedness Novelty/Exploration Effectance Biopsychological requisites	Elaborate I, I/Me, Me/I, Ideal/Self Regulation of temperament	Ucs – Cs Resolve compulsion to repeat Resolve disabling transferences Consolidate ego functions
Conservative Tendencies	Coping strategies (Cs & Ucs) Character armor (Ucs & Cs) Defense-transference (Ucs)	Coping strategies (Cs & Ucs)	Coping strategies (Cs & Ucs) Character armor (Ucs & Cs) Defense-transference (Ucs)	Ego defense mechanisms (Ucs) Transference (Ucs)

ongoing patterning of interactions with the inanimate world and ongoing patterning of transactions with the human world. Character is governed by temperamental characteristics such as activity level, rhythmicity, mood and affect fluctuation, which while inherent to the individual, can be modulated and shaped by the environment. The self domain is made up of three processes shaped in transaction with the environment which include the I-, the I/Me-, and the Me/I-processes and the ideal self. As will be described, this conceptualization of self processes highlights the convergent and divergent forms of inter- and intrapersonal relationships, and each self process denotes a particular form and configuration of relationship in the transactions of self and the world.

Our model also redefines a number of psychoanalytic concepts for the sake of clarifying the purported transactions within and across the domains and aims of the facets of the interpersonal and intrapersonal contexts. As will be explained, the repetition compulsion, for example, becomes the compulsion to repeat (intrapsychic facet); the ego ideal becomes the ideal self (characterologic facet); the concept of id is omitted as traditionally used, and rather, becomes that aspect of self that constitutes the I-process, and is encompassed, essentially, in aspects of the character facet, specifically the domain of regulation of temperament. In regard to the intrapsychic facet, conscious needs, desires, wishes, and fantasies belong to the developmental facet and its domains; unconscious needs, desires, wishes, and fantasies, however, aspects traditionally attributed to the id, remain discrete domains within the intrapsychic facet and are governed by the repressive action of the dynamic unconscious.

We have also attempted to refine and elaborate commonly held conceptualizations of defense and resistance. Thus, the ego defense mechanisms that psychoanalysis has identified are distinguished from what are identified here as coping strategies (Lazarus, Averill, and Opton, 1974). The ego defense mechanisms fall primarily within the intrapsychic facet of this model. Defense mechanisms protect the individual against conflict within the intrapsychic domains. The coping strategies are functions primarily of the systems, developmental, and character facets. Coping strategies help the individual's adaptation to and coping with undue stress by the environment. However, since all facets are influenced one by the other, ego defense mechanisms, which are by definition unconscious, will be present in the other facets, and conversely, coping strategies, which are primarily conscious or preconscious, will be present in the intrapsychic facet. To repeat, whereas defense mechanisms operate as functions of the dynamic unconscious, coping strategies may be conscious or operate as functions of the descriptive unconscious. We have defined a number of coping strategies, and these include: realistic appraisal and cooperation, compliance/submission, avoidance/distancing, externalizing/blaming, defying/fighting, disconnecting/fleeing, freezing/being immobilized, and affective transformation. (The second coping strategy after each slash is not a synonym for the first, but rather an intensified version of the first.)

Whereas part I of our model pertains to the multiple facets of psychological functioning, part II pertains to the multiple facets of therapeutic transactions and their attendant therapeutic bids. Thus, based on the assumption, principles, domains, and aims of psychological functioning described above, the theory of therapeutic transactions evolves from the multiple aims and facets of the theory of psychological functioning. When there is a disturbance (deficit, delay, arrest, or conflict) in any of the psychological facets, one looks toward the aims of the given facet or facets and more specifically at the disordered domains. One also looks at the domains that function well, for these, when properly isolated and addressed, fulfill compensatory functions for the disordered domains and promote healing. Finally, one looks at the conservative tendencies (the defenses, coping strategies, and character armor) the individual uses in order to protect him- or herself from the turbulence that any change requires in order for the person to adapt to new internal and environmental demands.

The principles of treatment involved are exploring, learning, understanding, and practicing (or working through). The aims of treatment are to restore balance in the affected psychological facets and the attendant domains. For example, the aim of treatment for a cognitively delayed youngster is to enhance his or her motivation to explore novelty and to become sufficiently self-assured so as to try to become effective in relating to the world of thoughts and things. Here we note that the primary disorder is in the developmental facet. The character facet is also affected, as may be the two other facets (the interpersonal and intrapsychic), but the disorder, at this time, is developmental. The major domains that require intervention are the cognitive domain within the developmental facet and the I and I/Me self-processes of the characterologic facet. The interpersonal, and intrapsychic facets, are presumed to be in the background, active but silent at this time.

Our analysis of each intervention has revealed component parts that entail specific therapeutic actions that we call therapeutic bids. Viewed in this light, an intervention shows itself to be multifaceted: it is played on the stage of one context against the background of the other context. It is directed toward certain aims that exist in a network of interacting aims, and it engages specific facets of functioning directly and indirectly. An intervention can be either a single therapeutic bid or a part of a complex of bids that highlights one facet of a multifaceted psychological sphere, but can silently engage any of the other facets and domains.

A therapeutic bid, or a complex of bids, then, can engage both contexts of functioning, the intra- and interpersonal, and the four facets of psychological functioning, the systemic, developmental, characterologic, and intrapsychic. A patient's response to a therapist's bid informs the therapist of the context or facet activated by the bid. This information enables the therapist to respond once again to the patient's response with another bid aimed at addressing the context and facet indicated in the patient's response. The reciprocal interactions of a therapist's actions, the patient's reaction, followed by the therapist's further reaction, constitute what we call a therapeutic transaction. Therefore, when a therapist treats an infant, child, adolescent, parent(s), or adult, each member of the therapeutic engagement is susceptible to influence by the therapeutic intervention's various facets. The influence of an intervention on any individual—the significance of any one or another facet of the intervention—will vary in degree according to the organizational needs and development of each individual participating in the treatment. That is, the complex of bids of an intervention assures that all participants are influenced by an intervention, but also that each participant is influenced in necessarily individual ways.

The therapeutic bids identified here, no doubt incomplete, constitute the universal grammar of the therapeutic language. As such, the therapeutic bids operate in all psychotherapeutic modalities (individual, dyadic, family group), and most therapeutic orientations (behavioral, cognitive, and psychoanalytic). They also cut across the particulars of chronological and developmental age or form of psychological disorder, though, of course, not all therapeutic bids are employed with equal frequency across all conditions and different clinical/theoretical orientations. The therapeutic bids include the following: receptive observation (including empathy, tact, and respect), mirroring/imitating, reflecting/labeling, probing, coaxing/encouraging, facilitating, didactic expansion, interpreting, containing (which includes inhibiting, delaying, and renouncing), disengaging/silence, and self-observation. (The second bid after each slash is not synonymous with the first, but rather is a stronger form of the bid before the slash.) The bids are part of a coding system we are developing to analyze the psychotherapeutic process. Observations leading to the development of the model also resulted in descriptions and definitions of a number of antitherapeutic bids (heretofore defined in the developmental research literature as variables pertaining to adverse parenting). The antitherapeutic bids include the following: overriding, underinvolvement, verbal seductiveness, verbal abuse, physical seductiveness, and physical abuse.

Recognizing and categorizing the contexts, facets, principles, domains, and aims of functioning and of therapeutic actions provides a therapist with a means of focusing and pitching a set of bids toward a particular facet, domain, and aim of psychological functioning. But the conceptual understanding and practical use of the therapeutic bids also help the therapist keep in mind that he or she can never know in advance the sum of influences an intervention can have on the therapeutic relationship or the corresponding therapeutic effects on each individual, for the intervention itself is an aspect of an ongoing transaction of mutually accruing influences.

In what follows, then, we hope the reader will share with us the necessary tensions of considering new possibilities for understanding. As Thomas Ogden (1989) suggests, "In attempting to learn, we subject ourselves to the tension of dissolving connections between ideas that we have thus far relied upon in a particular way" (p. 2). The reward for doing so is a deeper understanding of the object we study, or as Harry Guntrip (1969) suggested, "Everything in a given field cannot be seen from one point of view, and often a change of viewpoint leads to deeper understanding" (p. 171).

3

The Interpersonal Facet

The infant possesses considerable equipment at birth with all the human potentialities intact. But he or she cannot live without outside assistance. The infant, therefore, is the most altricial of creatures. Although the infant is very much guided by its own inner developmental push, it cannot conduct its affairs without protection, security, nurturance, and consistency provided by an emotionally receptive and regulating other. It is for this reason that the infant and caregiver together have been viewed as belonging to a unitary system, one governed by its own set of common assumptions and principles which draws on systems' theory. Infant and caregiver, like patient and therapist, function within an interpersonal context. Aspects of the interpersonal relationship become interiorized and represent the interpersonal facet of psychological functioning.

ASSUMPTIONS

The overriding assumption of the interpersonal facet is that the psyche of the infant or patient develops within an interpersonal and interactive context. The governing of the interpersonal transactional organization is best understood through concepts pertaining to the systems' theory perspective.

The specific assumptions of systems' theory posit that in a system in which the less mature member requires the assistance of the other, both members of the system aim simultaneously toward: (1) individual and mutual organization; (2) regulation; (3) integration; and (4) adaptation (Sander, 1975, 1987) in order to sustain psychological life. Sander (1987) has defined organization, regulation, integration, and adaptation as they operate for the infant–caregiver system. We believe they are equally applicable to all interactive dyads. Therefore, we adopt Sander's concepts as basic assumptions reflecting principles of operations described below.

TABLE 3.1
The Interpersonal Facet of Psychological Functioning

Assumptions: Transactionalism in organization, regulation, integration, adaptation
Principles: Feedback, tension, equifinality, disjoin

Domains	Aims	Conservative Tendencies

Mutual:
  Reciprocal
  Joint
	Balance between Autonomy and Independence	Coping Strategies (Cs and Ucs) [see Appendix A] Character Armor

Nonmutual:
  Asynchronous
  Parallel
  Unilateral
  Invasive
  Avoidant
  Clashing
		(Cs and Ucs) Defense-Transference

PRINCIPLES

The systems' principles that guide our understanding of the psychological functioning of infant and parents, or patient and therapist, include feedback, tension, equifinality, and disjoin.

Feedback is based on cybernetic and information processing theories (Miller, 1955; Sander, 1975, 1987) and their adaptation to human functioning. Mutual organization, regulation, integration, and adaptation may be viewed as being achieved through the principle of continuous feedback. Internal feedback within the individual (i.e., autofeedback), and mutual feedback in the interpersonal system occur over short and long periods of time, in the moment-to-moment feedback loops, and in the coordinations that endure over time between elements within the individual and between the partners of a system (Cohn and Tronick, 1988; Gianino and Tronick, 1987; Sander, 1975, 1987). From a systems' perspective, systemic feedback leading to alteration of behavior and perception is based not on optimal or identical feedback, which, in any case, is an impossibility between two live human beings, but rather, on the magnitude of discrepancy of the expected response (reflection) returned to the sender from the receiver. When the discrepancy is too great, the receiver may not be able to absorb the information. When the discrepancy is optimal, it tends to shake up a preexisting pattern of perception and thus can promote new learning, whereas identity (or sameness) of information can consolidate and reinforce one's newly achieved view of a given experience. When information feedback overemphasizes sameness, however, it leads to satiation or boredom. Thus, mirroring, as defined by Kohut (1977), Tolpin (1971), or Stern (1983) seems to be the key aspect within the feedback principle that accounts for the individual's building up of consistent and continuous representations of experience. When mirroring reflects the response of another human being, it validates the individual's sense of personhood and significance within an interpersonal context. When mirroring reflects the infant's sensorimotor-activated reactions of an inanimate object, for example, the infant touches a pedal or lever (even if only accidentally) and the mobile begins to move, the infant's sense of exploration and effectance is strengthened.

Developmentalists often refer to what psychoanalysts have labeled *mirroring* by another term, *contingency* or *contingent responsivity* (Ainsworth, Bell, and Stayton, 1974; Clarke-Stewart, 1973;

27

Greenspan and Lieberman, 1980; Beebe and Lachmann, 1988).
Thus, contingency is seen as an elicitor of social responsiveness
as well as responsiveness to the nonhuman environment (Papoušek and Papoušek, 1975). It is not, of course, contingency
alone that is the crucial factor; it is the quality of the contingent
responsivity that is of utmost significance. For if an infant touches
a lever which sets off a most unpleasant noise, the infant will likely
respond with displeasure and perhaps disorganization and is not
likely to return to touching that lever. Similarly, if a human contingent response is unpleasant, such as a slap, an injury, an unexpected insult or scolding, the person will not be inclined to
resume the behavior that apparently elicited the unpleasant reaction, and again, depending on the degree of unpleasant and unanticipated response, will withdraw, respond in some way that
puts distance between himself or herself and the punishing consequence, or become disorganized.

Research has demonstrated the functions of feedback operating through mutual coordinations; that is, states of attunement, mutuality, and reciprocity. While these states are
pleasurable and useful in facilitating the attainment of shared
goals, recent research indicates that these states of mutual coordination occur with relative infrequency (proportionate to the time
spent when such states do not obtain between two partners), and
are best thought of as states that function as essential motivators
for the search of human interaction.

Reciprocity, another form of feedback, has been defined as
complementary actions, behaviorally manifested by give and take,
turn taking, or attempts of one individual to fill in where the
other left off. Joint attention, as distinguished from reciprocity,
has been defined as an interactional engagement of and focus
on identical activities, meaning that the interests of interacting
individuals focus on the same object, event, or on one another.
Matching and imitation are aspects of joint attention that represent the convergence of two or more individuals pursuing together their inner and joint urges, needs, wishes, aspirations, or
interests. Finally, attunement refers to a process between two or

more individuals in which there is both reciprocity and joint attention. Attunement and mutuality, as the latter is defined by various researchers (Brazelton, Koslowski, and Main, 1974; Stern, 1977, 1985; Meltzoff and Moore, 1977; Cohn and Tronick, 1987; Beebe and Lachmann, 1988), appear to have essentially the same meaning. Attunement, then, represents a higher order concept abstracted from reciprocity and joint attention.[1]

Because the infant–parent system is made up of individual entities embarked on their singular pursuits while simultaneously requiring input from their sustenance-giving partners, it is inevitable that *tensions* will develop in the infant–caregiver system.

As Sander (1975, 1983, 1987) described, paradox and polarity are expectable manifestations of system entities which pursue the same goals at different rates and with their singular maturational, constitutional, and experiential capabilities. It is worth noting that the probabilities that the tensions resulting from the pursuit of identical goals by these singular entities will be "antagonistic" are no less than the probabilities that they will be mutually coordinated. Tensions signal mismatches in mutual coordinations. Seeking to repair mismatched coordinations creates a state that leads to the enlarging of the person's perceptual and organizing perspective and thus furthers growth.

Evidence from developmental research on the systemic functioning of the mother–infant dyad has led to more detailed descriptions of the underlying mechanisms of bidirectionality of interactional influences. Research by Fogel (1988) and Cohn and Tronick (1988) fine-tunes our thinking on the degree of mutual influence that has been hypothesized and found to exist within dyads. Cohn and Tronick (1988), for instance, find that bidirectionality does not affect the internal periodic cycles of gaze and

---

[1]At no time is there talk of merger between the entities of a system. There may well be attempts at overshadowing, overtaking, or retrenchment, or shrinking of function, but at no point can we accept, based on the logic inherent in biological and developmental principles, the nonexistence of individual psychological functioning. The concept of merger is, at best, a metaphor describing the clinical observation of optimal attunement, a process engaged by two willing partners. If merger is defined in terms of optimal attunement, then it does not mean losing one's self in another, but, rather, means two individuals pursuing identical or complementary goals for themselves, for one another, and with one another.

smiling of each member of a normal mother–infant dyad. Rather, the cycles of gazing and smiling seem to be governed by some inner mechanisms of the individual, whereas the bidirectional impact appears to be determined by the moment-to-moment reinforcements of the preceding behavior of the individual as well as by that of the individual's partner. Whether it is the individual's own behavior that proves to be reinforcing or that of the individual's partner cannot be predicted: "active processing of social signals by the young infant [is evident] . . . [I]nfants respond in specific and appropriate ways to their mothers' communicative displays" (Cohn and Tronick, 1988, p. 386). How this responsiveness comes about remains unknown, however, for Cohn and Tronick find that it is also evident that "[c]yclic behavior and bidirectional influence were unrelated" (p. 389). This is how the authors explain their findings:

> Bidirectional influence is achieved through the stochastic organization of behavior and not through mutual entrainment. Stochasticity means that a particular behavior cannot be predicted from a knowledge of the person's previous history of smile onsets [for example]. One cannot only talk about smiles having a certain probability of occurrence. . . . Some organismic or environmental conditions, however, can increase the inherent variability of a behavioral system past a critical value and attain an entirely different base rate. . . . In short, the variability of behavior is intimately tied to both its stability over specific time periods and its change over longer time periods [p. 389].

We will probably never be able to prove what takes precedence in determining an infant's response or initiation, his inner rhythms or his response as influenced by his need for the other. We can anticipate, however, that a behavior may occur. We would not know whether a behavior took place because of the individual's inner periodicity or because of the bidirectional influence that exists between two people who are significant one to the other. What we would know is that the behavior is the result of one *or* the other.

The finding implies that two lawful and independent processes occur within each individual: *that the individual's behavior is governed both by his or her unique cycles as well as by the responses of another.*

Thus, the findings of these researchers seem to lend support to the idea that we are indeed individual entities governed by our unique inner rhythms which are relatively uninfluenced by the environment, and that we are at the same time also subject to the rules of bidirectional influence which govern living systems.

Cohn and Tronick's (1988) research report gives further evidence for a more innovative perspective on the subject of mutual influence. As regards the extent to which infants and mothers are able to coordinate their behaviors, these researchers found that low-risk pairs spend 70 percent of their time in mismatched and nonsynchronous states. Even taking into account that the capacity for mother–infant coordination increases with age (Hunt, 1979), the researchers were surprised by the extent of the mismatched states. Earlier they had noted that disrepair in normal dyadic interaction is as ubiquitous as are synchrony and match (1987). Now, given the tilt of the proportion of asynchrony compared to synchrony, they are beginning to wonder as to the developmental function of nonsynchony. Could it be that normal dyadic development is more disjunctive than conjunctive? Could it be that disjunction, as well as conjunction, is necessary for human functioning?

Thus, if one were to ask what are the necessary and sufficient conditions for optimal functioning within an interpersonal context, one concludes that mismatch and nonsynchrony are as significant as are synchrony and match. States of mismatch, then, apparently represent the ordinary state of affairs in dyadic fit. This exciting empirical finding lends validity to the theoretical perspective presented here.

Psychoanalytic theories have begun to incorporate the interpersonal facet of psychological functioning as an essential element. In this regard we agree with Modell's (1984) argument that a two-person psychology is fundamentally complementary to a one-person psychology. We govern our own periodic cycles of affects, thoughts, sensual appetites as well as vital interests in out-side stimuli. And being aware of our need for "the other," we are influenced by that need for the other as much as by their need for us. Kohut's (1971) depiction of the human organism as the center of independent initiative, while beholden to the selfobject for the validation of personal centrality, also reflects the essence of this new position. Thus it can be said that human beings are governed simultaneously by their inevitable aloneness from which they cannot escape and by their need for one another without which they cannot survive.

The concept of *equifinality* holds that development can be fostered from differing initial conditions and through different pathways (von Bertalanffy, 1968). The concept of equifinality is an outgrowth of the notions of equipotentiality and multiple functions. Assuming that the goals of the system are inviolable, then we also assume that the individual and the interpersonal system will attempt to achieve their ultimate goals through a variety of pathways. This principle stipulates that, depending on the nature of the deficits, compensatory and inherent strengths in the entire system, ways can be found to facilitate the achievement of the goals. As a principle guiding our thoughts about evaluation, equifinality means that every aspect of the system, infant, child, adult, family, and environment, must be assessed in order to discern existing strengths and deficits. As a guide to intervention in the individual's system, equifinality leads us to consider that for any given problem there exist a number of possible avenues for solutions in terms of type of treatment approach (whether individual, dyadic, family or group), its sequence, and emphases (whether behavioral, cognitive–didactic or intrapsychic). How the problem will be resolved will depend on the psychological and financial requisites within the entire system.

In a groundbreaking theoretical paper, Sander (1975) intro-duced us to Ashby's (1958) principle of *disjoin*: "This mechanism of disjoin makes possible differentiated adaptation with the envi-ronment at the level of subsystems, so that perturbation of or in the 'disjoined' subsystem does not spread to the rest of the organism" (Sander, 1975, p. 151).

We reasoned that not only does a system require some insulation from perturbation in the various subsystems, but also each entity within a larger system requires insulation from perturbation, as well. How else would individuals maintain their uniqueness throughout life, given the principles that emphasize feedback, tension, and equifinality? "Ashby's argument thus provides the rationale that a 'self' or a self-organizing subsystem is essential to the regulation of adaptive behavior in a system at the critical level of complexity" (Sander, 1975, p. 152).

Our own experience led us to wonder how internal changes can occur in an individual or in a dyad, for example, the infant and the parent, when both are at all times influencing one another. Does it mean that no change can occur without the other being influenced by it? We had clinical evidence to the contrary. Infants turn away from their parents regularly; parents turn away from their infants. But if the infant's turning away is so predictable and repetitive it must also be peremptory. Research substantiates this observation (Brazelton, Koslowski, and Main, 1974; Beebe and Stern, 1977; Stern, 1977). Similarly, patients turn away from their therapists in their need to look inward so as not be subjected to external influence. Thus, we reasoned that the function of disengagement must serve the purpose of internal reorganization, while reflecting, too, that we are born as individual entities pursuing our own agendas as best we can.

To sum up the apparently contradictory principles that govern the parent–infant or patient–therapist system it is particularly appropriate to cite Winnicott. The Winnicott who offered that there is no infant without a mother who brings the world to her child (1963), is the same Winnicott who gave us the following thoughts: "At the center of each person is an incommunicado element... (p. 187). ... [a] private citadel of subjective reality held forever and inaccessible to public objective reality" (p. 182). With this he captured the essential duality of human existence—the mandatory holding environment and the reality of ultimate aloneness. "Although [it is a fact that] healthy persons communicate and enjoy communicating, the other fact is equally true, that each individual is an isolate, permanently non-communicating, permanently unknown, in fact unfound" (Winnicott, 1963, p. 187).

DOMAINS

The domains of the interpersonal facet follow logically from the principles of feedback, tension, equipotentiality, and disjoin. In the domains of the interpersonal facet one recognizes mutuality and nonmutuality. Mutuality is manifested by reciprocity in a dyad, a give-and-take, so to speak, or by joint interest, affect, activity or attention.

Nonmutuality is manifested by tension in assynchrony in a dyad when both members express competing tendencies to be with the other as well as to be elsewhere. Equipotentiality and disjoin are expressed in parallel, avoidant, unilateral, and clashing dyadic characteristics.

Specifically, mutuality includes reciprocity and joint attentiveness (as defined by Clark, Musick, Stott, and Klehr, 1980; Clark and Seifer, 1985). Mutuality characterizes a harmonious dyadic relationship in which both members of the dyad respond to one another or to an outside event with roughly equal attention and affect.

Reciprocity

Reciprocity reflects mutuality by turn taking and contingent responsivity. Therapist and patient, or parent and child, wait one for the other before responding. The response of one occasions the response of the other in a contingently responsive pattern of reciprocation.

Joint Attentiveness

Joint attentiveness reflects mutuality when both members of the dyad respond with equal interest to each other; that is, looking into each other's eyes if they are in the en face position, or listening and free associating to the patient's dream or to the story the patient has narrated. Both members of the dyad then reflect and think together about the multiple reasons and meanings of the dream, anecdote, or story. In the parent–child context the same joint attentiveness may be seen when they both view a TV program, listen to a story, or play a game, or are involved together in any other activity.

Nonmutuality is characterized by a lack of harmony in a dyad and includes characteristics of clash, avoidance, parallel experience, unilateral attentiveness, and asynchrony.

Dyadic Clash

A relationship characterized by dyadic clash is one in which both members of the dyad move toward the same object or goal with the intent of attaining one or the other only for themselves, excluding the other. For example, a young mother or father teases their young toddler by coaxing him to pick up a toy (truck) while simultaneously reaching for the truck themselves. At times a real tug of war ensues with parent and child vying for the same object. Within a different context a clash may ensue between therapist and patient about fees, time of session, or the like, each maintaining that their position is the one they had agreed on.

Dyadic Avoidance

A relationship characterized by dyadic avoidance is one in which both members of the dyad move in opposite directions with the intent of not coming to grips one with the other. For example, patient and therapist will intentionally avoid a subject about which they had clashed previously. Or a parent and child may turn away one from the other after an episode of clash.

Parallel Experience

This type of relationship looks different from the one defined in terms of dyadic avoidance in that each member of the dyad is interested in his or her own agenda. The parallel experience reflects a temporary disengagement from the other. In the therapist–patient relationship the patient may be musing or looking inward, and the therapist's mind may be wandering. In the parent–child relationship a similar situation may obtain.

Unilateral Attentiveness

A dyad is characterized by unilateral attentiveness when one member of the dyad seeks the attention of the other and the other avoids it. This can be seen in the patient–therapist relationship when one or the other member of the dyad seeks the other's attention but for unknown reasons is not responded to. Thus one or the other member is uninvolved. Often one observes this behavior with a parent and a young child, when the parent wants to read, write, cook, or the like and the child is clamoring for attention, "Look at me!" "Come and help!" or the like.

Asynchronous Transaction

An asynchronous transaction looks like one that could become synchronous at any moment, but is not. Reciprocity is not quite reciprocal, joint attention is not quite joint. An example of this situation is when the therapist and patient or parent and child is attempting to understand what the other is saying, but not quite getting it.

AIMS

In the interpersonal facet where each member is both entity unto him- or herself and responsive to the other in a profound way that transforms the other, even as both transact with one another, the aims of development entail achievement of both optimal *autonomy and interdependence* consistent with the maturational capabilities of each member of the system.

Autonomy

Autonomy emphasizes that the infant from birth on generates his or her own experience and knowledge because the individual comes into the world with a unique configuration of structures equipped to create psychological meaning from within.

Interdependence

Interdependence emphasizes that the infant from birth on derives the capacity to create meaning from his or her transactional association with caregivers. Interdependence also reflects the caregivers' dependence on their dependent infants or the therapist's need for his or her patients, to meet their needs for creativity and transmission, to continue their adult development.

CONSERVATIVE TENDENCIES

In the interpersonal facet, the conservative tendencies are principally interactional behaviors that emerge initially in infant–caregiver exchanges when the caregiver promotes or fails in his or her protective function of modulating stimulation and interacting reciprocally and in a coordinated fashion to help regulate the infant's tension states. When the protective function is promoted we speak of coping strategies; when there is failure in the protective function we speak of the development of maladaptive coping strategies. We observed and classified the following coping strategies aimed at promoting the protective function in an adaptive manner: realistic appraisal / engagement and agreement / cooperation. The armor of a dyadic system or of an individual determines how an individual or a system protects itself both consciously and preconsciously. Selma Fraiberg (1982) identified a number of maladaptive strategies that originate in infancy to cope with behavioral aspects of parental psychopathology that impede state- and emotion-regulating exchanges. These coping strategies include avoidance, freezing, fighting, transformation of affect, and reversal. Essentially, each strategy involves a perceptual–motor defense that obscures, blurs, or distorts the influence of the caregiver's misattunement to the infant's signals of needs and state. In our view, the crystallization of these behaviors as enduring aspects of the infant's interpersonal expectations and behaviors are engaged, and thus are defined and redefined, organized, and reorganized through action and transaction.

4

The Developmental Facet

Within the intrapersonal context of functioning, we distinguish three facets of psychological functioning, each informed by respective theoretical perspectives: the developmental, characterologic, and intrapsychic. Our view of psychological development is based on a combination of Piagetian and Vygotskyan theories and individual empirical researchers' thinking and findings. The assumptions underlying the developmental facet encompass the notions of epigenesis, continuity, and discontinuity over time. The characterologic and intrapsychic facets are based primarily on psychoanalytic theory, although new findings in developmental research and new conceptualizations about development, constitution, temperament, and maturation inform our view of the characterologic and intrapsychic facets. Each facet has its own assumptions, operating principles, and aims with respect to a number of domains.

The developmental facet is that the human being is a spontaneously active system in which internal activity rather than mere reactivity is fundamental. The autonomous functioning of the innate activities constitute the human organism's "drive" to perform certain activities and functions. At the developmental facet, the operating principles include organization, regulation, integration, and adaptation as defined by Sander (1987). These principles operate to yield continuity in and increasing differentiation and integration of goal-directed activities in the human being's ongoing attempts to realize developmental mandates while adjusting to the demands of the environment. The domains of the developmental facet consist of all the components underlying biopsychosocial adaptation, such as the neurophysical, motor, affective, cognitive, social relatedness, language, and fantasy, play and creativity. The aims of these principles are to fulfill biopsychosocial requisites, interest in novelty (exploration) and effectance, and the pursuit of social connectedness (see Table 4.1 for a summary of the developmental facet).

TABLE 4.1
The Developmental Facet of Psychological Functioning

Assumptions: Epigenesis, continuity, discontinuity
Principles: Organization, regulation, integration, adaptation

Domains	Aims	Conservative Tendencies
Neuromotor	Social connectedness,	Coping strategies
Cognitive	Novelty, exploration,	(Cs and Ucs)
Affective	Effectance and	[See Appendix B]
Social	biopsychological	
Language, Speech	requisites	
Fantasy, Play, Creativity		

ASSUMPTIONS

Three general assumptions pertain to the developmental point of view. Development is epigenetic, continuous, and subject to transformation.

The term *epigenesis* means that all aspects of development are subject to the governing maturational impetus of the individual. Within each phase of development, the developmental aims are tackled according to the maturational capacities that exist at the time.

40

The epigenetic assumption holds that each new phase of development embraces and integrates the previous phase(s) (Werner, 1948; Cassirer, 1955). Unresolved issues in the old phase tend to strain and made demands on the individual even as he or she attempts to meet the new emerging capabilities and the demands on adaptation they make. In this manner, the new tasks are met with the more or less integrated demands of the earlier ones and become imbricated in the new mode of adaptation.

The epigenetic assumption is anchored within a time dimension. However, both the sequence of developmental phases and the rate at which developmental capacities unfold tend to vary from individual to individual. Thus, even though crawling tends to precede walking, and gesturing tends to precede speech, there appears to be individual variability both in the sequence as well as in the rate of development. Within the confines of the dimension of time, ordinary development in infancy, as it is throughout the life cycle, is known to be uneven.

Theorists have identified a variety of progressive and stage-specific salient issues. We have drawn upon them all. From Freud's (1905) concept of psychosexual stages, Erikson's (1950) psychosocial developmental progression of intrapsychic and adaptive reorganization of ego structure, Spitz's (1959) progression of psychological organizers, and aspects of Mahler, Pine, and Bergman's (1975) progression of drive and ego structures as experienced within the matrix of self and other.

Greenspan's developmental model is particularly useful with regard to epigenesis (1975, 1979; Greenspan and Lourie, 1981). From his studies of infant and early childhood development, Greenspan has defined development in terms of a series of adaptive tasks that emerge with the maturation of physical and mental abilities in interaction with the environment. To grasp the complexities of the developmental progression, Greenspan has integrated behavioral, Piagetian, and ego psychological concepts to construct what he terms a *developmental structuralist* approach that anchors specific stages to phenomenologically derived observations. Moreover, Greenspan's stage theory integrates the individual's subjective and dyadic experiences from the point of view of both the infant and caregiver who promotes the achievement of developmental tasks. Greenspan's stage theory is consistent with Sander's (1975) observations that place emphasis on stage specific dyadic issues that accompany the infant's developmental transitions from one stage to another.

Stern's (1985) model is also developmental and relates to the epigenetic assumption. He focuses on the developmental progression of subjective experiences of self that unfold in the context of interpersonal transactions. The progression of subjective experiences of self creates a multilayered self organization in which each phase (layer) emerges diachronically but then operates synchronically with other phases of organized subjective experiences of self. Stern's (1985) model posits an organization of self that develops in an orderly temporal sequence from the emergent self (onset at birth), through the core self (onset at about 3 months), and the subjective self (onset at about 10 months), to the verbal self (onset at about 15 months). True to the epigenetic assumption, Stern maintains that each successive subjective organizing perspective requires the preceding one as a precursor. Once formed, however, all the domains of self and other-relatedness remain active during development and the life span. As Horner (1986) notes:

> While Stern emphasizes that the infant develops within domains of interpersonal relatedness, the subjective sense of self is there, pre-wired, *in statu nascendi*. By sense of self Stern means simple, non-reflexive awareness, an awareness that is presumably mediated by the perceptual–cognitive mechanisms which in turn yield, as development proceeds a sense of *organization, agency, physical cohesion, continuity and . . . transmitted meaning* [p. 7].[1]

---

[1] The substantive difference between Stern's and the other epigenetic models centers on three significant issues: The first is the nature of the central organizer within the human being; namely, it is a structure called the self. The second is the timetable of the earliest developmental and psychological capacities; all four forms of self development occur within the first 18 months. The third addresses how these capacities, whether in their emergent or fully symbolic forms, impinge on current functioning, whether these capacities can be apprehended in their original infantile forms, and whether they are transformed through further maturation and experience. Stern seems to imply that they are both subject to transformation but that they also can be expressed in their original

Continuity holds that developmental aims have their origin within the genetic and constitutional repertoire of the human organism. From birth on, then, the individual is guided by powerful genetic repertoires. Twin studies and temperament studies tend to corroborate the inherent stability of genetic influences (Plomin, 1986). Continuity and stability are also influenced by the constancy of the individual's general external environment and the constant patterns of the specific primary caregiver relationship with the infant. The relative constancy patterned relationship points to the significance of a transactional perspective. In this regard, Emde (1988a) writes, "continuity can be understood . . . in terms of consistency in the product of organism-environment interactions" (p. 28). Researchers agree (Stern, 1985; Sroufe and Fleeson, 1985; Beebe and Lachmann, 1988; Emde, 1988a) that it is not the individual characteristics of the infant that endure, but, rather, it is the interiorized relationship that endures and leads the maturing and developing individual to organize experience in ways consistent with expectations derived from interiorized patterned relationships. Thus early relational styles and patterns organize sensations, perceptions, affect, and states, which "get activated in similar relationship contexts throughout life" (Emde, 1988a, p. 28). Stern (1985) goes a step further in offering an explanation of the mechanism by which interactions become interiorized and yet may not be specifically retrievable. His concept of Representations of Interactions that have been Generalized (RIGs, p. 97), underscores that the mind generalizes experiences, and it is this generalization that accounts for the tenacious stability and continuity over time in spite of the diversity of experience. Unlike Bowlby's (1988) concept of "internal working models," which appear to be accessible to experience and seem to have a more straightforward reversibility, Stern's RIGS, because they are experiences that are generalized, cannot easily be broken down into their original parts and consequently cannot be thought of as easily retrievable.

---

infantile forms. Stern, then, holds to a modified view of epigenesis, which seems to be corroborated by our clinical observations.

Since organization of experience begins at birth (if not before), all experience is powerfully guided by precedent even when one takes full cognizance of the influence of maturation and transformation. In other words, how one has organized and organizes sensations, percepts, and thoughts together with their attendant affects, determines how one takes in and absorbs the next experience. As such, the more the individual changes, the more the individual nevertheless remains bound by the continuity of his or her experiences, simply because the manner in which ongoing experience is organized is based, in large part, on the way in which experience has been organized in the past. Thus, there develops a powerful interplay between the continuity of experience and the transformation, or discontinuity, of experiences.

Discontinuity, or transformation, in development is accounted for by maturation and experience which take place within the biobehavioral and the neurophysiological domains of functioning, as well as in consequence of the gradual unfolding and activation of genetic markers on the genetic map (Emde and Harmon, 1984). Transformations also take place at the intrapsychic and characterologic levels of functioning through processes of maturation as well as through mechanisms of repression and potential alterations of defenses, and coping strategies, and removal of resistances.

The individual, however, as a continuous, physically cohesive entity imbued with intentionality as agent in his or her modes of adaptation, remains the overall architect, primarily unconscious and in small part conscious, of whatever transformations take place at those levels of experience and behavior. As such, all transformations take place within the continuity of the individual (Stern, 1985, p. 6).

PRINCIPLES

The principles which seem to best explain human functioning from a developmental perspective are those defined by Sander

(1987) as organization, regulation, integration, and adaptation. Sander proposed these principles which we paraphrase as follows:

1. *Organization* is the individual's inherent biological capacity that predisposes him or her to organize experience into hierarchies both cross-sectionally and over time.

2. *Regulation* governs both temporal events, as they are apprehended, and states of the individual. Included in the principle of regulation are the "concepts of equilibrium as well as the autoplastic alloplastic modifications necessary to reach regulation" (p. 215).

3. *Adaptation* is related to the specific and mutual modification between the individual and the environment as well as to the achievement of enduring coordinations.

4. *Integration* rests upon a wide range of mechanisms such as intermodal mapping and amodal perception. Infants appear to experience a work of perceptual unity, which enables them to have a global perception regardless of the modality by which the perception is ordinally apprehended. [This capacity occurs within the neurophysiological domain where the enormous proliferation of cortical arborization in the immediate postpartum period achieves its peak at the end of the first year of life and gradually tapers off up to the fourth year (Huttenlocher, 1982). This intense activity at the cortical level is associated in the infant with high susceptibility to afferent stimulation, and therefore may be responsible for overriding specificity in hemispheric functions and for prompting the fluency of cross modal functions.]

It may be useful to point out that the above principles of development are consistent with Piaget's principles of accommodation, assimilation, and equilibration as regards cognitive functioning (1952). As defined by Sander (1987) and employed here, however, these principles are generalized and viewed as governing all aspects of human biological and psychological functioning.

45

DOMAINS

The domains of the developmental facet are classified here as the neuromotor, cognitive, affective, social, language (speech), play, fantasy, and creativity. Many developmentalists have contributed with their knowledge and research to elaborating on these empirically and clinically observed domains. We draw on Piaget (1952), Knobloch and Pasamanick (1974), Uzgiris and Hunt (1975), Hunt (1979), Izard, Huebner, Risser, McGinnis, and Dougherty (1980), Emde (1983), Demos (1984), and many others to define these domains.

Neuromotor

In the domain of the neuromotor one recognizes the gross and fine motor behaviors as they develop epigenetically and maturationally from headlifting when lying in a prone position, looking at a rattle, and taking a swipe at the rattle (at 3 days of age) to skipping, running, and coloring within the lines in a coloring book (4 years, 6 months). The physical motor coordination of an adolescent or an adult, can also be observed by the patterns of gross and fine motor movements, from the disjointed, erratic nature of movements to their easy, graceful, and well-coordinated flow.

Cognition

The cognitive intellectual domain can be seen in its earliest manifestations as the goal-directed neuromotor behaviors such as taking a swipe at a rattle (3 days). Rapidly the infant moves from beginning to coordinate various schemes of circular reactions to practicing means–end relationships, to developing the concept of object permanence. By the time a child has reached the age of 4, mental representations have come to stand for absent things or events. Language is the necessary tool for symbol formation and for the beginning of classifying objects, ideas, or events into meaningful categories. The capacity for seeing relationships between objects, ideas, and events continues to evolve through childhood, adolescence, and adulthood. Symbolic thinking leads to ever more complex forms of abstract thinking.

Affect

Affect is seen as a neurophysiological amplification of experience (Tomkins, 1980) or an expression of emotional experience (Emde, Gaensbauer, and Harmon, 1976; Izard, 1978). Very early in the human infant's life (from birth to 2 months) one recognizes signs and expressions of distress, rage, tension, pain and finally the appearance of the social smile. Soon (3–6 months) content-mediated affect appears (as in pleasurable assimilation, or disappointment and frustration when there is failure in assimilation). Laughter also appears as an excitatory process (Sroufe, 1979). By 7 months, interest, surprise, curiosity, excitement, apathy, listlessness, and disgust have joined the affective repertoire. By the time a child has established relationships (2–3 years), empathy, love, contempt, hate, jealousy, guilt, provocativeness and defiance have been added to the repertoire (a larger list of affects can be found in Appendix A).

In childhood, adolescence, and adulthood, these same affective experiences, together with seriousness, sensual, erotic and sexual excitement, as well as envy, terror, panic, and fear are also found. Thus the roots of a great many affective expressions can be traced to the age of 3, if not before, and most others to the age of 5 or 6. These emotional experiences become deeper and more developed with the development of cognition, social relatedness, language, and life experience.

Social Connectedness

Social connectedness is referred to here as the prewired inclination of the human infant to respond preferentially to its own kind (such as the human face, Fantz [1961]). While social connectedness cannot be separated entirely from social relationships, the attempt here is to define the person's capacity for engaging in social relationships by delineating certain attributes inherent in the human repertoire from birth on and what develops over time.

Of note is the infant's visual preference for the human face and the appearance of the social smile (birth to 2 months). The infant's reaching toward the human face, breast, arm, and fingers appear next. The capacity to show preference for the primary attachment figure (usually mother or father) is followed by manifestation of some distress at the appearance of a stranger (4 to 8 months). Some separation anxiety from the primary attachment figure appears subsequently between 9 to 18 months (Spitz, 1965; Mahler et al., 1975; and Emde, Gaensbauer, and Harmon, 1976). Disengagement from social connectedness also appears early in human development (Stern, 1974) and this tendency to disconnect can be seen as an attempt of the young infant at differentiation and further reintegration not only in the capacity to think, but also in the continued evolvement of social connectedness. Thus the "look at me" admiration seeking phenomenon (which appears at around 15 months and continues until greater social understanding has been achieved) is a manifestation of a new level of striving toward social connectedness associated with the development of autonomy (interpersonal facet), which Mahler, Pine, and Bergman (1975) call the separation–differentiation phase and the beginning of rapprochement.

The view presented here is that social connectedness is one of the developmental domains prewired and inherent in the individual and constitutes the foundations for social relationships. The kernels of social connectedness can be observed from infancy through adulthood.

Language

Language, defined as communication through vocalization, gesture, and speech, has been studied by many developmentalists (Bates, O'Connell, and Shore, 1987). Language is associated with cognition and intellectual functioning, with the modulation of affect, and the deepening of social relationships. Language is manifested through crying, vowel-like vocalization, and cooing (from birth to 3 months). The repertoire of vocalizations becomes enlarged by babbling and combines with consonants by 6 months. From 9 to 12 months, the infant has word sounds such as *mama* or *dada* and understands words like *no, stop,* or *all gone.* From 12 to 24 months, the vocabulary expands to include more single words and to understand simple instructions. From 2 to 3 years, the child acquires the capacity to use prepositions, such as *in, on, under, beside,* as well as the words *what, when, where,* and *why,* which form the foundation for furthering concrete and symbolic speech. From 3 to 5 years, the child has acquired the capacity to identify colors, shapes, numbers, and letters, can follow directions, and begin to talk about meaningful experiences.

Language and cognition are the two developmental domains that evolve and become ever more complex from early childhood through adulthood. It is beyond the realm of this book to address the expanding complexity of language and thought. For our purposes, it is sufficient that the clinician be able to recognize and identify these domains as modes and contents of therapeutic communication.

Play, Fantasy and Creativity

The child's play begins early in infancy with the repetition of movements, sounds, and games that have a predictable sequence and outcome, as well as an effect on others. Imitation is a significant component of early play; pretend activities (beginning at age 2) and symbolic play develop thereafter and form the underpinnings of fantasy which is defined as internalized play. While the functions of play and fantasy are to meet the aims of biopsychosocial requisites, social connectedness, and the pursuit of novelty, exploration, and effectance indirectly and symbolically, they can also result in the direct and concrete achievement of these aims. This happens especially when the energies of play and fantasy are directed toward the creation of a project, scientific, literary, artistic, or the like, that is shared with others or exists solely for the satisfaction of its creator. Much has been written on the subject by developmentalists and psychoanalysts alike such as Piaget (1952), and Winnicott (1971) among many others. Suffice to say here that these domains are also recognizable from earliest infancy through adulthood as modes and contents of therapeutic communication reflecting the internal preoccupations of the patient.

AIMS

If human functioning is internally motivated and goal-directed, and if all the elements of human capabilities are present from birth on, albeit in their most rudimentary forms, then the developmental agenda can be stated in universal terms, and one can say that what changes as a function of maturation and experience is the specific content of the agenda, but not its form. This is significant because without an equivalence in inherent motivations and goals, people would be unable to understand one another, parents would be unable to guess at the needs of their babies, strangers would be unable to intuit each other's states, and, for all intents and purposes, communication would be impossible. The common lexicon of communication between people, then, is based on a common developmental agenda. Based on the findings of research and the numerous clinical observations of infants, including our own, we have broadly classified the aims of psychological development into three large categories: the fulfillment of biopsychological requisites, the pursuit of social connectedness, and the search for novelty, exploration, and effectance. Others (e.g., Emde, 1983; Lichtenberg, 1989; Connell, 1990) have classified motivational systems into somewhat different categories, but all agree that a number of motivational systems operate simultaneously within each individual and guide behavior toward certain aims. Most of the proposed motivational systems include the three categories abstracted here.

Fulfillment of Biopsychological Requisites

At core, the human organism is governed by its biology, which becomes psychologically meaningful through the mediation of the affective, sensory, perceptual, and cognitive systems. Thus, the regulation of sleep cycles, respiration, gastrointestinal activity, elimination, circulation, and states of alertness lie within the individual's self-generating rhythms. The ebb and flow of affect, sensual pleasures, sensory perception, thought, language, and fantasy reflect psychological rhythms anchored in physiological correlates, and all are within the individual's organizational and regulatory capacities.

To be sure, the caregiver contributes to the infant's fulfillment and regulation of basic biological and psychological requisites, but the tendency toward organization and self-regulation is inherent within the infant's organism (Emde, 1983; Stern, 1985; Tronick and Gianino, 1986; Sander, 1987). Moreover, insofar as infants, as well as all (more mature) human beings, spend proportionately more time alone than with others, the task of internal regulation of biopsychological requisites remains essentially the task of the individual.

Pursuit of Social Connectedness

Emphasizing the reality of the infant's aloneness in no way diminishes the reality of the infant's total dependence on other human beings for survival. Research and evolving attachment theory

51

strongly support the view that humans at birth are prewired to seek social connectedness with other humans. The inherent attraction of one's own kind serves species preservation (Ainsworth and Bell, 1969; Bowlby, 1969), but the interest in the caregiver serves not only to seek provision for biologically based needs, but also to elicit response to an inherent need for social communication (Fantz, 1961; Carpenter, 1974; Sander, 1975; Bennett, 1976; Stern, 1977; Emde, 1983). Moreover, theoreticians like Winnicott (1960) and Bion (1962) have written evocatively on the clinical meaningfulness related to the significance of the mothering person as holder, container, and translator of experiences in the physical and psychological development of the infant. Thus, infants need their parents to recognize and meet their urges, needs, and wishes for human contact and relatedness as much as they need them for the recognition and gratification of various appetites and for the regulation or fulfillment of biopsychological requisites.

Pursuit of Novelty, Exploration, and Effectance

Interest in novelty, exploration, and effectance is a developmental aim demonstrated in the stimulus-seeking nature of humans from birth on (Hendrick, 1942; Piaget, 1952; White, 1959, 1963; Roffwarg, Muzio, and Dement, 1966; Korner and Thoman, 1972; Mahler et al., 1975). Capable of attentiveness, curiosity, and exploration through sensorimotor modalities, infants show pursuit of novelty through heightened alertness to novelty and through attempts at producing effects on the novel aspects of the object that have captured their interest. They respond to distal and proximal stimuli with a variety of behaviors, which include the physical musculature as well as the response variations available through the affective, verbal, cognitive, and social domains.

These three developmental aims are universal. What we wish to emphasize here is that the pursuit of these aims can be observed in humans from birth, and that these aims give impetus and direction to interpersonal interactions. The developmental aims are subsequently facilitated or constrained by the mutual influences of interpersonal transactions to configure the unique aspects of the characterologic and intrapsychic facets of the individual's psychological functioning.

This is how the three-pronged developmental aims intersect. In normal to moderately problematic infants, it is possible to observe that regardless of their developmental state, infants almost always show the pursuit of the three developmental aims. Only severely impaired babies may show a relative absence of one of the developmental aims. Very often the three aims function in complementarity, as can be seen, for example, when the infant moves smoothly between hungrily sucking on a nipple, playing with mother's bracelet, and looking into her eyes. At various points, however, the pursuit of one of the aims may be disrupted (e.g., then mother moves her arm, for example, or disrupts the mutual gaze by turning toward another object, or by removing the breast or bottle from the infant's mouth), leaving the infant to decide, based on what is available, what she or he will pursue next. The infant may clamor or cry for the nipple, or grasp at the bracelet. In any case, the disruption entails conflict; it may be a conflict between having and not having the nipple, or it may be a conflict of competing aims, such as wanting to look into mother's eyes, and wanting to play with the bracelet. How the conflict will be resolved will depend on the infant's own resourcefulness and on the response of the environment. If mother returns the gaze and coos, for example, that may satisfy the infant's achievement of social connectedness and temporarily diminish or efface the pursuits of novelty and effectance and of attempting to assuage the wish to be fed. If mother puts the infant down and leaves the premises altogether, the infant will be faced with a dilemma: it will either have to do without the mother, the bracelet, and the breast or bottle. What developmental aim will the infant then pursue? Perhaps the infant will look around the room and fix on a toy or mobile, or perhaps find its thumb and suck on it, or perhaps "fall out" into wailing, thrashing, and looking in the direction of the door, and manifest no evidence of curiosity or novelty seeking. Nothing will help until the infant either finds an object to fix on, or until mother returns with more feeding. With these examples, it can be seen that at times the infant will be able to pursue goals autonomously, fixate on new objects, and suck its thumb, and at other times it will require the assistance of the mother to resume the feeding, or perhaps burp and rock the baby to sleep.

In sum, these developmental aims are universal and cut across stage-specific theories such as identified by Freud (1905), Erikson (1950), Piaget (1952), Mahler et al. (1975), or Greenspan and Lourie (1981).

CONSERVATIVE TENDENCIES

The conservative tendencies that maintain organismic integrity threatened in the pursuit of their developmental aims include coping strategies and ego defense mechanisms. Coping strategies are primarily conscious or preconscious adaptations to internal or external demands. They serve to protect the fulfillment of biopsychological requisites, the need for social connectedness, and the thirst to learn, explore, and affect the environment. These coping strategies are the same as those mentioned in the interpersonal facet and those in the character facet (see definitions in chapter 5). Namely, realistic appraisal/engagement, agreement/cooperation, compliance/submission, externalization (flight), freezing/immobilization and transformation of affect.

Ego defense mechanisms come into play in cases where physical or psychological trauma and intrapsychic conflict have created developmental deficiencies or arrest. The ego defense mechanisms are elaborated on in the discussion of the intrapsychic facet.

5

The Characterologic Facet

We noted before that a transactional orientation provides a perspective from which to understand how an individual both changes and remains the same. In this connection, our perspective on character theory addresses the "constitutional" complementary aspects as well as the ongoing, continuous influence of the human being's initial patterning of behavior, emotional tone, attitudes, and values that constitute enduring interpersonal contingencies and attitudinal expectancies in interpersonal interactions. The organization of interpersonal contingency relations and behavioral as well as attitudinal expectancies as related to self experience and self-with-other experience remains influential throughout development in constructing novel experiences in familiar ways (Sroufe and Fleeson, 1985; Stern, 1985; Sander, 1987; Beebe and Lachmann, 1988; Emde, 1988a).

ASSUMPTIONS

Character theory takes account of the individual's constitutional endowment, his or her temperamental characteristics and maturational givens (Abrams, 1992; McLean, 1992; Schlesinger, 1992). In his *Introductory Lectures on Psychoanalysis* (1916–1917), Freud clearly expressed the idea of the complemental series in which factors of constitutional endowment are balanced against factors of experience and development. Most psychoanalytic contributions have focused on experiential or developmental factors, but recently the constitutional aspects of the genetic point of view have received increased attention. To paraphrase Schlesinger (1992, p. 228), the infant's temperamental characteristics, in particular the activity level and rhythmicity (Thomas and Chess, 1980), can be seen as behavioral manifestations of his or her attempt at self-regulation, in relation to the fulfillment of developmental biopsychosocial requisites (sleep, hunger, elimination, soothing, etc.), as well as in relation to intrapsychic needs, wishes, and fantasies, and in relation to the outside world, the world of people and things. In spite of much emphasis on character traits, fixations, and pathology (e.g., Abraham, 1921, 1924; Kohut, 1971; Kernberg, 1976), psychoanalytic theory does not have a theory of character, with the exception of Reich's (1949) work on character analysis and Melanie Klein's (1935, 1940, 1946) conceptualizations of the paranoid–schizoid and depressive positions that represent her effort to discern principles of personality organization (Schlesinger, 1992). We believe that based on the findings from infancy work, we now have many of the building blocks necessary to construct a character theory that informs our view on the character facet.

We believe Emde (1988b) is referring to the issue of character when he surmises that what we might regard as "constitutional," reflects the influence of the infant–caregiver relationship experience on motivational structures to yield a *unique bias on experience that is pervasive and resistant to later change in experience.* Sander's (1987) view on the bases of life-cycle continuity in self-experience is particularly relevant:

> Each infant–caregiver system constructs its own unique configuration of regulatory constraint on the infant's access to awareness of his or her own states, and on initiatives to organize self-regulatory behavior. These configurations then become a repertoire of enduring coordinations or adaptive strategies between the interacting participants and represent patterns unique to, and

characteristic for, each infant–caregiver system. These strategies set the conditions in the system by which infants can re-experience a knowing of, or recognition of themselves. Construction of experiences in which one recognizes oneself in terms of reexperiencing familiar states is the vehicle by which a sense of continuity of self is conveyed. The experience of self-recognition in these recurrent experiences constitutes a parameter that biases the infant's later construction of an ecologic niche in which these same strategies can be employed, which promises continuity in familiar inner experience [p. 218].

Thus, the individual is biased by his or her earliest experiences to "re-create situations for continuity and familiarity—with or without smoothness or pain and with varying degrees of openness to new experience and to new possibilities" (Emde, 1988b, p. 289). Character, then, denotes the parameters that bias the individual's ("constitutional") scope and complexity of involvement with internal and external stimuli. In general terms, character is defined in terms of resilience and strength: "resilience" refers to elasticity and the ability to rebalance one's subjective and objective orientation in confrontation with destabilizing change, and the ability to recover from unexpected assault to the organism; "strength" refers to pregnability yet firmness in maintaining general ideals and values, needs, wishes, hopes, aspirations, and ambitions (i.e., conserving all of one's interests) while pursuing a particular goal (see Table 5.1 for a summary of the character facet).

PRINCIPLES

Because character issues involve the continuity of experiences in relation to people and things based on constitutional and temperamental givens from birth on, the principles of organization that conserve the integrity of character are the same as the laws or principles of organization that govern interpersonal systems, which included *feedback, tension, equifinality, and disjoin.*

Table 5.1
The Character Facet of Psychological Functioning

Assumptions: Genetic, constitutional–biophysical and temperamental givens in interaction with the environment create character from birth on.
Principles: Feedback, tension, equifinality, disjoin

Domains	Aims	Conservative Tendencies
Self-Processes I, I/Me, Me/I, Ideal self Temperament regulation (Activity, Rhythmicity)	Elaborate on Self-Processes I, I/Me, Me/I, Ideal self Regulate temperament	Coping Strategies (Cs and Ucs) [See Appendix B] Character armor (Ucs and Cs) Defense-Transference (Ucs)

But the emphasis in character theory is on *how* the individual maintains the interpersonal, developmental, and intrapsychic aims. In this regard, the domains and aims of the character theory differ from the interpersonal systems theory.

DOMAINS

The domains of the characterologic facet are first and foremost the domain of regulation followed by forms and transformations of self experience, which entail what has been referred to as the subjective or experiential self (Jacobson, 1964; Kohut, 1971; Lewis and Brooks-Gunn, 1979; Pine, 1982; Emde, 1983; Stern, 1985; Horner, 1986), which we refer to as the sense of *I* and the self as it relates to the interpersonal world and is informed through engagement with or disengagement from that relationship, which we term the sense of I/Me and the sense of Me/I.

The Sense of I

The sense of I emerges from the infant's organization of unfolding sensorimotor, perceptual, cognitive, affective, social, and verbal domains of experience. Experientially, these encompass the physical, emotional, and cognitive products of the developmental aims and are inextricably part of the domain of self-regulation in all biopsychosocial spheres. The sense of I is the core of subjectivity informed by the developmental domains in the pursuit of biopsychological requisites, social connectedness, the pursuit of novelty, exploration, and effectance. Hoffer's (1949) "body ego," Kohut's (1977) "nuclear self," Pine's (1982) "experiential self," Lewis and Brooks-Gunn's (1979) "existential self," Emde's (1983) "pre-representational self," and Stern's (1985) "sense of emergent self," all refer essentially to the sense of I as conceptualized here.

The Sense of I/Me

The sense of I/Me develops in the process of identifying one's self in and with the transacting other. The development of the sense of I/Me is a two-step process of assimilation in which the infant first projects its feelings or sensations of self onto the parental figure, which the parental figure in some sense feeds back to the infant who, in turn, reinternalizes that feedback as conveying an aspect of "meaning" to the feeling—behavior that accompanied the projection. This process operates, in fact, like the mechanism of projective identification as first defined by Melanie Klein (1946).

The Sense of Me/I

The sense of Me/I represents an alternating process of the infant's perceiving of his or her own image as reflected in the response of the significant other. Whereas the I/Me process is prompted by the infant's search for identity in the other, finding one's own kind, as it were, and thereby establishing object-relatedness in the self, the Me/I process represents the alternating moments in which the reflected image the infant perceives in the other is incongruous with the infant's sense of I. When the infant finds himself or herself in the parent's mirroring response, it finds a selfobject as defined by Kohut. When the infant perceives an imperfect, distorted, or incongruous reflection of its state of being, a discrepancy or mismatch occurs. This discrepancy interrupts the I and I/Me identity, creating instead a sense of estrangement, disidentity, followed by disengagement. Given that this disidentity occurs in contrast with the I/Me function in the pursuit of a self-with-other (Stern, 1983) or selfobject relationship (Kohut, 1971, 1977), the disidentity or estrangement is from one's own sense of subjective self, I and I/Me. The alternation of the I/Me and Me/I processes generate a dynamic tension. The sense of disidentity motivates a process of accommodation in the renewed search and pursuit of identity. To the extent that the infant experiences consistency in refinding the sense of I/Me, it will move progressively toward an awareness and appreciation of the otherness of the other and, simultaneously, will move forward in the internalization of a dialogue, and, as such, the development of an observing ego. That is, the infant will come to understand that the incongruity between perception and expectation reflects the differing perspective on the self of the interacting other, and may learn that taking that perspective may provide an empathic route to understanding one's self through promoting a harmonious relationship that refinds the desired self state and sense of I/Me identity. The harmonious relationship is initially pursued through an external relationship, but with development the relationship is pursued both through external relationships with others and through internal relationships between an objectifying or observing ego and subjective states of I. In short, the elaboration of this process allows one to look at one's self as though through the eyes of the other. And the process contributes to the creation of an "observing ego," and constitutes the underpinnings for the capacities to develop a "therapeutic split" between self-observation and self-experience. All this occurs in the more or less average, normal processes of infant–other relationships.

To the extent that the infant experiences inconsistency in refinding the sense of I/Me in the parental figure's response, its sense of estrangement continues. But congruity-incongruity is never an either–or proposition, for perfect "mirroring" is impossible; every response has aspects that are incongruous with expectations. Whether the sense of Me/I estrangement shapes a healthy sense of isolated aloneness or an unhealthy sense of insulated loneliness (Winnicott, 1963) may depend upon the extent to which the parental figure's incongruous response is felt by the infant to be more an assault or intrusion than a misunderstanding or lack of understanding. The perception of assault or intrusion would force the infant's sense of I into hiding to preserve itself, as is the case with children who are abused but manage to grin at their victimizers for the sake of self-preservation. Furthermore, the perception would also distort and burden the accommodative processes of the sense of Me/I to function as proxy for the I/Me. In sum, the I, I/Me, and Me/I processes evolve, alternate, and complement one another in an ongoing dialectic of personal and social meaning making.

The Ideal Self

The concept of the ideal self is based on Freud's (1914a) early concept of the "ego ideal" and Chasseguet-Smirgel's (1976) elaboration of it. But the term *ideal self* replaces *ego ideal* to reflect, in our view, the origin of the function it denotes in the primary formation of the infant's character and sense of self.

The ideal self receives its impetus from the evolving I and I/Me processes, which involve the infant's projections of I onto the parent. The ideal self derives form and image from the Me/I processes, which represent the parent's interpretive reflections of the infant's needs, wishes, and aspirations. The parent's interpretations always include an aspect of mismatched attunement—one adaptively based on an appropriately progressive view of the infant's emerging potentialities (e.g., Vygotsky's [1978] "zone of proximal development") or maladaptively based on the parent's egocentric view of the infant as mere extension of the parent's self-needs, wishes, and aspirations (parent's I/Me). The infant internalizes the reprojections from the parent onto the infant to constitute a *parental imago*. In other words, the part played by the I/Me processes in developing the ideal self derive from the infant's narcissistic, exhibitionistic, and grandiose projections onto the parent, which are understood by the infant-child as reflecting characteristics of the parent. But the "parent" is actually a parent–infant relationship that represents something the infant "creates" to contain and shape its creativity. The sense of Me/I that represents alternating moments of mismatch between the infant's state of being and his or her perception of the caregiver's reflecting gaze signals object loss. Initially, the lost object is a desired state of being, later it is the loving and facilitating parent, and later yet it is the parental imago that functions as an internal caregiver of the I. The Me/I disengagement creates a gap between self and object (other), a loss of connection and identity, and thus creates a psychological space that the infant-child may fill with preconceptual symbols, such as the objects of "transitional phenomena" (Winnicott, 1953). The sensorimotor–affective symbols embody the core experiential elements of the infant's nascent aspirations, ambitions, and hopes, and the symbols constitute the early formation of the ideal self. The world belongs to the infant, but, as represented in the parent's reflecting responses to the infant's creative projections, it is a world with an ever-expanding horizon: "I create the world that is my/other (mother) who provides me the world to create." The core of the ideal self represents the parent's empathic recognition of the infant's unfolding potentialities and promise of fulfilled ambitions, engendered in the infant by I/Me experiences that identify and satisfy but elude permanent attainment. The ideal self serves as a beacon to orient the direction of pursuit in resolving tension between the I/Me and Me/I processes. It might be said that the ideal self constitutes the space between the I/Me and Me/I senses of self, a space within which the I creates itself and the world.

AIMS

The aims, then, of the characterologic principles center on the development and elaboration of self-processes into a coherent sense of self and self-awareness, creation of coherent and consistent meanings grounded in reality and informed by personal fantasy and inventiveness, and the development of a character armor (Reich, 1949) that has sufficient resistance to ward off environmental overstimulation or malignant environmental influences, but also has sufficient flexibility to absorb new and necessary input to assure adaptive connection with the outside world. The characterologic aims also shape and reshape the ideal self.

CONSERVATIVE TENDENCIES

The conservative characteristics of the characterologic facet include coping strategies as well as resistances that take the forms of character armor (Reich, 1949) and defense transference (Schlessinger and Robbins, 1983).

At the core, coping strategies which were listed in the discussion of the interpersonal facet signify the individual's attempt to adapt and accommodate his or her sense of self to the exigencies of the human or nonhuman environment. We will expand on coping strategies here.

Coping Strategies

We have defined coping strategies according to the definitions offered by Lazarus, Averill, and Opton, Jr. (1974), who emphasized the mediating cognitive processes of appraisal, or the perceptual processes of infancy, as did Fraiberg in 1982. According to these observers, coping strategies distinguish the potentially harmful from the potentially beneficial, or irrelevant. Lazarus et al. do not view coping behaviors as responses designed to reduce an emotional mediator, but rather as responses "to the perception of some threatening condition and of potential avenues of mastery" (p. 259). That is why they represent, in our theory, the primary conservative tendencies of the character facet, as well as of the interpersonal and developmental facets, since they deal with the commerce between the inner experience of appraisal and the perception of an external environmental or interpersonal condition. Also, we agree with these theorists that the coping strategies are not subject to the dynamic unconscious (repression), but we suggest that they belong to the purview of the descriptive unconscious, as in unawareness, as well as to the conscious adaptive and maladaptive repertoire of the individual.

In our clinical experience, we have observed the following coping strategies in the diagnostic and treatment process. These are by no means exhaustive and represent a mere beginning at classification. What we can say, with a degree of assurance, however, is that we have observed them in a wide array of patients, from infants to adults, and across the gamut of psychopathology (see also Appendix B).

Realistic appraisal, engagement: being able to assess a situation without distortions and with a sense that one's perceptual apparatus has taken in the situation, and therefore has become engaged in it.

Agreement, cooperation: to have appraised a situation, agreed with it, and engaged one's efforts to collaborate with it.

Avoidance, disengagement: to remove oneself from a situation and focus one's attention and percepts elsewhere.

Externalization, blame: to attribute one's own mishaps, negative acts, feelings, thoughts to the outside, and attribute responsibility to others.

Defiance, fight: to challenge another's acts, thoughts, wishes, opinions, and develop a quarrel or battle (Fraiberg, 1982).

Disconnect, flight: to break off contact from a situation or person and run away (Fraiberg, 1982).

Freezing, becoming immobilized: to come to a halt, a total standstill, due to an all encompassing danger and fright (Fraiberg, 1982).

Transformation of affect: to manifest an opposite feeling on one's face than one experiences internally (Fraiberg, 1982).

Resistances signal conflict in interpersonal transactions or with the world of things, and aim to protect the individual's sense of continuity within the self processes. In this connection, Reich's (1949) conceptualization of "character armor," and, especially, Schlessinger and Robbins' (1983) conceptualization of the "defense transference," are relevant to our views on characterologic resistance. The character armor can be flexible and permeable allowing for the absorption of new experiences, leading to new solutions in relation to intrapsychic conflicts and developmental competing tendencies, experience, knowledge, and subsequent change; or it can be inflexible and impermeable so as to ward off and turn away from new experience and knowledge. The character armor tends to be preconscious, as in the meaning of the "descriptive" unconscious; in this definition, disavowal would be the main defensive maneuver. Coping strategies may be more conscious, insofar as they reflect the individual's awareness of the efforts and methods employed to balance assimilative needs and accommodative demands for adaptation.

Reich's notion of character armor describes a rigid protective shield that armors the ego against internal and external stimuli that threaten disruption of smooth, pain-free functioning. Formulated in the terms of Freudian drive theory, Reich's concept describes the armoring of the ego through identification with frustrating reality (caregiver), turning the anxiety-inducing aggression stimulated by the frustrating caregiver back onto the self, and the formation of reactive attitudes by the ego to ward-off expression of sexual impulses for fear of punishment. Reich believed that character armor made every patient inherently resistant. (Accordingly, he advised a "systematic resistance analysis" as the first line of intervention in every psychoanalytic treatment.)

Schlessinger and Robbins (1983) developed a concept of what is essentially character resistance in what they term *defense transference*. They link their concept to Mahler's (e.g., Mahler et al., 1975) theory of separation-individuation, and suggest that defense transference reflects the individual's solution to the object relations conflicts of separation and individuation. This can only be a temporary solution in psychoanalytic treatment, but may be a necessary one in protecting the individual from unmanageable tension states. And this internalized pattern of interpersonal tension-regulation "establishes the limits and distortions of and the necessary support systems for the developing ego functions" (p. 205). Schlessinger and Robbins emphasize that the defense transference is meaningfully defined primarily in relation to its influence on determining the conditions for the later development of oedipal anxieties and psychoneurotic problems, though they do not extend their concept to describe character pathology, per se. For our purposes, their concept is most useful in identifying an individual's developmental patterning of character constrictions that grow out of interpersonal conflicts. The latter set the balancing point around which the individual must attend to the conservative concerns of self-protection on the one side, while being free to attend to the progressive concern of pursuing developmental strivings and ambitions on the other.

6

The Intrapsychic Facet

Our view of the intrapsychic facet, of course, derives largely from psychoanalytic theories. The perspective on this facet attempts to understand the individual from within, becoming acquainted with the individual's unique structuralization of needs, wishes, fears, anxieties, and conflicts, which are manifested (and structured) through personal expressions in interpersonal exchanges (nonverbal as well as verbal), ruminations, reminiscences, dreams, fantasies, and defensive phenomena. This perspective provides a means by which the therapist can attempt to learn the language of an individual's inner meanings, a language that entails a dialogue and dialectic between the objective knowledge of formal reality (secondary process) and the symbols of a subjective personal reality and unconscious processes (primary process).

ASSUMPTIONS

Psychoanalytic theories are based on three broad assumptions: unconscious processes, psychic determinism, and multiple function.

It is a psychoanalytic tenet that psychological experience and action are governed by *unconscious processes*, that is, processes operating mostly outside of conscious awareness. This is how Freud (1923) defined the descriptive unconscious. Basch (1988) refined Freud's concept to define the descriptive unconscious as representing the activity of the brain of which one is not aware. Basch's definition might be broadened to include one's unawareness, inattentiveness, and inability to know about the inordinately complicated processes within the brain that dictate decision making at the most elemental level of functioning. The dynamic unconscious arises out of intrapsychic conflict, and is governed by the rules of displacement, condensation, and symbolism. Whereas the descriptive unconscious processes are present from birth on, the dynamic unconscious processes develop with the acquisition of symbolic communication and language combined with conflict deriving from *competing tendencies* (a term developed by Klein [1976]) within or between the developmental aims, the self processes, the ideal self, and the ego and superego processes (for a summary on the intrapsychic facet see Table 6.1).

The concept of *psychic determinism* is the bedrock of psychoanalytic thought (Waelder, 1936; Arlow and Brenner, 1964). Together with the assumption of unconscious processes, psychic determinism constitutes the most powerful thesis affirming that the contents of human feelings, thoughts, and behaviors are psychically determined and psychologically meaningful.

As introduced and defined by Waelder (1936), the concept of *multiple function* speaks to the complexity of divergent and convergent influences that impel the individual's action. As such, the concept denotes the assumption that any given behavior can be expected to serve several functions: the behavior represents a response to many pressures from within and without, and it can reflect a solution to a number of adaptive tasks. Whereas psychic determinism emphasizes the significance of psychological meaning that underlies and determines our sensations, perceptions,

TABLE 6.1
The Intrapsychic Facet of Psychological Functioning

Assumptions: Unconscious processes, psychic and multiple determinism
Principles: Compulsion to repeat, transference, construction and reconstruction of personal reality and meaning

Domains	Aims	Conservative Tendencies
Ego Superego Ucs wishes, needs, imagery, fantasies	Make the Ucs, PreCs, Cs Resolve: Compulsion to repeat, Disabling transferences, Consolidate ego functions	Ego defense mechanisms (Ucs) [See Appendix C] Transference (Ucs)

and attributions, and impels our actions, multiple function emphasizes that many determinants underlie the psychological meanings the individual attributes to experience.

PRINCIPLES

The operating principles of the intrapsychic facet consist of the compulsion to repeat, transference, and the construction and reconstruction of personal reality and meaning. Like all the operating principles described with respect to the other facets of psychological functioning, these operating principles are related to one another in that they share in common a more general organizing principle that encompasses conservative and progressive processes.

Because we see a need to emphasize the progressive side of the organizing principles, we prefer the expression *compulsion to repeat* (c.f., Freud, 1914b; Yahalom, 1993) over the term *repetition compulsion* (Freud, 1920). The principle of compulsion to repeat emphasizes this progressive inclination. Freud's (1920) concept of the repetition compulsion emphasized a pathological aspect of the conservative tendency of the human organism, a principle of conservation (or constancy) that he located in the realm and purposes of the death instinct. Hartmann's (1939) elaboration of the concept linked it to the Zeigarnik (1927) effect, which, in essence, identifies a human tendency to hold in mind, as it were, tasks that have been partly completed and carry tension (in memory) associated with the pleasurable results promised with their completion. Hence, the repetition compulsion can also be understood to carry a progressive tendency within it. However, because the term continues to connote psychopathology, we prefer the expression *compulsion to repeat*. Thus, we view the compulsion to repeat in terms of an individual's inclination to return to those activities which carry the unfinished business and promise of partially successful strivings that have been repeatedly blocked from completion by impeding organizations of experience derived through the transactions of developmental aims and interpersonal transference-laden contexts.

Transference, as defined by the American Psychoanalytic Association's *Glossary of Psychoanalytic Terms and Concepts* (Moore and Fine, 1968), is "the displacement of patterns of feelings and behavior, originally experienced with significant figures of one's childhood, to individuals in one's current relationships. This unconscious process thus brings about a repetition, not consciously perceived, of attitudes, fantasies, and emotions of love, hate, anger, etc. under many different circumstances" (p. 92).

In Freud's papers on technique (1911–1915), he works through the puzzlements of transference to a solution that encompasses both the conservative and progressive aspects of transference (e.g., 1912a, 1914b). The conservative aspect entails assimilating contemporary circumstances to repeat (rather than remember and report) an early patterning of a wish-bound object relationship. But the repetition of an earlier relationship in a current relationship activates the wishes attached to the earlier relationship to define the current relationship in intrapsychic reality. It is the accommodative nature of wishes that provides the progressive potential in the transference activity—wishes seek satisfaction and will follow the most expedient and immediate route to their realization and resolution. This, of course, provides an opportunity for their refinement and elaboration under the guiding as well as constraining conditions of contemporary external reality.

The *construction and reconstruction of meaning* refers to the changes that take place within the individual's unconscious ideas and fantasies, or within the infant's specific or generalized (e.g., Stern, 1985 [RIGs]), affective, sensorimotor memories. In this connection, Modell's (1990) clarification of Freud's concept of "Nachtraglichkeit" is particularly relevant, for his reexamination of the concept emphasizes the active nature of memory and meaning making. In this view, memory is not a mere matter of retrieval, but, rather, a matter of retranscription of past experience and attached meanings. Past experience and attached meanings are stimulated by current circumstances and are rearranged in accordance with current circumstances. This concept, then, highlights how the pursuit of continuity entails change; "memories" and meanings are revised in the process of a reconstructed and reconstructing recollection. (Piaget's concept of assimilation-accommodation describes this process too, but in terms of an individual's construction and reconstruction of logical reality.)

INTRAPSYCHIC DOMAINS

We include a separate section here on the domains of the intrapsychic dimension to clarify our particular uses of and elaborations on traditional conceptualizations of these domains. The domains of the intrapsychic dimension are the familiar ego, superego, and all the wishes and needs engendered by the developmental domains and expressed in the sense of I, the classical concept of the id (Freud, 1923) without its drive component, and the ego psychological concept of autonomous ego functions (Hartmann, 1939). The character domains of the sense of I and the ideal self are transactional conduits to the intrapsychic facet of functioning.

Ego

We use the concept *ego* in the way it has evolved in, primarily, psychoanalytic ego psychology advanced through the work of Hartmann (e.g., 1939), pursued by Rapaport (1967) and his followers at the Menninger Clinic, and elaborated and refined in the recent work of Greenspan (1979, 1989). Greenspan has integrated clinical and research findings on infants with a psychological theory that itself integrates Piagetian and ego psychological views. The concept *ego* refers to functions that serve to synthesize internal tensions between competing tendencies of the developmental domains as manifested by needs, wishes, fantasies, and dreams.

Superego

Our use of the concept *superego* is fairly conventional. The superego represents internalized moral–ethical parental and societal standards in what is commonly referred to as conscience. We should mention in brief the differentiation we make between our concepts of the ideal self and the superego, however. Whereas the ideal self represents one's sense of self-affirmation and evolving identity through an affectively attuned interpersonal recognition of desire and ambition, the superego represents one's sense of responsibility in integrating internalized personal strivings with an attuned awareness of societal requisites to maintain civilized standards. Disturbances of the ideal self make one vulnerable to shame and experiences of persecution, anaclitic-type depressions, or manic-like flights into an illusory state of self-sufficient omnipotence. Disturbances of the superego make one vulnerable to guilt and ("introjective") depression, as well as the compromise solutions expressed in obsessive–compulsive, hysterical, and phobic psychoneurotic disturbances and character neuroses.

AIMS

The aims of the intrapsychic facet and its domains consist of strengthening and expanding the ego's functions, strengthening and diminishing where necessary the superego's functions, making the unconscious conscious, resolving disabling compulsions to repeat and disabling aspects of transference inclinations.

CONSERVATIVE TENDENCIES

We refer to the conservative tendencies to maintain personality integrity within the intrapsychic facet as defense mechanisms. These are the ego's defense mechanisms as defined by Anna Freud (1936) (denial, repression, projection, reaction formation, and the like) that have been amply explored and described by psychoanalytic investigators. (For a more complete list of defenses see Appendix C.) Defense mechanisms are by definition dynamically unconscious attempts at adaptation.

SUMMARY

In sum, we believe our theoretical model of psychological functioning is necessary to grasp the complexities of interpersonal and intrapersonal transactions in the individual and in psychodynamic psychotherapy, as well as in parent–infant transactional therapy. This model allows one to view the simultaneous effects of a given intervention within a number of contexts and facets of functioning, the intervention assuming different functions depending on the developmental levels of the participants, and being understood by each according to his or her emotional and cognitive capabilities. That is, insofar as the infant and parent(s) operate as a unit, one can view the ongoing transactions of the relationship as manifestations of the psychic structure of each individual, as well as a manifestation of their relationship as a larger system.

7

Regarding Diagnosis: Deficits, Delays, Arrests, and Conflicts

Psychological treatment obviously requires some understanding of the problems a patient presents if treatment planning and strategies are to be effective. As commonly construed, treatment is to diagnosis what an answer is to a question or what a solution is to a problem. In psychodynamic treatment, diagnosis and treatment evolve first diachronically and then synchronically and reciprocally. That is, therapists usually draw diagnostic formulations from an initial phase of evaluation and then plan and initiate treatment strategy accordingly. Once treatment proper has begun, diagnostic considerations are woven into the treatment process by virtue of interventions that stimulate activity that refines the patient's and therapist's understanding of the nature of the problems. The ongoing refinement of understanding of the nature of the problems, is itself an integral aspect of the therapeutic effect of psychodynamic treatment.

Like all clinically oriented psychodynamic theories since Freud's, the theory of psychological functioning presented here was substantively shaped by diagnostic questions that pursued understanding of behavioral and mental disorder through exploration of innate and experiential influences and processes that deviate from normalcy to engender disordered functioning. The resulting theory, in turn, gives direction in indicating how psycho-pathology seen through a multifaceted prism on psychological functioning can be understood and classified with a view toward remediation through treatment.

Psychodynamic clinicians strive to understand and diagnose the presenting problems of patients through evaluation of the patient's overall personality functioning, including healthy as well as deviant attributes, within which presenting problems manifest themselves. The complexity in the diagnosis of personality organization is reflected in the absence of agreement within the mental health field, in general, and psychoanalysis, in particular, as to what constitutes the best organizational framework or criterion for diagnostic assessment.

Since 1980, which followed the pioneering efforts of the GAP (Group for the Advancement of Psychiatry, 1966), the American Psychiatric Association's editions of the *Diagnostic and Statistic Manual* (DSM-III, DSM-III-R, DSM-IV) have emphasized an empirical–descriptive orientation that focuses on manifest symptoms clustered and classified in terms of observable behavior (APA, 1980, 1987, 1994). Psychodynamic clinicians find the approach inadequate insofar as it emphasizes manifest behaviors, signs, and symptoms to an extent that tends to reduce the significance given to the individual's personality organization within which the manifest disturbances arise as just that, disturbances often reflecting personality organizational difficulties in managing some transactional combination and conflict of internal and external forces. For the psychodynamic therapist, a simple phobia manifested in an individual suffering from a severe personality disorder entails a very different problem with very different treatment implications than a simple phobia manifested in an individual whose overall level of adaptive functioning is relatively intact. (Greenspan and Polk [1980] have a more detailed discussion of the limitations of an empirical–descriptive approach in delineating the developmental and psychostructural aspects of functioning necessary to place manifest symptoms in therapeutically meaningful and useful contexts.) With regard to personality organization, psychodynamic clinicians often find the empirical–descriptive approach to personality disorders (axis II) provides insufficient support for or guidance in treatment planning. The atheoretical DSM approach now eschews the psychoanalytic assumptions that brought these disorders to light and which link and group these disorders by spectrum or continuum of psychostructural as well as psychodynamic issues. (In this connection, see, for example, Kernberg's [1984] discussion on the problems in classification of personality disorders.)

Consequently, psychodynamic diagnosticians typically supplement their DSM-based descriptive formulations with assessments and formulations of some combination of developmental, psychodynamic, psychostructural, and perhaps family systems issues. The diagnostician's choice or emphasis on these various perspectives on diagnostic evaluation generally depends on her or his theoretical bent. But a psychodynamic perspective hosts an array of theories, none entirely compatible with the others and each tending to highlight different aspects of psychological experience. Different diagnosticians favoring one or another of the theories of Freudian/ego psychological, Kleinian/Bionian, British object relations, self psychology, and the like, would select and order observations on the same patient to construct diagnostic formulations that differ in what they focus on and emphasize as the most salient issues underlying the patient's disordered functioning. Grotstein (1988) articulates both the strength and weakness of the various theoretical perspectives available to the diagnostician–therapist when he likens the use of psychoanalytic theories to the tissue and cell stains used by bacteriologists, histologists, and pathologists to highlight specific features in the microscopic field but at the expense of other features necessarily eclipsed to allow the sought-after element to be exposed. Whereas, however, a bacteriologist is aware of the limitations of a particular tissue stain, psychoanalytic clinicians may not be as inclined to acknowledge limitations in the use of preferred theoretical perspectives, for each of the psychoanalytic tissue stains, as it were, theoretically can make sense of and understand all data from all patients. Increasingly, however, owing to the integrative efforts of psychoanalytic thinkers like Grotstein, psychoanalysis has begun to move toward a generative integration and synthesis of different perspectives. (See, in this regard, Solomon's [1992] encyclopedia of reviews on psychoanalytic writings contributing to a movement toward multiple-model perspectives.) As such, some clinical theorists have advanced models that advocate listening perspectives that make use of the different effectiveness of a variety of theoretical orientations to raise into high relief different aspects of human experience (e.g., Hedges, 1983; Pine, 1988, 1990; Chessick, 1989). Other theorists have integrated psychoanalytic theories as well as findings from infant research, cognitive psychology, neuroscience, and psychopharmacology to construct theories that advance development of an interdisciplinary approach in psychodynamic theory and diagnostic and therapeutic practice (e.g., Gedo, 1979, 1981, 1988; Greenspan, 1979, 1981, 1989; Grotstein, 1980, 1983, 1984a, 1984b, 1988).

We believe the multifaceted theory of psychological functioning can provide a framework that enhances the comprehensive diagnosis of the facets and domains of experience relevant to understanding psychopathology in the individual and in the individual's relationships. As is the case with most other psychodynamic approaches to diagnostic evaluation, our model is used to supplement the descriptive approach (DSM). After all, one must be able, no matter the differences, to maintain a common language within our common field. We should reiterate, however, that the focus of this book is on therapeutic transactions. What follows, then, is not an attempt to construct a model of psychopathology, nor is it an attempt to apply the theory to any or all specific classifications of forms of disorder. Rather, the effort will focus on use of the model for evaluating the relative strengths and weaknesses in the multiple dimensions and domains of psychological functioning relevant to understanding the influence of the patient's psychological organization in shaping the manifest symptomatology.

FORMS OF DISTURBANCE

Forms of disturbance can be categorized into deficits (defect and/or deficiency), delays, arrests, and conflicts. Deficits refer to a missing or inadequate capacity in any one or more aspects of functioning that hinder the pursuit of interpersonal, developmental, characterologic, or intrapsychic aims within the interpersonal and intrapersonal contexts. A deficit may reflect a defect (lack or failing) in the biological substrate, owing to congenital or to anatomical–neurochemical alterations induced by physical or psychological trauma. This creates a deficit in capacity for attention, concentration, information-processing, regulation of state, and affective arousal contributing to learning disorders, attention-deficit disorders, endogenous major affective disorders, some forms of drug addictions, and at least some variants of schizophrenic illness, to name a few. Defects, of course, engender deficiencies (insufficiencies), but not all deficiencies entail defects. That is, deficiency emphasizes psychological and social implications. A child who grows up in an environment severely impoverished in the instrumental and emotional support it provides, is vulnerable to suffering deficiencies in psychological organization that reflect the deficiencies in the facilitating environment. Deficit by deficiency seems to imply greater possibility of reversibility than does deficit by defect. But as the literature on stress, vulnerability, coping, and resilience indicates, early experiences in adequate nurturing and nurturance lowers vulnerability and increases resilience to stress, but does not significantly distinguish between deficit by defect or by deficiency. Findings from therapeutic interventions indicate that deficiency generally requires stimulation of dormant capacities, whereas defect requires activation and generalization of use of intact compensatory capacities (Garmezy, Masten, and Tellegen, 1984; Rutter, 1985, 1987; Anthony, 1987; Cohler, 1987).

Delays are maturationally or emotionally based lags in functioning in which there is evidence, based on physical and psychological tests or on clinical observations that causes one to surmise the existence of intact constitutional or genetic bases of functioning. Delays point to biopsychosocial deficits, that may reflect arrest by trauma or inhibition by inter- or intrapersonal conflict.

Arrests entail the temporary or permanent cessation of development of one or more aspects of psychological functioning because of physical or psychic trauma that also involves aspects of inter- and intrapersonal conflict. Conflicts entail problems that ensue with competing or incompatible aims, and they typically involve and perpetuate deficiencies arising, for example, from problems in "goodness of fit" (Thomas and Chess, 1980) between child and parent. These engender deficiencies in reciprocal communications necessary to facilitate self-regulation in inter- and intrapersonal commerce that activates, encourages, and promotes progress in the pursuit and achievement of the aims of the various domains of psychological functioning.

The initial diagnostic evaluation and profile of a parent–infant dyad or of an individual patient may emphasize one or another of these forms of disturbance, but with the onset of treatment and the deepening of the therapeutic process, aspects of each, deficit, delay, arrest, conflict, are likely to emerge. Any of these forms of disturbance may take foreground prominence within either context and within any dimension of functioning at any particular time of treatment. Identification of the most salient form of disturbance at any particular moment is important for selecting the appropriate therapeutic intervention. That is, the therapist applies small therapeutic interventions (bids) on a moment-to-moment basis, so it becomes important to consider what aspect or form of a disturbance is being addressed when choosing a particular bid. On the other hand, the kinds and relative frequencies of bids used spontaneously by the therapist can provide important information as to the presence of deficits, delays, arrests, and conflicts and their location in the inter- and intrapersonal context.

Deficits require interventions that tend to emphasize modeling and contingent responsivity in the forms of imitating, reflecting, and labeling, and sometimes containment, as well as didactic and expanding modes of intervention that enlarge the individual's knowledge and skills (the interventions will be described in detail in chapter 9). Delays are typically treated as deficits until it can be determined whether the delay entails most predominantly a deficit, arrest, or conflict. Interventions, then, would be pitched to address the contributions of these forms of disturbance on the delay. Arrests are associated with traumas that bring development within certain domains (affect, cognition, social relatedness, physical motor patterning, language, play, and creativity) to a halt. As such, arrests are treated as both deficits and conflicts. Reflective and didactic bids that address deficits are supplemented by internally integrating and insight-orienting modes of intervention that point to and make use of what is new in the present situation in order to recast and thus reintegrate knowledge derived from the past. When addressing an arrest, then, the therapeutic response may highlight deficit aspects, intervening with teaching, modeling, and contingent responsivity, but at other times, the therapeutic response may highlight conflict aspects, intervening with self-observation, probing, and interpretation.

As can be seen, categorizing disturbance into deficits, delays, arrests, and conflicts does not divide them into mutually exclusive conditions. We agree with Greenspan (1989), who contends that deficits, for example, are not products of only prerepresentational levels of psychological organization, and that conflicts are not created only with the establishment of representational or symbolic capacities. Deficits create conflicts and conflicts create deficits. A frequently cited example in the clinical literature drawn from infant research may be illustrative. An infant at play with a parent will normally look away briefly from the parent (disengage) and then look back (reengage). The infant's looking away functions to lower the level of stimulation (external) so as to lower the level of arousal (internal). If the parent reciprocates in a complementary manner by lowering his or her stimulating activity, the infant has accomplished an interactive regulation simultaneously with self-regulation. If, however, the infant's looking away evokes the parent's "chasing," stimulation is not reduced but heightened as is arousal, so the infant reacts by "dodging" (gaze aversion) the parent's efforts to maintain direct, uninterrupted interaction. Conflict is clearly evident while the child also experiences deficiency in self-regulating functioning.

Were this interaction repeated frequently enough, the infant would come to anticipate and expect the interactional pattern, which could engender a patterned experience of habitual avoidance, which would contribute to deficits by virtue of taking the infant "out of the game," as it were, and reducing the possibilities for engaging the challenges of novel experience. As behavioral psychologists (e.g., Skinner, 1938) have demonstrated, the potentially maladaptive side of negatively reinforced behaviors, those increased in frequency by their effectiveness in removing aversive stimuli, is that they obscure or preclude recognition of altered circumstances that would make the behaviors unnecessary, entailing a problem of maladaptation through generalization of negatively reinforced behaviors.

Similarly, a deficit in the infant's functioning may contribute to difficulties in "goodness of fit" that engenders conflict. That is, the infant may have innate vulnerabilities and sensitivities in sensorimotor affective processing that make regulation of arousal (internal) and thus regulation of stimulation (external, parent's interactive behavior) especially difficult, and thus makes the parent–infant interaction vulnerable to conflict, which in turn, perpetuates the negative affects of the deficit in adding to the infant's deficiencies in psychological functioning. This infant–parent paradigm can be easily applied to the patient–therapist paradigm. An individual patient in treatment with a therapist who holds a multifaceted, psychodynamic orientation may find himself or herself avoiding certain disturbing issues in order to lower the therapist's anticipated negative reaction. This anticipated reaction may be based on transference if the patient does not know how the therapist will react to the patient's material. Or the anticipated reaction will be based on interpersonal experience with the therapist, not necessarily transference, if the patient has had experience in bringing up certain disturbing issues and the therapist has responded negatively so consistently as to be predictable, thereby shaping the character of the therapeutic dyad in an avoidant–chasing pattern. No matter what his or her intentions, the therapist may respond with criticism and become consistently overriding, uninvolved, or verbally harsh and abusive, thereby contributing to a therapeutic impasse that will almost certainly follow.

One can see, then, the limitations of any attempt to order the forms of disturbances into hierarchical patterns, at least at the microgenetic level. Generally, psychoanalytic theories have contended that deficiencies in structural organization underlie preoedipal disturbances, whereas conflicts between and among structural organizations indicate oedipal disturbances (Gedo and Goldberg, 1973). Gedo, however, has changed his position over the years. He has come to articulate that a patient fully engaged in psychodynamic treatment responds "unhierarchically" out of many levels of intrapsychic experience (Gedo, 1988). Our multifaceted psychodynamic perspective holds that the so-called preoedipal disturbances or disorders of the self represent deficiencies in the basic capacities to regulate the I-processes, the basic biopsychosocial "spine" of the self, as it were, as well as in basic capacities to use the human object to regulate adaptively a sense of social interdependence. Thus we have no need to grapple with the now almost anachronistic dual drive theory that emphasizes the role of inherent conflict in psychological functioning, nor do we engage in the debate about the various disorders of the self that tend to emphasize deficiencies related to environmental or selfobject shortcomings.

On a moment-to-moment basis in psychotherapy, the psychotherapist must remain cognizant of the interactive nature and transactional influences of deficit and conflict in the individual's psychological organization of functioning. In this connection, one can see the relevance of didactic interventions in addressing issues related to deficits. Psychoanalytic investigators (e.g., Kafka, 1984; Grotstein, 1986; Gedo, 1988; Greenspan, 1989) have observed that patients, as well as psychodynamic therapists, frequently perceive self-regulating and interpersonal deficits as secondary to the effects of negative feelings and desires. In fact, however, the dysregulated feelings and their negative personal and interpersonal effects arise from primary defects in the biological substrate or in the "constitutional" (Emde, 1990) organization of self-regulating processes in inter- and intrapersonal functioning as derived from early parent–infant interactions (constituting a biopsychosocial substrate). In such cases, the therapist helps the patient detail the components of the deficit to understand its impact on the patient's functioning (for example, discerning a learning disability and sizing up its impact in terms of impeding a cohesive organization of sense of self and others under particular conditions). Alternately, the therapist may be required to facilitate the patient's learning of unacquired skills or knowledge through didactic intervention (see, in this connection, Gedo's [1988] approach to "apraxias" and our classification of didactic expansion bids discussed in chapter 9).

Owing to the transactional nature of psychological functioning, when certain facets or domains are affected by trauma, certain nonaffected areas may also be compromised. On the other hand, other aspects of the person's functioning may remain intact until such time as the affected area becomes exposed, engaged, and activated through maturation, development, or the treatment process. We are referring here to the situation in which the patient has conducted life in a way that employs coping strategies and defense mechanisms to prevent expression of perceived weaknesses. But as the patient matures and develops and is thereby faced with increasing demands and responsibilities, there is an increasing threat that the weaknesses will be exposed. When activated, even the earlier noncontaminated aspects of functioning may become affected and symptomatic. Hence, psychodevelopmental arrests are typically treated as though they entail both deficits and conflicts, and are treated in the manner prescribed before. As can be anticipated given our multifaceted and transactional perspective, we have generalized the notion of conflict from the specific conflicts within the intrapsychic dimension (between ego, superego, and a host of needs, wishes, and fantasies) to the notion that conflicts are generated from birth within and between all dimensions and their respective domains. Thus, in agreement with George Klein (1976), who first articulated these ideas, conflicts are associated with a host of ambivalences and ambitendencies. These stem from incompatibilities or opposing aims between, for example, the wish to explore—novelty, exploration, and effectance—and also to stay close to mother—social connectedness which would be opposing tendencies between two domains within the developmental facet. Alternately, there may be conflict within and between facets and several of the domains. Take, for example, a little 14-month-old's wish to go after a toy at the end of a room in a neighbor's house. The child craves the toy (novelty, exploration) but looks anxiously back toward the mother (social connectedness). This spells conflict within the developmental facet in that both the wish to explore the novel toy and the wish to stay close to mother are two domains within one facet. But now the mother encourages her child to go ahead and find the desired toy; her smiling face urges him on. Or instead the mother may discourage her child by a frown. Thus she conveys disappointment because she fears her child's apparent request for "permission," as it were, is indication that the child will turn out to be like, say, her timid husband, father, or brother. This reflects the influence of transference on her perception of and actions toward her child. Noting the mother's tense affect, which complements the child's own internal conflict between leaving mother or finding an exciting new toy, the child now begins to cry. As described, the conflictual transactions between mother and child are within the interpersonal facet, and represent conflict within the dyad expressed in the form of asynchrony between the aims of autonomy and interdependence.

When conflict is in the foreground, the individual's capacities for developing structural hierarchies, for tolerating delay, postponement, frustration, and self-denial, become engaged. Differentiating between the concrete and the abstract is associated with conflict, as is learning to shift between what is real and what is fantasy; what is real from one perspective and fantasy from another; playing with different levels of reality and fantasy; differentiating between what is happening inside and outside oneself; between one's needs for dependence and autonomy; for aloneness and togetherness; for what is possible and impossible; what is allowed or forbidden. As stated before, conflict is present from the beginning of life, although the complexity of conflict as represented in the intrapersonal context of functioning certainly increases as the maturational and developmental processes unfold.

THE CHARACTER OF THE DYADIC SYSTEM

Given our emphasis on transactionalism, our diagnostic as well as treatment focus is on the interactive and transactional operations of dyadic systems, whether parent–infant or patient-therapist. The focus on the dyadic system is consistent with the psychoanalytic emphasis on interpersonal and transference phenomena. But in diagnostic analysis of the character of the dyadic system, especially during the course of individual treatment, we understand the therapist's or parent's use of positive and negative interventions as contributing substantively in affecting the entire character of the dyadic therapeutic relationship, and consequently the character formation of the patient as an individual. As such, the actual character of the individual and the dyadic relationship is formed over time by the transactional dialogue between the therapist and patient, or between parent and infant in parent–infant interactions. The character of the dyadic system is determined by how the members of the dyad relate to one another, the *how* as well as the *what* of the communication in the dyad. Aspects of the early interpersonal relationships become internalized and are relived in relation to significant others later on as syntonic or dystonic transferences. These internalized relationships become imbricated aspects of the self processes and are unconscious or preconscious. Other aspects of the early relationships become part of the individual's view of the social world; these are either preconscious or conscious attitudes the individual holds, which to the extent that they interfere with his personal and social functioning will be addressed in treatment.

The character of the dyadic system may be diagnostically ordered by classification of observable dyadic attributes that define the dyad's relational patterns. These patterns include the following: mutuality (which includes reciprocity and joint attentiveness), mutual clash, mutual avoidance, parallel experience, unilateral attentiveness, and asynchronous interaction (see Table 3.1, under Domains of the Interpersonal Facet).

Obviously, no dyad can be characterized by only one of these patterns of interactive functioning. Diagnostically, one would look for the predominance of mutuality or nonmutuality, and the relative proportions of activity and influence of the various forms of dyadic interaction. In work with parent–child dyads, the diagnostic assessment of these characteristics of the dyad would provide direction for further diagnostic probing of the parent's use of negative interventions (see chapter 9) and management of growth-promoting tasks. There are also the transactional influences of, say, the infant's self-regulatory capacities (character facet) entrained with the parent's own self-regulatory capacities and intrapsychically organized transference experiences. With regard to individual treatment, these classifications of the forms of dyadic interaction describe dyadic relations at a lower level of inference than transference paradigms described by psychoanalysts in efforts to conceptualize the essential psychodynamic or psychostructural features of disturbed functioning in patients (e.g., Kohut's [e.g., 1984] conceptualizations of mirroring, idealizing, twinship, and merger of selfobject transferences from the perspective of self psychology on disorders of the self; Kernberg's [e.g., 1991, 1992] conceptualizations of infantile, psychopathic, paranoid, and depressive transferences from perspective of ego psychology/object relations perspective on disorders of borderline narcissistic personality organizations). As with the diagnosis of the character of parent–infant transactions, the diagnostic assessment of these forms of interaction can further direct the therapist to diagnostic probing of the what, when, where, and why of mutuality in relating (strengths in psychological functioning), and derailment in relating (weaknesses in psychological functioning reflecting deficits, delays, arrests, or conflicts).

COPING STRATEGIES, DEFENSE MECHANISMS, AND AFFECTS

Diagnosis of the character of the dyadic system would be elaborated by assessment of the coping strategies and defense mechanisms employed by the individual patient or parent and infant as cooperating individuals in interactive treatment. As we define them, coping strategies serve conservative functions in promoting self-regulating and interactively regulating processes across the interpersonal and intrapersonal developmental and characterologic facets. Coping strategies have observable behavioral components but may operate consciously or preconsciously (descriptive unconscious, in Freudian terms). Our classification of coping strategies includes realistic appraisal/engagement, agreement/ cooperation, compliance/submission, avoiding/disengaging, externalizing/blaming, defiance (fight), disconnecting/flight, freezing/immobilized, and transformation of affect. We discussed in chapter 5 the derivation of this classification of coping strategies and the conservative functions they serve. Here we will emphasize that realistic appraisal (thought organization) connotes sound reality testing, unimpaired formal thought processes, and capacity to perceive and tolerate a wide range of affects without disruption of perceptual (reality testing) or cognitive processes (thought organization). These as well as the coping processes of cooperation and accommodation indicate essential capacities for flexibility in personal and interpersonal functioning. Compliance/submission, externalization/blame, disconnection, and the like, on the other hand, indicate compromises in the individual's capacities to maintain an even balance in achieving a sense of autonomy through interdependence (interpersonal facet); a sense of social connectedness while also pursuing personal effectance (developmental facet); and a harmonious sense of self through the dialectics of the I, I/Me, and Me/I and ideal self processes (characterologic facet).

When the patient's compromising coping strategies show themselves in near spontaneous or knee-jerk reaction to stimuli that apparently threaten autonomy, effectance, or self-regulatable maintenance and coherence of the sense of I and aspirations of the ideal self, one can think diagnostically in terms of signs and indications of character armor (Reich, 1949) or defense transference (Schlessinger and Robbins, 1983). Character armor or defense transference embody elements of both deficit and conflict, and encompass as well, perhaps, the effects of delay and arrest. Coping strategies constitute something of a shield against perceived vulnerabilities in interpersonal relating and transactional communications of bidirectional influence. Thus, therapeutic interventions usually must first address these strategies to provide access to and an avenue for the symbolized description and elaboration of their intrapsychic representations of conflicting aims expressed in the construction of the personal narrative (i.e., the domains and aims of the intrapsychic facet of functioning).

The ego defense mechanisms derive from psychoanalytic theory and by definition (e.g., A. Freud, 1936) are dynamically unconscious; in our theoretical schema the ego defense mechanisms operate across the characterologic and intrapsychic facets. Many defense mechanisms, particularly the so-called primitive defense mechanisms (e.g., projective identification, splitting, denial), have their origins in behaviors negatively reinforced in the sensorimotor affective period of development within the parent–infant dyad. These defense mechanisms serve intrapsychic functions but operate interpersonally (see, for example, Ogden's [1982] exploration and conceptualization of projective identification). More advanced defense mechanisms (e.g., intellectualization, rationalization, reaction formation) make use of higher level cognitive processes that provide conservative functions through operations of reversibility on the plane of thought, as described by Piaget's model of cognitive development (Greenspan, 1979). The dynamic operations and functions of defense mechanisms have been extensively studied and elaborated on in the psychoanalytic literature. On the whole, the defense mechanisms entail a higher level of inference guided by psychoanalytic theory (controversies about definitions and clinical applicability abound) than the coping strategies we have defined here. As such, a clinician's diagnostic detection and therapeutic approach to defense mechanisms requires supervised training in clinical work in conjunction with extensive self-knowledge and knowledge of the literature (e.g., Giovacchini [1987] and McWilliams [1994] for summaries; Anna Freud [1936] and Fenichel [1945] for "classic" views on defense from Freudian ego psychology perspectives; Kernberg [e.g., 1975, 1987], Ogden [1982], Sandler [1987], and Scharff [1992] for contemporary views on so-called primitive defenses involving projective and introjective processes).

Affective expression also carries diagnostic implications (for a list of affects see Appendix A). From infancy on, affects are displayed through, and readily observable from, facial, vocal, and bodily expressions (e.g., Tomkins, 1962–1963, 1980; Oster and Ekman, 1977; Stern, 1977, 1985; Emde, 1983; Demos, 1984, 1988), which have a universal basis in pattern of expression and recognition across the life span (Emde, Kligman, Reich, and Wade, 1978; Izard, Huebner, Risser, McGinnis and Dougherty, 1980) and culture (Ekman and Oster, 1979; Izard, 1971). As Emde (1983) notes, display and recognition of discrete emotional expressions are part of our biological heritage and indicate a preadapted readiness for emotional expression for affective communication. Stern (1985) adds that the "vitality" dimension of affect operates in conjunction with the categorical dimension of affects in communications of emotion. Vitality affects refer to the dynamic and kinetic aspects of feelings as experienced in surging, fading, fleeting, explosive, crescendo, decrescendo, bursting, drawn out, and the like. Diagnostically, affects have importance in signaling the state of the individual. Affective monitoring (Emde, 1983) serves to orient the individual's self-regulation according to what is pleasurable and unpleasurable. For the infant, affective monitoring serves a simultaneous interactional regulatory function in guiding the responses of the parent. Similarly, the patient's affect expression may serve to orient the therapist's understanding of the patient's state and instruct the therapist with regard to appropriate intervention. In this connection, it is important to keep in mind that affect expression may communicate meaning in the nonverbal channel that is cut off from organization and expression in the verbal channel, as in the case of the dynamic interplay of repression and disavowal (Basch, 1983; Levin, 1991).

DIAGNOSTIC CONSIDERATIONS OF DISTURBANCES IN THE INTERPERSONAL DEVELOPMENTAL, CHARACTEROLOGIC, AND INTRAPSYCHIC FACETS

The discussion on the various facets of psychological functioning detailed a number of diagnostic considerations of disturbance in the facets and domains of the interpersonal and intrapersonal contexts of psychological functioning. Here we will offer a sample of the diagnostic implications of the use of the model.

Interpersonal Facet

Formal classification of disturbance in the systemic dimension is mostly confined to relationship disorders manifested in the interactional behavior of the infant and toddler. The notion that a disorder can be specific to a particular interpersonal relationship is significant with respect to the infant and toddler insofar as the young child's disturbed relational functioning in the developmental, characterologic, and intrapsychic dimensions may be clearly attributable to the parent–infant interaction and its primary influence in psychic structuralization. *Diagnostic Classification: 0–3* (Zero to Three/National Center for Clinical Infant Programs, 1994) provides descriptions of useful classifications of relationship disorders (e.g., underinvolved, overinvolved, anxious-tense, angry-hostile, and so on). Disturbed interpersonal functioning in the older child, adolescent, or adult would necessarily involve contributions of patterned structuralization of developmental, characterologic, and intrapsychic aims. That is, disturbed interpersonal functioning in the older individual could not be adequately understood with respect to only the particular disturbed relationship. Dyadic clash, as it were, between a therapist and patient would reflect a clash of the developmental, characterologic, and intrapsychic particulars of each individual as brought to bear on the interpersonal stage of transaction. In the diagnosis and treatment of older children and adults, then, attributes of the character of the therapeutic dyad (see above) are discerned and employed to explore deficits, delays, arrests, and conflicts in the developmental, characterologic, and intrapsychic facets and domains.

Developmental Facet

Disorders in the developmental facet include deficits, delays, or arrests in the domains of cognition, affective expression, social relatedness (e.g., autism, PDD), neuromotor organization (sensorimotor vulnerabilities), language or speech, and fantasy, play, and creativity. The domain of fantasy, play, and creativity includes elaboration of dynamic affective themes identified in psychoanalytic concepts of epigenetic sequences of development (e.g., separation–individuation, psychosexual, psychosocial, and the like). Deficits or delays in the domains of the developmental facet involve what Gedo (1988) terms *apraxias*. Intervention requires attention to a didactic approach combined with encouragement, facilitation, containment, and reflection to bolster the patient's sense of self-efficacy in reaching to mobilize activity in his or her emergent capabilities (zone of proximal development).

Characterologic Facet

Disorders in the character facet essentially involve disturbed self-regulation of affective arousal and self-esteem in pursuit of cohesiveness and continuity of identity. The child or adult may show disturbance in this dimension by responding to internal and external stimuli with habitual overemphasis on coping strategies that entail rigid adherence to concrete reality, compliance/submission, defiance (fighting), externalization/blame, and so on, aimed at maintaining the shielding functions of character armor.

Characterologic maladaptation may be a response to developmental deficit or delay, "constitutional" patterning of an early interpersonal relationship, or crystallization of defense against intrapsychic conflict, all of which emerge and operate through transactional influence. Disorders in the characterologic facet involve the confluence of biospsychosocial elements that engender psychosomatic and somatopsychic dysregulated functioning manifested in, for example, major affective disorders, personality disorders, and substance abuse disorders.

Intrapsychic Facet

Disorders in the intrapsychic facet are signaled by symptoms representing wish/need-defense conflicts among the intrapsychic domains of ego, superego, and needs and wishes. Disturbances include obsessive-compulsive, hysterical, phobic and somatic symptoms, as well as perversions (e.g., fetishism, voyeurism, exhibitionism, sadomasochism), and reactive depressions. A distinction is made here between state and trait disturbance parallel to a distinction generally made between psychoneurotic symptoms and character neurosis. The latter would reflect disturbance in the character facet, indicating, in part, organization of an intrapsychic conflict into a characterologic trait that chronically constricts the individual's organization of experience. Similarly, intrapsychic conflicts can engender inhibited growth in the developmental facet and can create perceptual distortions (through skewing effects of transference) in interpersonal interactions.

Neurotic symptoms may emerge in pathology spanning the continuum from the relatively severe to the relatively mild. As such, neurotic symptomatology is probably better thought of in terms of psychic state expressions of encapsulated intrapsychic conflicts, whether expressed at a neurotic, borderline, or psychotic level of personality organization.

CASE ILLUSTRATION OF ARREST, DELAY, DEFICIT, AND CONFLICT[1]

A clinical example will be presented here to illustrate how psychological trauma led to psychological arrest in the intrapsychic facet, deficits in the character facet, delays in the developmental facet and disordered functioning in the interpersonal facet. Then in Chapter 8, the same case will serve to describe the treatment process itself illustrating the functions of the therapeutic bids and the psychological facets they seem to change.

Part I: The Diagnostic Profile

The patient was 50 years old. He had survived the Holocaust as a young child and seemingly managed life well enough into adulthood. He had married, raised a family, and reached a stable position in his profession as an investment advisor in a large corporation. He sought treatment as a result of a midlife crisis prompted by a failure at work, which led him to question his capabilities, and experience a loss in self-esteem and a general state of anxiety and depression. Moreover, he was also reacting to the "loss" of his children, who had left home to attend various colleges and universities. Thus he sought professional consultation which led to a lengthy therapeutic analysis. As part of a diagnostic evaluation he told the following life narrative.

He was born in a Western European country, and was 5 years old when the Second World War began in 1939. His parents were interned in a concentration camp within days of the war's outbreak, and were killed shortly thereafter. He and his older brother survived the years of German occupation by living under assumed names, first with Jewish relatives, then in hiding, with several non-Jewish families, and finally in a Catholic orphanage.

---

[1] In order to maintain anonymity of other clinicians associated with the diagnostic evaluation of this patient, and for the sake of didactic illustration, the senior author, CHR, claims sole responsibility for the diagnosis of this case.

Each new place of refuge was prompted by the advance of the German armies into yet another Western European country. Each change required a move to a different country, learning a different language, and separating from the people who had provided some sense of security, even if temporary. Yet the patient told his story as though he were retelling a series of difficult adventures, but adventures nevertheless. For example, he prided himself for his adaptability. When he and his brother first left their home after the traumatic loss of their parents they were smuggled to a nearby country to live with their Jewish relatives. Upon their arrival at this strange new place, his brother was sad and morose, whereas he immediately befriended his new family, regaling them with Jewish songs and stories taught to him by his mother and father. Soon, however, he had to assume a new identity, live with a new name, new parental names, birthplace, and the like since they were now living with false papers. He also had to go to a school with children whose language he did not understand, pretend he was Christian at school and on the street, and continue to live his home life as a Jewish child. Whereas he seemed to manage quite well so far as maintaining his sense of humor at home and passing for gentile on the outside, he was unable to concentrate on learning when he got to first grade. While his teacher commended him on the lovely songs he sang, the poems he managed to learn and remember (all these in a foreign tongue), she called him a dreamer and sent him home repeatedly with papers that were crossed out and marked VERY BAD. Clearly he had trouble learning and he was failing in reading, writing, and arithmetic. By the year's end he was told that he would have to repeat first grade. This failure singed the child's self-esteem greatly for he had managed not to face his tragedy and had leaned on his interpersonal adaptive skills and his temperamental qualities, in order attend to his emotional needs, which his new family seemed to have met. But his failure in school indirectly underscored his difficulties in dealing with the loss of his parents, for his brother, sad though he was, and not nearly as well liked by the new family, had done well in his first year in the new school. The brother, 4 years older, was naturally more capable in coping with the tragedy of their loss and therefore also more able to learn immediately after their first displacement. The patient, as a child, was unwilling and unable to recognize the developmental differences between himself and his brother for he apparently needed his sense of superiority (if not grandiosity) in order to continue functioning. As a result, the patient only remembered feeling hurt and envious that he was not as capable as his older brother.

But since these were war years, he was soon "rescued" from having to face his difficulties due to the continued advance of the Germans; and even those who lived on false papers could not escape their growing restrictions and careful selections. This meant a new escape. This time the family enforced on the child the importance of his learning all the family members' false names, identities, places of birth and so on, for he, as the youngest, would most likely be taken in for interrogation. In fact, when they reached the border, he was taken in for a lengthy interrogation and he managed not to reveal anyone's identity. Of course he was celebrated by all, but inside of him he knew he still had to reckon with his inability to read, write, and count.

After this second escape, the patient and his brother were separated from their newly found family, and placed with a non-Jewish family, on a farm, in a new country, having to learn yet another language. In the first telling of his accounts of the war years, the patient placed hardly any emphasis on those multiple separations. Instead, he was very proud to report that he had learned yet a third language, when alone in the bathroom, the only place in which he was able to find some privacy on the farm, where, for reasons of security, he was confined to the house. He was so proud of his achievement that he promised himself that henceforth he would become a good study, learning whatever had to be learned, adapting and coping as best he could, so as to avoid the earlier humiliation and danger associated with not being smart. Indeed, later on, when still another move to another country was required, this time to a Catholic orphanage, he became a fine altar boy, learned all his Latin prayers, as well as a fourth language, and was able to enter the confessional with the most devout of his newly found Catholic friends.

With the end of the War he and his brother were reunited with members of their family who became the caretakers of the boys into adulthood. The patient, with the exception of a few turbulent rebellious adolescent years, became a stellar student in spite of tempting fate by never studying until the very last moment, as though he needed almost to relive his earlier school failure but rescue himself out of it at the very last minute. He, in fact, dropped out of high school for no apparent reason (for he was a straight A student), and did not return to college until he separated from his family and left home, to come and live in the United States. Here he managed to finish college in record time (one year and ten months), then applied to graduate school where he finished his MBA also in record time.

He was married, had a good job, and fathered four children. His midlife crisis coincided with two major issues in his life: the first was associated with intellectual failure, for his failure at work related to having made a serious error in judgment regarding an investment issue, which led to the loss of a significant client for the corporation. The second was associated to his children leaving home, going off to school at considerable distances from home. He who had always encouraged separation and autonomy was now astounded at his reaction to the separations.

During the course of a lengthy therapeutic analysis he revealed many of his secrets. For example, in his adult life he habitually flew into violent rages at home, had spanked and beaten his children when they were little and became rambunctious, wild, disruptive, and disrespectful to him or any other adult. With his wife he had many shouting matches, but since she never crossed the limits that he would find offensive, and also because she genuinely loved him and had great empathy for him, he trusted her completely; his behavior toward her, however, was replete with verbal abuses and hardly matched hers toward him. Sexually, he was not the most attentive of lovers. Here he was uneven in his ability to attend to his wife's needs. When life was good to him on the outside, or when he felt good about himself, he was a giving and potent lover. However, when he experienced doubts or conflicts, or worried about his competence, he became either oblivious to his wife and perfunctory in the sex act, or completely impotent. Interpersonally, his friends and acquaintances knew him for being the life of any party, but also for being capable of creating dissension and strife at a gathering, seemingly at will. His moods were not predictable because they were dependent on the response he got from others, as if the lines of communication between what he thought and felt were totally dependent on the feedback he received from those around him.

Thus he was diagnosed according to the DSM IV (1994), as follows:

Axis I: Anxiety Disorder and Dysthymic Disorder (300.2 and 300.4)
             Post-Traumatic Stress Disorder Chronic (309.81)
Axis II: Narcissistic Character Disorder (301.81)
Axis III: None
Axis IV: Severe, when past trauma is reactivated
Axis V: Vacillates according to external stress between 91 and 70

According to the multiple facets perspective on diagnosis, the patient manifested delays and deficits in development, deficits and conflicts in the character and intrapsychic facets, and irregular patterns in the interpersonal facet. For example, he remembered being told that as a young child he was a lively, temperamental baby who cried and smiled easily. He was said to have been willful, demanding, and given to tantrumming when he did not get his way. But he was also said to be sweet, responsive to love and praise, and had a great wish to please. As an adult he also vacillated between these two poles. With acquaintances and colleagues he tended to be pleasant and calm; most often he did not lose his composure, except when he felt unlistened to, or when his opinions were denigrated. With family and friends, however, when he felt unjustly criticized, devalued, or the like, he tended to lose control, fly into angry outbursts that were as intense as they were brief. While he strove for mutuality in interpersonal relationships, he was so sensitive to the slightest criticism that he tended to see others as overriding his ideas, as being uninvolved with him, depreciative, if not emotionally abusive to him. Consequently, relationships were characterized by asynchrony, unilateralness, avoidance, and clashes unless he himself was in charge of the situation; then he used his undamaged capacities to identify with the plight of others in order to be helpful and supportive to them.

Developmentally he was endowed with above average to superior cognitive capacities, the language domain being one of his most highly developed domains, the creative and play domains being almost as high. He remembered that as a child he played alone for hours on end, with little stones, salt and pepper shakers, pieces of discarded dominoes, and developed the most complicated symbolic plots for his "characters." He was exquisitely attuned to social interactions, driven no doubt by the necessity of keeping a watchful eye on others, lest his own fate be jeopardized. The affect domain had a wide range, was deep and intense, but not well modulated. The developmental goals of curiosity, exploration, and effectance were highly motivated. The social connectedness goal was equally strong. On the other hand, in the sphere of biopsychosocial requisites he showed dysregulation: while he seemingly had stable sleep patterns, he had respiratory problems, was highly allergic, had asthma, showed feeding and eating difficulties, and was prone to dermatological problems, perhaps as a result of being undernourished. Cognitive blocking and delays were probably the result of the posttraumatic stress disorder. He overcame these blocks as a result of resorting to the defense mechanisms of denial and disavowal, and coping strategies such as externalizing and blaming. These mechanisms helped bolster the other domains associated with cognition (such as language) and thus helped compensate for the delays. Eventually he caught up cognitively and even exceeded his own expectations, but even into mature adulthood he remained vulnerable to cognitive failure as manifested by one of the first precipitants that prompted his anxiety and depression and led him to treatment.

Characterologically he was equally complex. For example, as noted earlier, on the one hand his capacity for self-regulation, activity level, and rhythmicity, as well as affective balance were remarkably uneven. On the other, his tenacious persistence and his capacity for perseverance were his strong suit from early on, from the time he first learned songs and stories on his parents' lap, to when he had to learn dozens of strange names, places of birth, and then taught himself new languages, and finally when he decided to learn at the university. (These are aspects of the self-processes we refer to as the I.) In addition, his need to project himself onto others (I/Me), to control them with what he himself felt, thought, and wished, prompted him to make easy connections with other people, for he had the characteristics of being appealing and good looking, thus he had a kind of "draw-appeal" that others responded to favorably. However, when his intense need to be responded to was not reflected back to him (as it would be by a caring parent reflecting his Me/I) he became emotionally unsettled, irritable, angry or rageful.

As regards his ideal self, he had maintained a strong set of ideals throughout life that, while unmodified and therefore at times unrealistic, had served him well in maintaining a strong sense of identity with his community and past history. This ideal self, he and his analyst surmised, were the parental ideal selves projected onto him, which he, in turn, had taken in. But in him they remained unmodified, because they had not been subjected to the common erosion of everyday life which under ordinary circumstances leads to a more realistic set of ideals. Thus often he did not distinguish between realistic possibilities and wishes, hopes, and aspirations. For him everything was possible if only he wished it so, or if it was the right thing to do. Of course, somewhere he knew that this could not be so (because he also was a pragmatic individual), but he also did not know it, because he experienced a true sense of inner confusion between what could and could not be. As a result of this deficiency the patient had a defect in reality testing and self-appraisal. When he experienced success, whether at work, play, or in lovemaking, he was ecstatic. When he experienced failure, his self appraisal was uncommonly low. Alternately he tended to externalize the reason for failure and blame others for his defeats, or to turn on himself with unmitigated vengefulness, destroying any vestige of self-esteem. The numerous coping strategies already cited also included those of cooperation, as well as submission, both when he was still little (pretrauma), as well as later. Fight, flight, avoidance, and blaming were common coping strategies he had used in interactions with his parents and brother, as well as later throughout childhood and adulthood, in interpersonal interactions.

Intrapsychically, his ego functions lacked firmness as regards his capacities to mediate internal needs and wishes and external reality. Nor were his superego functions intact. Lacking consistent parental figures to help guide him through the maze of chaos and inconsistencies of the war societies in which he lived, his conscience was always nagging at him. He tended to be overly strict about infringements on honesty, justice, equality, and the like, but he also was tormented with notions that if he were less adamant in his stance, he could be a criminal (thus, reaction formation). For example, he knew that lying is not acceptable; but as a child, he was presented with situations that made lying to his close and intimate ones unacceptable, yet to strangers necessary if he wanted to preserve his life. Another example, in the postwar environment in which he grew up, the people he cared about tended to cheat heavily as regards the paying of taxes. Though he knew it was wrong, he felt he understood their sense of postwar entitlement. Not until he emigrated to the United States was he able to feel at ease and pay his taxes without thinking that he would be laughed at for doing so. Nevertheless to this day he feels that he could cheat on his taxes, and if he did, someone would applaud him for his cleverness. Yes, he thought, he could be a criminal.

Within the intrapsychic facet, as would be expected, the greatest emphasis lay on the nature of his defense mechanisms, paramount amongst which were the mechanism of disavowal and denial. He and his analyst speculated that he had responded to the death of his parents with shock, for he had no memory of the events that happened either immediately before or after they were led away from home; nor did he recover any memories of these events in the course of his analytic treatment. But memories of subsequent events had not been erased. Thus he and his analyst assumed that the mechanism of repression had served him well, causing him to avoid the pain of the loss of his parents, and helping him to adapt to the strenuous demand that life made on him. In addition, the underlying dynamics were seen as resulting from oedipal strivings and ego conflicts which were unresolved due to early parent loss. (In regard to the effects of early parent loss, see Altschul [1988].) The characterologic manifestations actually antedated the traumatic events of this boy's life, since they were seen by the patient and his analyst as originating in the bosom of his admiring parents, where his sense of self had alternately swung between being the object of parental admiration to being the subject of perceived rejection for being the youngest in the family, the littlest one, the baby, so to speak. His self-esteem was deeply injured when after admiration he was also the object of belittlement. Not understanding that these insults are part and parcel of the daily family life transactions with a younger child who also happens to be smart and appealing, his cleverness, charm, seductiveness, brooding, and temperamental outbursts became the mark of his infantile character. The character coping strategies, however, were first called into massive action when the patient had to face the first of his traumatic life events, namely, the loss of his parents, which at his young age he experienced as abandonment. Later on, the coping strategies proliferated and became entrenched with the accumulation of subsequent traumatic life events. (In regard to the cumulative effects of stress on coping, resilience, and indirectly on character, see Rutter [1981, 1985, 1987].) Thus the characterologic coping strategies were intertwined with the defense mechanisms of disavowal, denial, projection, projective identification, reaction formation, rationalization, intellectualization, and sublimation.

In sum, we believe we have shown that while the existing diagnostic nomenclature captured the essential features of this man's conflicts and character, analysis of his functions according to the defined interpersonal, developmental, characterologic, and intrapsychic facets and their respective domains, substantially enriches our view of him as a complex, multifaceted human being and leads to a better understanding as to how to approach his treatment.

PART II

The Facets of Therapeutic Transactions

8

An Integrated Theory of Therapeutic Transactions

The therapist attempting to employ developmental, psychodynamic, and analytic techniques confronts the difficult task of having to sort out and grasp the purposes and applications of a wide array of theoretically divergent interventions derived from principles of abstract theories. Recommendations on "what works" therapeutically depend on conceptualizations of how the mind functions generally and on the etiology and expressed manifestations of psychopathology specifically. Psychoanalysis is represented not by a single theory, but rather by many theories, which are often at odds with each other regarding the essentials of the mind and its processes. As theories differ so do their respective recommendations for technical aspects of treatment.

Clinical findings, of course, have always informed theoreticians' constructions of psychoanalytic theories of the mind. On the whole, however, the abstract theories of mind have generally advanced well ahead of theories of treatment and the evolution of psychoanalytic technique.[1] Psychoanalytic theories in the first

---

[1]Gray (1994) observes, for example, a "developmental lag" in the Freudian and ego psychological assimilation of advances in knowledge of unconscious ego defenses to develop a technique that focuses on analyzing resistances rather than on trying to overcome or bypass resistance through use, essentially, of the authoritarian role patients vest in their analysts.

half of this century developed elaborate models of psychopathology, while leaving descriptions of treatment technique relatively unelaborated. For example, Freud's writings on technique included only a few papers (1912a,b, 1913, 1914b, 1915). Interpretation, the basic technique of making the unconscious conscious, evolved as the central and defining method of psychoanalysis. The advance of ego psychology and object relations theories, particularly those emphasizing "deficiency" in nurture as a primary cause of disturbed functioning, led to exploration of the analyst's role in remediating deficiencies in psychic structuralization, and thus developed more elaborate models of treatment. The thrust of many of these models has furthered attempts to delineate forms of therapeutic communication that go beyond interpretation to address preverbal or preoedipal disturbances in self development. These forms of therapeutic communication address integrative ego or self-organizing functions that have been arrested or distorted to an extent that undermines the use of, for example, observing ego capacities necessary to take part in an interpretive process. Not surprisingly, then, infant research, particularly that which has focused on forms of communication between parent and infant in both normal and disturbed interactional patterns of relating, has been viewed increasingly by psychoanalytic theoreticians as offering important insights into the basic forms of communication necessary to foster development within the dyadic psychoanalytic situation. We have taken this tack and have classified the components of these forms of communication as "therapeutic bids." The classification of these communication components provides something of a lexicon of patterns of communication that can help the clinician devise and track movements in treatment from moment to moment, as well as session to session and phase to phase.

Evolving Theory of Therapeutic Transactions

Before describing our theory of therapeutic transactions, we will provide a more detailed but brief review of the development of psychoanalytic theories of therapy. In this way we can locate our place in the evolution of therapeutic psychoanalytic techniques.

Freud's earliest theory of therapy derived from his treatment of hysteria (Breuer and Freud, 1893–1895). Symptoms were viewed as representing a repressed memory in conflict with censorship, and the goal of treatment was to make the unconscious conscious. To bring these unconscious memories to light, Freud initially employed hypnosis, then tried to employ the power of suggestion through applying pressure to the patient's forehead. Eventually he came to understand there could not be a complete or lasting cure if the patient's resistances to remembering were merely bypassed through hypnosis or mere exploitation of the therapist's authoritarian role. In short, Freud came to realize that resistances to remembering were very much a part of the symptoms that treatment must address. His papers on technique written between 1911 and 1915 emphasized that transference entailed both a representation of the repressed in the form of an enacted repetition (i.e., transference neurosis) as well as a resistance to remembering through the repetition. Analysis focused, then, on encouraging (essentially by not discouraging) the development of the transference neurosis which then could be analyzed and interpreted as a resistance to remembering, but a resistance that also made evident in its form and content that which was being repressed. Ostensibly, the therapist need only turn the patient's attention to manifestations of resistance to reveal aspects of functioning that remained outside the patient's awareness (unconscious) but active in overt expressions of symptom formation. The psychoanalyst's observations were interpretations, informed as they were by hypotheses and theory about the workings of the mind and its forms of communication in disguising expressions of desire.

Freud's further exploration of resistances contributed to his revision of his topographical model of the mind; he conceptualized the tripartite structural model (1923), in part, to better describe the dynamic relations of unconscious ego defenses against desires of the id deemed unacceptable. The structural model that divided the mind into the three agencies of id, ego, and superego represented something of a developmental, hierarchical scheme. The ego was viewed as evolving through its development of executive service in providing a reality gate and conduit for the pleasure-dominated id. The superego was conceptualized as emerging as a split-off aspect of the ego that represents internalizations of parental injunctions as a resolution to the Oedipus complex and develops in its service of providing moral supervision over the ego in its attempt to balance the demands of the id with the exigencies of the external world. Interpretation now addressed the dynamic interplay of intrasystemic conflicts between the id (unconscious by definition) and unconscious, defensive operations of the ego and the unconscious supervisory aspects of the superego.

Freud's structural model stimulated significant debate and theoretical revisions about the curative action of psychoanalysis as related to the analyst's interpretive activity. Sterba (1934) advanced the notion that the therapist interprets to the patient's observing ego, the rational aspect of the patient's functioning that constitutes the basis for a reality-based ego alliance. In this view, the patient maintains a therapeutic split between ego as observer and ego as experiencer. Strachey (1934), by contrast, focused on Freud's as well as Melanie Klein's ideas about the introjective and projective processes that construct the superego. He posited that the curative action of the analyst's interpretations effected a modification of the patient's superego. The "mutative interpretation" is necessarily an interpretation of an emotionally immediate transference experience that the patient introjects in the form and function of the analyst's superego attitude. Functioning as a modifying introjection, the interpretation provides, essentially, a more benign view of or attitude toward the patient's transference expressions of self-alienated desire. Strachey's concept of interpretation was influential in opening the theoretical path to an affect-dominated, relationship-oriented view of interpretation that would appear to contrast markedly with the affect-free, cognitively oriented concept of interpretation advanced by Sterba. That is, Strachey argued that an interpretation involves something of the therapist's actual relationship to the patient, and it is that relationship aspect of the interpretation, which blends cognitive and emotional understanding, that the patient internalizes.

Sterba and Strachey may be viewed as representative of early movement in psychoanalysis toward a diversification of theories on psychological functioning and treatment techniques. One path was ego psychology, which followed Freud's lead in his development of the tripartite structural model to focus on ego processes that functioned in interfacing both the external and internal worlds. Anna Freud's (1936) detailing of ego defense mechanisms and Hartmann's (1939) exploration of the function of the ego in adapting to reality and of the intrapsychic relations of autonomous and defensive functions of the ego, were early advances in ego psychology. These advances were expanded upon in the many and ongoing refinements contributed by the triumvirate of Hartmann, Kris, and Lowenstein (1946; Hartmann, 1964), and in the theoretical reformulations of David Rapaport (1960, 1967) and his followers.

The operations of the defensive ego in contributing to the patient's resistances became the focus of analytic interpretation. Kris noted in 1951, however, that ego psychology did not depart significantly from the technical approaches outlined by Freud, who, following the development of the structural model, had advanced the idea that ego analysis must parallel id analysis; Freud had emphasized the treatment principles of surface to depth analysis and the importance of interpreting resistance before content. Bibring (1954), however, made an important contribution to the explication of psychoanalytic treatment methods in a seminal paper that details five groups of basic techniques: suggestive, abreactive, manipulative, clarifying (drawn from Rogers [1951]), and interpretive. These techniques actually compose something of a hierarchy of therapist–patient interactions of which the first four are largely preparatory to interpretation. Suggestion, manipulation (similar to suggestion), clarification, and interpretation are actions of the therapist, while abreaction, reciprocal clarification, and then assimilation and reorientation in response to interpretation represent the patient's actions. In our view, Bibring's approach is important for furthering the conceptualization of the moment to moment dynamic interplay between therapist and patient. But Bibring's approach also highlights the extent to which the Freudian/ego psychological theory of therapy continued to maintain the significance of the analyst's authoritative position in effecting change. Gray (1994) argues that the Freudian/ego psychological reliance on the analyst's authority has never been given up, and represents a "developmental lag" in the actual integration of the appreciation of unconscious ego defenses into a technique that truly focuses on analyzing resistances rather than trying to override them by the domination of the analyst's beneficient authority.

In this connection, the question of how the analytic therapist deals with the patient's resistances was, in part, addressed through the development of the notion of the working or therapeutic alliance (Greenson, 1965; Zetzel, 1970). Ego psychologists' advances in conceptualizing a model of ego development derived in large part from theoretical refinements on Freud's (1923) concept of the ego's synthetic functioning (e.g., Rapaport, 1960) and from increasing respect for the role of autonomous ego functions in developing and maintaining conflict-free, rational, and integrative adaptive functioning. The notion that conflict-free, rational ego functions coexist with conflict-laden (defensive) ego functions provided analysts with an ally within the patient's own functioning that could be employed to overcome resistances while accommodating to the unique aspects (nontransference) of the analyst and the analyst's interpretations. The analyst's relationship with this "ally" in the patient became the working or therapeutic alliance (Greenson, 1965; Zetzel, 1970). Psychoanalysts differ in their views of the usefulness of this concept. It can be argued, for example, that the view represents an assumption about the patient's collaborative effort that should not be assumed. Moreover, it might be construed as an attempt to remove the notion of the analyst's authoritative stance as a necessary component of treatment technique, but nevertheless bypasses the issue of analyzing the resistances that pervade the patient's presentation by assuming that a collaborative bent in the patient's efforts reflects a working alliance (collaboration, after all, could be a defensive compliance). We find the concept to be useful if understood to be a part of the goal rather than a mere means of treatment. The therapeutic alliance is one measure of the interplay of the patient's intrapsychic and interpersonal dynamics that is brought to bear in constructing the treatment situation. As the therapeutic bids operate to expand and strengthen the patient's interpersonal and intrapsychic facets of functioning, they also operate to strengthen the therapeutic alliance.

Another approach to the conceptualization of mental functioning and theory of treatment was pioneered in the work of Melanie Klein. Employing psychoanalysis in her extensive work with young children, Mrs. Klein saw and heard things in her patients' play that led her to revise basic tenets of Freud's theory. At the heart of her revision was a redefinition of the nature of instinctual drives. In her view, instincts were represented in object-related phantasy (i.e., unconscious phantasy, which represents the satisfaction of an instinct by an appropriate object, is the representation of the instinct). In this view, instincts are understood to be experienced in the emotional terms of love and hate, and the person from birth on as separate self (ego) struggles to balance the forces of love and hate (e.g., greed and envy, paranoid concern about self-survival, depressive concern about the object's survival) through interchanges with its objects. As such, Melanie Klein's theory brought object relations to center stage in describing the drama that constitutes the analytic patient–therapist interaction. What requires emphasis here with regard to a theory of therapeutic transaction is Klein's focus on projective and introjective mechanisms. These mechanisms entail interactions between self and object that structure the ego's capacities as it structures an internal model of the emotional world of human relationships. For Klein, the configuration of the internal world (e.g., paranoid–schizoid versus depressive positions) is predetermined by the predetermining structuring influence of unconscious phantasy, namely, instinct. Interpretation remains the essential and defining technique of Kleinian analysis as with Freudian/ego psychological analysis. But the Kleinian analyst interprets the dynamic exchanges between ego and internal objects as reflected in the patient's activation of these dynamics in his or her immediate relations with the analyst. In this view, transference is not merely the repetition of past experiences with external objects in the present relationship with the analyst, but rather the presentation of the here-and-now dynamics of the patient's internal world of ongoing relations between internal objects as revealed and expressed in the relationship with the analyst. Everything the patient brings into treatment is viewed in terms of transference, so that the analyst focuses attention on how the patient uses the analyst, including communications that go beyond the content of the patient's report (e.g., Joseph, 1989). Concepts such as the transference neurosis or working alliance are not particularly significant in the Kleinian view. There, transference is operative immediately, and communication between patient and analyst is framed in terms of introjective and projective processes which highlight the significance of emotional rather than mere rational understandings. Indeed, Klein's (1946) conceptualization of projective identification gained prominence as a focal issue of clinical research by her followers, and was eventually understood as manifesting itself not merely as a pathologically induced defense but a basic mode of communication between self and its objects. As such, projective identification can be construed as a defense which occurs within a normal developmental process as well as one which represents a manifestation of underlying pathology.

In this regard, contemporary Kleinian psychoanalysis is strongly influenced by Bion's (1962) elaboration of the concept of projective identification into the notion of the "container and contained." Bion makes explicit the importance of the actual environment (mother) in viewing projective identification as an interpersonal as well as intrapsychic process. Optimally, the mother–analyst recipient of the infant–patient's projective identification contains or processes the evoked feelings, thereby giving them meaning and returning them to the sender for reintrojection in a more manageable and better integrated form and integrating capacity (see also Ogden, 1982, 1986). Bion's model of the container and contained is a model for interpretive technique, but one that emphasizes both the verbal and nonverbal transactions of communication that combines cognitive and emotional facets in the process of understanding or "knowing."

The centrality of an object relations view in theory construction emerged fully in the independent theorizing of a number of British analysts, of whom the most prominent were W. R. D. Fairbairn (1954), Harry Guntrip (1961, 1969), Donald Winnicott (1965, 1971), and Michael Balint (1968). Guntrip (1961, 1969) attempted to advance Fairbairn's theory and, later, to integrate it with Winnicott's, reflecting the influence of Melanie Klein's ideas as well as their attempts to revise or correct what were viewed as faults or limitations in her ideas. With regard to these theorists' contributions to the theory of therapy, each was influential in emphasizing the role of the external world of human relationships, the actual parent–infant relationship, as fundamental to the psychological development of the self. Their focus on actual relationships represented a shift in emphasis from Klein's focus on phantasied construction of formative internal object relations. In concentrating on the importance to psychic structuralization of the vicissitudes of the earliest infant–parent relationships, the British object relations theorists, like Melanie Klein and her followers, gave increasing significance to preoedipal issues (as defined in the Freudian/ego psychological developmental scheme) as paramount for healthy development. In the views of these object relations theorists, pathological development resulted from the failure of primary caregivers to provide the kind of environmental responses necessary to facilitate the child's healthy development of self. As such, their views have been construed as postulating a deficiency model of psychopathology that contrasts with the Freudian and Kleinian conflict model. Although these writers were far from hasty in recommending treatment techniques that challenged the centrality of an interpretative approach, their views implied that interventions aimed at understanding took precedence over interventions aimed at explaining. In the analyst's relation to the patient, "understanding," as it were, emphasizes the role of attachment in fostering integration, a "being with," rather than a "being separate," that is reflected in the analyst's objectifying cognitively couched explanation.

Fairbairn and Winnicott's views prefigured much of the essence of Kohut's (1971, 1977, 1984) theory of self psychology. Kohut's study of narcissism and narcissistic pathology led him to an identification and classification of selfobject needs and selfobject relations. As defined by Wolf (1988), a "selfobject is neither self nor object, but the *subjective* aspect of a self-sustaining function performed by a relationship of self to objects who by their presence or activity evoke and maintain the self and the experience of selfhood" (p. 184). Selfobject relationships are defined in terms of their functions: those identified include mirroring, idealizing, alter ego, and twinship. Failed selfobject needs create a deficiency in selfobject needs in the development of the self that is revealed in transference relationships identified in terms of selfobject relationships. Kohut (1984) makes explicit that treatment techniques must emphasize understanding over explaining ("explaining" representing interpretation by an objectifying and thus separate other, hence perceived as distant or perhaps even persecuting or alienatingly misattuned). The therapist, then, approaches the patient with an empathy-based understanding (vicarious introspection) that attempts to resonate with, and thus confirm and affirm, the patient's selfobject needs. To a significant extent, Kohut followed a trend begun by Fairbairn in advancing a psychoanalytic psychology and theory of treatment that divorces itself from classical theory and its elaborations in contemporary ego psychological/object relations theories, as represented most prominently in Kernberg's views (e.g., 1975, 1984) and as highlighted in debates (e.g., Kernberg, 1974) over the validity and efficacy of their respective theories and treatment approaches to narcissistic disorders. In short, the work of Kohut, as with the British object relations theorists, underlined the significance of the therapist's necessary (and inevitable) participation in the therapeutic relationship as a whole person. The therapist provides the patient with an affect-laden attunement and responsiveness to foster and support the renewed development of psychological functions rendered deficient by caregiving inappropriate to early needs. In this view, interpretation, at least in the classical sense, is no longer held to be the most efficacious intervention for patients suffering preoedipal disturbances. Rather, emphasis shifts to interventions in which the therapist shares or reflects back to the patient understandings obtained through empathic resonances with the emotional appeals of the patient struggling to overcome deficiencies in his or her self-organizing capacities.

The thrust of the object relations and self psychology perspectives was to shift focus from a one-person to a two-person perspective (Modell, 1984). As such, the shift in emphasis began to move psychoanalytic technique beyond interpretation.

Perhaps the most significant nodal point in the development of contemporary American views on a psychoanalytic theory of therapy was expressed in the work of Hans Loewald. His seminal paper, "On the Therapeutic Action of Psychoanalysis" (1960), is an integrative and integrating work that employs, while substantially revising, the framework of Freudian metapsychology to synthesize drive theory principles with a refined understanding of the role of object relations. His conceptualizations provide a view toward integrating interpersonal and intrapsychic dynamics and as such anticipate, for example, much of the transactional treatment principles derived from infant research and the refinements in developmental psychology made by subsequent psychoanalysts through their incorporation of Piagetian and Vygotskian theories of cognitive development. His conceptualizations also address and give direction to the understanding of concerns that led later to the development of self psychology, as well as to the development of hermeneutic and intersubjective perspectives. In his paper on therapeutic action, Loewald assigns himself the task of making a "first attempt to correlate our understanding of the significance of object relations for the formation and development of the psychic apparatus with the dynamics of the therapeutic process" (p. 16). As such, he makes explicit use of the parent–child relationship as the model for the therapeutic relationship. His is a developmental view that emphasizes the transactional nature of human relations that underlies individual development. In a nutshell, the child–patient's developmental reach is both facilitated and extended by the parent–therapist's future–looking, higher level integrating view that reflects back to the child–patient a vision of what he or she is, as perceived, in part, in terms of what he or she might become. The child–patient introjects, as it were, an integrating perspective that melds acceptance of what is with expectation of what can be. Loewald, then, highlights the developmentally progressive thrust of transference manifestations. In effect, the activation of an alienated desire expressed in the transference also represents the renewal of hope for a better solution to an aborted developmental striving. The therapist's interventions aim to foster the patient's exploration and elaboration of the wish and thereby serve to extend the patient's reach, as well as to provide integrative functioning that the patient models to reinforce and strengthen his or her own higher level integrative process. In effect, the patient internalizes a higher level integrative process, initially embodied in the therapist's integrative functions, as an other to whom he or she can speak to obtain interpretive understanding (i.e., development of self-reflective perspective).

One must not do disservice to theoreticians by blurring important differences, and thus unique insights in the conceptualizations of each, when looking for continuity or similarity across their views. But with regard to the psychoanalytic evolution of therapeutic principles and techniques, we think it is worth noting that important elements of Loewald's notions on the curative forms of interactive communications is not dissimilar from the general thrust of Bion's notion of the "container and contained," or from Kohut's subsequent emphasis on empathy as a method of therapeutic understanding and communication.

Indeed, Robert Emde (1990) finds much in Loewald's work that is supported in the subsequent research on infancy that, in turn, can be applied fruitfully to an understanding of the therapeutic action of empathy in promoting the developmental thrust Loewald identifies. For Emde, Loewald's work is exemplary in providing a developmentally oriented theoretical framework that infant research can now flesh out to promote a more detailed description of therapeutic action. In this regard, Emde (1990) has made an important contribution to the evolution of a theory of therapy by making use of the findings of infant research to describe the therapeutic action of different forms of empathic availability that mobilize fundamental modes of development. Emde's aim is toward balancing a psychoanalytic therapeutic focus on the patient's pathological or regressive developmental tendencies by describing how a therapeutic action mobilizes in the patient a biologically prepared, positive developmental thrust. His classifications of forms of developmentally mobilizing aspects of empathy and availability are quite similar to some of the therapeutic bids identified in our work and described in this book.

Emde is representative of another strand of influence in the evolution of psychoanalytic theory of therapeutic transaction, namely the developmental approach. This approach has most recently made use of the laboratory to expand and revise observations previously obtained through clinical, ethological, and anthropological studies of Spitz (1945, 1946, 1959), Provence and Lipton (1962), Mahler, Pine, and Bergman (1975), and Bowlby (1969, 1973, 1980), amongst others. Emde is one of a number of psychoanalyst/infant researchers who have attempted to enhance psychoanalytic theory of therapy by exploring the implications of research findings on parent–infant interactions for therapist–patient relationships. Louis Sander (1975, 1987), Daniel Stern (e.g., 1977, 1985), Stanley Greenspan (e.g., 1981, 1989), and Virginia Demos (e.g., 1988), to name a few, have brought research on early development to bear on psychoanalytic theory. Their work sheds light on what the infant–child/patient responds to and looks for in the external world to promote a self-creative and self-creating integration of personal striving with the exigencies of the external world. Simultaneously, their work sheds light on parental-therapeutic responses and initiatives that promote the infant-toddler/patient's developmentally integrative processing. The views of these research theoreticians have been employed increasingly by psychoanalysts to elaborate and reformulate psychoanalytic theory of the mind and theory of therapy (Basch, 1977, 1988; Lichtenberg, 1983, 1989; Sanville, 1991). Obviously, such work has had a great influence in orienting our perceptions and shaping our conceptions in developing an integrated theory of psychological functioning and in classifying infant–patient/ parent–therapist interactions into a lexicon of therapeutic interventions.

But the incorporation of infant research findings into psychoanalytic views is only one aspect of a psychoanalytic movement toward an interdisciplinary orientation in the construction of a theory of the mind and of treatment. Stanley Greenspan (1979, 1989), for instance, has integrated psychoanalytic ego psychological hypotheses with Piaget's cognitive theory, empirical findings on infants, and biological psychology, to develop a stage theory of ego development. In detailing and conceptualizing the somatic, behavioral, and representational levels of functioning that develop diachronically but then function synchronically, he is able to describe therapeutic means of addressing deficiencies and conflicts expressed at preverbal as well as verbal (representational) developmental levels. Greenspan argues and demonstrates the importance of psychoanalytic treatment being attuned to somatic and preverbal manifestations of functioning. He also emphasizes devising the interventions aimed at addressing somatic and behavioral issues that influence representational levels of functioning. This in turn gives meaning to these influences while providing them with access to the organization and deliberation of consciousness (in the traditional sense) created by representational functioning. Similarly, John Gedo (1979, 1981, 1986, 1988) has progressively detailed a psychoanalytic developmental model based on his conceptualization of an epigenetic unfolding of core issues represented in five stages of development. Gedo initially constructed the model in collaboration with Arnold Goldberg (Gedo and Goldberg, 1973) in an attempt to build a comprehensive psychoanalytic theory that integrated the developmental paths outlined in diverse psychoanalytic theories into a unified model that placed these developmental paths in a hierarchical scheme. Since then, Gedo has gone on to develop his model of a hierarchy of personal aims with support from his integration of evidence from infant studies, progress in the neurosciences, and the data he has obtained from use of the model in clinical psycho-analysis.[2] Mode I of his model entails unifying ego nuclei, developmentally motivated by the need to avoid overstimulation. Mode II entails achieving self organization through development of self awareness, with the ability to formulate needs and wishes and to prioritize them in a manageable organization, developmentally motivated by the need to organize self around real interpersonal interactions. Mode III entails achieving self regulation that balances competing wishes without resorting to defensive disavowal and persistence of narcissistic illusions, developmentally motivated by concern with critical archaic selfobject functions. Mode IV entails developing the ability to renounce wishes that threaten disruption of an adaptive equilibrium, developmentally motivated by oedipal issues. Mode V entails increasing development of symbolic capacities, developmentally motivated by the need to adjust a hierarchy of attitudes and goals throughout the lifespan. Each mode in the hierarchy requires specific kinds of environmental responses, and evidence in the treatment situation of problems in any particular mode signals needs for particular interventions: "pacification" (mode I), "unification" (mode II), "optimal disillusionment" (mode III), "interpretation" (mode IV), and "introspection" (mode V). Gedo, then, also advances the view that noninterpretive interventions are necessary to go beyond interpretation to provide the patient models of psychological skills deficient in the patient's functioning, deficiencies Gedo (1988) terms *apraxias.*

Gedo's approach is also representative of the movement toward a multiple model perspective in the evolution of a psychoanalytic theory of therapy. This movement reflects the view that the various psychoanalytic schools of thought on theory and treatment point to and articulate important aspects of human functioning and forms of psychopathology, but that none is comprehensive on its own. Pine (1988, 1990) suggests a treatment

---

[2]Rodgers (1994) provides a concise review of Gedo's model with respect to its place in advancing a multiple model perspective in psychoanalysis. Levin (1991) reviews and employs Gedo's theory with respect to its place and utility in advancing the integration of neuroscience into psychoanalysis.

approach that adopts Freudian, object relations, ego psychology, and self psychology perspectives to orient the therapist's attunement to the patient's expression of issues best understood within the respective languages of drive, ego, object relations, and self experience. Chessick (1989), too, endorses the notion of the therapist approaching patients by listening with an ear attuned to expressions best captured through flexible use of the perspectives of Freudian theory, object relations theory, phenomenology, self psychology, and interactional theory. Chessick cautions that the therapist must use this kind of flexible listening with the understanding that the perspectives themselves are derived from theories that are incompatible or at least unintegrated with one another. Chessick's observation points to a critical question in the use of a multiple model perspective: How does one determine on a moment-to-moment basis choices of and shifts between perspectives? We believe that our integrated model advances the solution to that problem, and that direction in determining movement within and between interpersonal and intrapersonal facets is provided by the initiatives and responses revealed in and through employment of the therapeutic bids.

There have been, of course, other psychoanalytic points of view that influenced our thinking that were not cited in the preceding review. We have simply tried to describe, in admittedly an oversimplified way, those lines of inquiry and solutions that address treatment concerns as we see them from our contemporary perspective. One line of thinking that was not reviewed is that of structuralism (Piaget, 1970) or a systems theory view (von Bertalanffy, 1968). The principles of systems theory orientation were described in chapter 1. Here, we will make use of those principles to summarize our view of the implications of the trend in the theory of therapy described above.

Treatment techniques are intended to promote change, of course. In psychoanalytic theories, resistances to change can be understood from the perspective of structuralism or systems theory to reflect the conservative tendencies of mental functioning, conceptualized in terms of structures and substructures of mind. Structures are necessarily identified through their operations, or processes, which entail transformational actions (syntax or rules of organization) that function to maintain the stability of structures in the face of perturbations that threaten destabilization. Broadly conceptualized, structures develop through exercise of functions that reactively rebalance equilibrium (conservation) upset by the impact of forces, internal or external, that push the state of organization the structures seek to maintain to a state of disorganization or imbalance. A flexible structure is one that changes or modifies itself to maintain its stability by expanding its transformational actions to handle a wider and more diverse array of internal and external stimuli. The expansion and elaboration of transformation actions is commonly referred to as learning. Psychoanalysis refers to these processes and the functions served for the inferred structures in terms of refined wishes, sublimation, neutralization, differentiation, integration, internalization, and the like. A rigid or weakly developed structure is one that maintains stability by excessively excluding internal or external stimuli that cannot be handled by the capacities of transformational actions of the structure and thus would disintegrate the structure. Promoting change therapeutically, then, requires engaging the processes of structures, fostering the exercise of their functions. For the patient, the therapist or the therapeutic relationship becomes the object the patient's structures attempt to structure. In being worked on, as it were, by the processes of the patient's structuring activity, the therapist can foster, through reciprocal action, the patient's expansion in capacities of transformational actions to maintain structural integrity (conservation of purposes) while handling a wider and more diverse array of internal and external stimuli. That the patient does necessarily bring his or her structuring processes to bear on the therapist and therapeutic relationship should highlight appreciation of the accommodative (hence, progressive) thrust in the patient's transference (assimilatory) activity, a point emphasized by Piaget (e.g., 1952), Loewald (1960), and Emde (1990), amongst others.

Rigid or weakly developed structures are more easily identified owing to manifestations of limited adaptation as measured on some form of developmental continuum. Insofar as psychoanalysis has largely developed theories of the mind through exploration of psychopathology, the structures of mind conceptualized in psychoanalytic theories reflect the identification and classification of transformational actions, yielding rigidity. As such, psychoanalytic theories of the mind have, arguably, gone farther in describing what prevents change than what promotes change. This development is not surprising. A flexible structure, after all, is one that hardly reveals itself owing to the fluidity and fluency of its adaptation to internal and external demands. The search for what promotes change might be better sought in normalcy. But, then, how can those elements that foster adaptive change be identified in normalcy when the structures or suborganizations of the healthy mind are apparently concealed (blended or integrated, more accurately) by the flexibly fluid and fluent processes that serve the functions of those structures? The obvious answer would seem to be that an integration of a theory of mind and a theory of therapy necessarily require conceptualizations of both structure and process and comparative study of human functioning in both psychopathology and health.

Psychoanalysis has, of course, studied human functioning as expressed in both psychopathology and health, though far more with psychopathology than health. Still, psychoanalytic theories seem far more secure in describing what prevents change than in describing what promotes it. As noted before, psychoanalytic theoreticians have offered fewer conceptualizations and well-articulated theories of therapy than theories of the mind. From Freud on, psychoanalytic writers have devoted most attention to illuminating disturbed states of mind, assuming, one might suppose, that the more one understands about the transformations of mind in states of derailed functioning, the more treatment interventions become self-evident as corrective measures. Put simplistically, to discover how something is bent or broken is also to discover how that something is to be unbent or put back together.

More accurately, however, psychoanalysis during Freud's era and the period immediately following it operated on the principle that psychopathology, especially neurotic pathology, varied in form and certainly content, but shared the characteristic of disclaimed knowledge having a toxic influence on conscious experience and adaptation. The corrective intervention, then, required helping the patient to reclaim what had been disclaimed. Technique centered on interpretation, which aimed at analyzing and thus removing resistances and defenses while making connections between past and present experiences, all with the aim of making a pathogenic unconscious force conscious and thus available to alteration and transformation by the more mature, rational functions of the ego.

The widening scope of psychoanalysis included more severely disturbed patients whose functioning revealed other kinds of "not knowing," as it were. For these patients, the problems centered not on disclaimed knowledge, but rather on knowledge that had never been acquired or claimed to begin with. Consequently, the theoretical focus shifted from observations and descriptions of the dynamic interplay between the larger structures of experience conceptualized in terms of Freud's (1923) tripartite model, to observations and descriptions of the processes of structure formation. This shift in focus was paralleled by a shift in significance assigned to attachment, that is, to the role of interpersonal relationships in the development of intrapsychic structure and the subsequent influence of that structural organization on later emotional, cognitive, and interpersonal functioning. Object relations theories and self psychology emerged with this shift in focus. Freud had emphasized the role of attachment in treatment as being necessary to yield the kind of wish-driven relationship that would reveal what the patient had disclaimed and thus needed to reclaim. The transference neurosis describes that aspect of the therapeutic relationship that highlights the representation of a self-alienated past. The technique of interpretation reintegrates in the present what had been disintegrated in the past. With patients for whom "not knowing" reflects lack of development of knowledge and skills, attachment itself, or the development of the relationship itself, something Freud more or less took for granted, becomes more prominent as not merely the means but rather a goal of treatment. Psychoanalysts learned that focus on constructing a viable therapeutic relationship requires the therapist to put aside notions of functioning as only a reflective observer of the patient's use of him or her as a substitute or replicate (displaced) object defined by the patient's desire. Instead, the therapist has to foster a therapeutic situation that provides the means for the patient to develop, in the actual present, organizations of experience that had been foreclosed in the past. Treatment interventions aim, then, to integrate in the present what has remained unintegrated from the past.

Thus, new techniques emerged from revised theories of mind on the processes of intrapsychic structuralization. Terms such as *holding environment* (Winnicott, 1960), *container and the contained* (Bion, 1970), and *empathy* (the later term used by everyone, really, but especially identified with Kohut [1971]) are three such interventions that have become as important as curative measures, in the views of many, as interpretation.

These terms represent conceptualizations of parent–infant interactions adopted as treatment techniques. The terms themselves clearly convey that structure lies in a relationship. Moreover, the terms also convey the processes of those structures: the environment ("mother"/therapist) holds, the container ("mother"-therapist) contains, and the empathizer ("mother"-therapist) emotionally resonates understanding. The terms have an evocative appeal carried through an emotional tone that is absent in the notion of interpretation. An analyst who interprets is separated from the patient through the cognitive activity of interpretation, whereas an analyst who provides a "holding environment" is both part of the infant/patient unit as well as a separate individual providing a supporting background or facilitating container for the infant–patient's exploration and organization of experience. Although interventions termed as *holding environment* or *empathy* have a warmer, friendlier, and more intuitively familiar ring than interpretation (which may easily convey a notion of daunting responsibility for presumed knowledge and precise application), these interventions are no less defined by reference to the abstract theories of mind from which they are derived; that is, these techniques are principles, not specified procedures.

As such, we are brought back to the problem stated in the first sentence of this chapter. A therapist's skill with therapeutic and psychoanalytic techniques depends upon his or her grasp of the theories of mind from which they derive as principles for promoting change. Moreover, therapists learn quickly that theories of the mind are not templates that can be laid over a patient's actions to organize data into objective or objectifying configurations that can signal the application of interventions defined more in terms of principles than specified procedures.

At the outset of our project, it seemed possible to us that therapeutic interventions could be better defined and classified by referring both to psychoanalytic principles of treatment and to our observations and those of other infant researchers on the grammar and syntax of parent–child transactions that operated to facilitate or impede child development and parent–child communication. We looked for and tested similarities and congruence of transactional patterns found in parent–infant interactions with those discerned in therapeutic treatments of older children, adolescents, and adults. Consequently, we developed a view of what seemed essential in facilitating growth-promoting transactions which, in turn, shaped the psychological theory of functioning discussed in part I.

INTRODUCTION TO TREATMENT AIMS AND PRINCIPLES

The theory of therapeutic transactions is informed by the interpersonal and intrapersonal theoretical perspectives and the facets of psychological functioning delineated in part I. These multiple perspectives orient the clinician's attention to the diverse influences of a particular intervention or combination of interventions as they impinge on the intra- and interpersonal transactions. This multifaceted orientation prompts the clinician into a self-questioning of, "What did I or might I expect a particular intervention to do?" Holding the different facets in mind may appear at first sight to be quite difficult, but we find that most clinicians do subscribe to a number of theoretical points of view in working with their patients. As we saw, psychoanalytic clinician-theoreticians are increasingly advocating multiple model perspectives (e.g., Hedges, 1983; Pine, 1988, 1990; Chessick, 1989). We have tried to develop a comprehensive yet comprehensible multimodel orientation that articulates and defines in as much detail as possible the various theoretical lines and their behavioral–psychological facets that inform our approach.

We take the infant–parent–therapist therapeutic transaction as the paradigm for the treatment relationship because it contains something elemental that is inherent in any patient–therapist relationship. The infant represents the kernels of all universal human strivings, while the parent represents the modicum of strivings that have been modified by realistic appraisal and organized into an interrelated system of needs, wishes, aspirations, and ideals. The infant in the parent is reawakened by the external infant, and the parent in the infant is in the process of formation from birth on, if not before, when the parent becomes the repository of the infant's yearnings and emissions. As such, from the onset of life, it is part of the infant's mandate to become the nurturing, containing parent. While these caregiving functions are, of course, first assumed by the parent, it is clear that part of the parent's agenda includes the transfer of nurturing and containing functions to the child.

Let us begin with an illustration: Suppose, in this instance, that the clinician observes a parent–infant play interaction that becomes a chase-and-dodge affair (Stern, 1977). The infant displays gaze aversion to reduce the immediate impact of the parent's overstimulating behavior, but the parent pursues (chases) the infant to maintain a full-face alignment, to which the infant responds with more rapid dodges of gaze aversion. When the infant begins hiccupping and then curls knees to stomach with a grimace and bubbling spittle at the corner of his mouth, the therapist infers that the infant is displaying difficulty in meeting some basic biopsychological requisite (be it gastric comfort, or the need to sleep) which may well reflect a conflict in coordination between biopsychological and social connectedness aims. The infant's problems lie within the developmental facet of psychological functioning. The therapist does not know the basis for the parent's apparent insensitivity, but may assume that, insofar as the parent is not attuned to the infant's current needs, the parent must be responding to something else. Perhaps the parent is attributing motives to the infant that are impossible developmentally and reflect the parent's projections of his or her needs or wishes (projective identification). Perhaps the parent is seeing the infant as representing a significant person in the parent's early life (transference), a significant person for whom the parent continues to search (compulsion to repeat). In effect, then, the parent's unaware preoccupation with needs and expectations derived from an earlier relationship now patterned in an internalized relationship, obscure and override his or her view of the here-and-now infant's developmental aims in the here-and-now. The parent's problems, then, may involve problems in the intrapsychic facet that contribute to problems in the interpersonal facet and thus exacerbate the infant's problems in the developmental facet. But the infant's derailed developmental aim in dysregulated somatopsychic functioning is the point of urgency, as it were. Assuming, then, that the infant's inherent push toward meeting his or her biopsychological requisites (of hunger, sleep, digestion, and the like) requires a supportive interpersonal (caregiving) matrix, the therapist chooses to intervene from a systems perspective. The therapist might employ therapeutic bids such as observing receptively, as well as mirroring and reflecting aloud, to note that the infant appears to be physically uncomfortable, while also wondering tactfully what the parent might do to comfort the infant. The receptive observation, mirroring, which reflects and labels the infant's discomfort, provides the parent with a cognitive scaffold that might help reorient him or her from an internally derived transferential response to the here-and-now actuality of the infant's behaviors. The therapist's probing intervention might prompt the parent to explore openly for a more satisfactory response to the child (rather than to pursue the "chasing"). If the parent arrives at a satisfactory response, such as patting the infant gently on the back without chasing the baby to capture eye contact, the parent might experience the pleasure of mastery over significant competing internal tendencies in the presence of the infant and therapist. This time around, then, everyone in this triad will have arrived at a satisfactory solution.

If, however, the parent cannot respond to the clinician's therapeutic bids of receptively observing, mirroring, reflecting, labeling, and probing, and persists in the chase-and-dodge pursuit, the therapist will intervene with another therapeutic bid. This might be a didactically expanding statement, that directly indicates to the parent a response that might help the child. Next, to promote better understanding of the parent's need for gaze responsivity, the therapist might probe into the parent's own associations about this particular need. This might lead the parent to tell the therapist, in the presence of the child, of his or her own experience with parental rejection, for example. The parent might then elaborate on how much he or she expects this baby to make up for the difficulties the parent has endured during their own childhood. The presence of the receptively observing therapist provides the parent with a new or renewed experience of being watched and listened to by a receptive other. The therapist might become, at that moment, the refound other the parent has been seeking in his or her interaction with the infant. The presence of the infant, whether now sleeping peacefully or still manifesting discomfort, enables the parent to distinguish at that moment between his or her transferential distortion and the actual baby in the here-and-now. The infant certainly does not understand the content of the parent–therapist conversation, but becomes part of that conversation, as it were, in hearing a different tone and rhythm in the parent's voice, or perhaps the sound of experienced sadness and pain, and perhaps, too, the sound of pleasure for having mastered, this time, something he or she had been unable to resolve previously. In similar future episodes, the parent–infant transactions may well take a different course (see the findings of Condon and Sander [1974], which demonstrate that early infant movement is synchronized with adult speech; Cramer and Stern [1988] also describe infant changes as the parents are able to express themselves verbally to the receptive clinician).

TREATMENT AIMS

Here we shall summarize the general treatment aims as seen from the conceptualized contexts and psychological facets. Within the interpersonal facet the aims of treatment are to achieve an optimal balance between autonomy and interdependence. Within the developmental facet, the aims of treatment are to achieve an optimal balance between fulfillment of biopsychological requisites, social connectedness, and novelty-exploration and effectance. Within the character facet, the aims of treatment are to elaborate on the I, I/Me and Me/I self-processes and the ideal self and to flesh out character structure. Within the intrapsychic facet, the aims of treatment are to make the unconscious conscious, to resolve the compulsions to repeat, disabling transferences, and to consolidate ego functions (see Table 8.1 for an outline of treatment aims).

To illustrate, the treatment aims represented in the clinical example described before may be identified as follows:

1. Interpersonal facet:
   (a) Helping the parent learn about and understand the infant's autonomous striving for satisfaction of biopsychological regulation and social connectedness in relation to and with the assistance of the parent.
   (b) Helping the parent to perceive the infant as an interdependent yet autonomous entity, not as an entity that exists only as an extension of the parent's internalized past personal experience.

TABLE 8.1
The Multiple Facets of Therapeutic Transactions

Treatment Principles: Exploring, learning, understanding, practicing/working through

	Interpersonal Facet	Developmental Facet	Character Facet	Intrapsychic Facet
Aims	Achieve balance between Autonomy and Interdependence	Achieve balance in the pursuit of social connectedness Novelty, Exploration, Effectance, and Biopsychological requisites	Elaborate on Self-processes, Ideal self, regulate temperament	Bring unconscious processes to consciousness, Resolve compulsions to repeat and disabling transferences, Consolidate ego functions
Issues	Focus on interpersonal issues of mutuality and nonmutuality, e.g., such as asynchrony, invasiveness, unilateralness, parallel avoidant and clashing relationships. Focus on aversive bids such as overriding, uninvolvement, verbal and physical seduction, verbal and physical abuse and sexual abuse	Focus on competing and antagonistic tendencies as well as delays and deficits in the developmental domains of neuromotor, cognition, affect, language, social, creativity, play	Focus on disordered view of self-processess, unrealistic Ideal self (delays, deficits, arrests, conflicts) Disordered temperament (such as inhibited, disinhibited, uneven)	Focus on conflicts, arrests, and deficits in ego, superego functioning, as well as in needs, wishes, and fantasies

TABLE 8.1 (continued)
The Multiple Facets of Therapeutic Transactions

Therapeutic Bids and Categories

Basically Humane	*Supportive*	*Insight-Orienting*	*Learning*	*Containing*	*Internally Orienting*
Receptive/ Observation	Mirroring/ Imitating	Probing	Facilitation	Inhibiting	Disengaging/ Silence
Empathy	Reflecting/ Labeling	Coaxing/ Encouraging	Didactic Expansion	Postponing	Self-Observation
Tact	Praising	Interpretation		Renouncing	
Respect					

2. Developmental facet:
   (a) Helping the infant, via the parent, to regulate her bio-psychological needs; in this case, helping the baby with gastric regulation.
   (b) Helping the infant to satisfy needs for social connectedness; in this case, helping the baby recognize that she wants to be close to mother, but not too close.
   (c) Helping the mother recognize her own needs for internal regulation, to which she attends by seeking closeness with her baby.

3. Character facet:
   (a) Helping the infant to experience herself as I, namely by the parent's mirroring, reflecting, and labeling that she, the mother, feels the baby's stomach gurgling, and thinks the baby needs some gentle patting, but that the baby does not want to be looked at, or to be played with at this time.
   (b) Helping the parent to see the child's multiple I goals, namely, that the child has needs which include attending to her gastrointestinal discomfort as well as to temporarily disengage from mother.
   (c) Help the parent to observe her own multiple self-processes (I, I/Me and Me/I); namely how she turns inward at the insistence of her own internal bodily cues (I), how she can realistically expect that her baby will react in a similar manner (I/Me), but that does not mean that the baby is rejecting her (by turning way), or that she, the mother, is rejecting the baby. The sense of being a "bad" rejecting mother comes from the mother's own negative Me/I (the source of which was her perception of her own mother's rejection of her).

4. Intrapsychic facet:
   (a) Helping the infant to begin learning about her own personal ways of communicating, in this instance, identifying for the baby her ways of curling up, salivating from the mouth, and crying. (Here the intrapsychic facet corresponds with the developmental domain of language and communication; as well as the character of the I).

(b) Helping the mother understand the connection between her own personal history of her difficult early experiences in being parented and feeling rejected and her tendency to repeat the experience of her early rejection with her baby at those moments when she feels the baby is not meeting her needs (this is expressed through her insistence on playful visual proximity); namely, the mother's insistence on visual connection prompts the baby's turning away (losing the object).

(c) However, the insistence and compulsion to repeat serve a dual purpose: in the first instance, the repetition keeps alive the mother's poor sense of Me/I (for she knows no other identity). In the second instance, the repetition kindles the hope that this time her baby will *not* turn away from her which will also mean to her that this time she has reversed her past; namely, she can now believe that her mother did not turn away from her. This is the essence of the transference distortion which can be remedied through treatment work with the mother.

TREATMENT PRINCIPLES

The general treatment principles underlying any of the clinical interventions involve exploring, learning, understanding, and practicing or working through. Exploring involves the process of becoming curious about oneself and one's environment through trial and error and free association or free play. Learning involves the acquisition of new knowledge through contingent responsivity, through trial and error activity, and through symbolic representation that constructs and encodes abstractions from experience that differentiate and integrate sensations, perceptions, emotions, and sensorimotor and sensori-affective patterning of goal-directed pursuits. Our views on exploring, learning, understanding, and working through derive primarily from our understanding of Greenspan's model of three levels of learning (1982), a model that integrates behavioral principles, Piaget's theory of cognitive development, and ego psychological concepts on the dynamic processes of psychic structuralization (1979, 1989). Greenspan delineated three kinds of learning and corresponding levels of experiential awareness. *Somatic learning* is the earliest, most basic level of learning, which has to do with the regulation of somatic states of arousal, autonomic nervous system patterns, psychophysiological regulatory capacities that both promote and are promoted by interest in and engagement with the human world. This level of learning and awareness points to the significance of Sander's (1982) proposition that the ego is a state ego (and affect ego) before it is a body ego. States themselves serve as primary goals that entail maximizing positive affects while minimizing negative affects (Demos, e.g., 1988). *Trial-and-error exploration* is also part of the first level of learning, since from birth on, not all learning is purely somatic, but also involves attraction to pleasant stimuli, some with human and other nonhuman attributes. The second level of learning is behavioral consequence learning, which involves the kind of means–ends learning ascribed to operant learning paradigms (Skinner, 1938), as well as the kind of learning described in Piaget's concepts of sensorimotor development (Flavell, 1963). Learning and awareness at this level are in the language of behavioral action and affective gesture. The third level of learning is representational–structural learning. It is at this level that mental imagery and symbols are forged and used to organize experience at a fully psychological level. The individual can become conscious of self at this level; that is, aware of having feelings and ideas that are one's own, as it were. The three levels of learning evolve diachronically, but as each develops out of the other, each level of learning and experiential awareness functions synchronically with the others to generate a dialectical structuring of experience (Ogden, 1988).[3]

---

[3]Thomas Ogden's (1988) concept of three modes of experiential organization that constitute what he conceptualized as the "dialectical structure of experience," appears to correspond well with Greenspan's concepts of three levels of learning and of awareness. The three modes, autistic-contiguous, paranoid-schizoid, and depressive, also refer to somatic, behavioral–affective, and symbolic levels of organization. What is particularly interesting in this correspondence of views is that neither writer refers to the other's work, and indeed, their conceptualizations stem from different schools of psychoanalytic

The principle we label *understanding* entails the evolving process that generates self-reflective narration and explanation. It is a process carried out on the representational–structural level of learning and awareness. The process of understanding involves the coordination of two interrelated processes. The first involves elevating somatic, trial-and-error exploration, and behavioral–consequential experiences to the level of symbolic representation. The symbolic representation of experience abstracts concrete aspects of experience to create ideas representing a conceptual whole that relates, and thus becomes greater than the sum of its concretely perceived parts. The second of the interrelated processes of understanding involves resorting and reintegrating old knowledge with new experience. Resorting and reintegrating knowledge is a process of reconstruction that may be cortically based. In this connection, Gerald Edelman's (1987) neurological theory of memory (as described by Modell [1990]) is relevant. As summarized by Modell (1990), Edelman's theory posits that:

> [M]otoric action is essential for perception; perception consists of the refinding of categories held in memory; this refinding requires repetitive action during which the environment . . . is periodically sampled and tested so that when novelty is encountered there is a *retranscription* of memory in a new context . . . memory is no longer seen as a passive registration of experience in which there is an isomorphic correspondence between the event and the memory trace. What is stored in memory is not a replica of the event, but rather the *potential* to generalize or refind the category or class of which the event is a member [p. 64].

Modell employs Edelman's theory to advance Freud's concept of Nachträglichkeit, which, through Modell's elaboration, comes to emphasize the inherently forward developmental thrust of the transference experience. That is, any representational actualization of (past) experience necessarily involves recontextualizing

---

thought and developmental–clinical research. Greenspan's orientation is ego psychological; Ogden's perspective is object relational, primarily an extension and elaboration of the views of Klein, Bion, Winnicott, and Meltzer. Though one cannot infer "scientific" validity from the congruence of their concepts, one can reasonably think in terms of a validity in clinically derived wisdom.

that experience in the context of immediate experience, the present takes its meaning from the past, but, simultaneously, the past refinds its meaning in the context of the present, so that refinding is reconstructing.

The notion of understanding has multiple meanings, of course. We emphasize understanding in terms of its potential for enhancing self-reflective narration and explanation. But understanding also implies affective sensitivity and empathic resonance. Taking into account, for example, Edelman's (1987) theory of memory and its implication for transference phenomena makes apparent that the kind of understanding that fosters change may operate at prerepresentational levels, too. In this regard, the therapist's empathic availability can mobilize modes of development (Emde, 1990), for no matter how assimilatory a transference enactment may seem, it cannot be enacted without some accommodation to or recontextualization within current circumstances. It is within the accommodative or recontextualizing aspects of patterned experience, that is, of transference that the therapist's empathic availability has influence; that is to say transference at the somatic, trial-and-error exploration, behavioral–consequential, or representational–structural levels of learning and awareness.

In the transactional modes of treatment the clinician helps the patient to become observant of the various processes in which the patient is engaged. This is done through the use of therapeutic bids (see chapter 9 on Therapeutic Bids). The goal of this work is to transfer to the patient the clinician's modes of becoming observant and to help the patient to be able to understand and observe the past, present, and hopes for the future.

Here, then, we will offer a brief summary on what we think constitutes understanding when organized according to specific issues that derive from the interpersonal and intrapersonal contexts and their respective facets. The modes of learning that lead to understanding and working through apply to understanding within specific situations. Practicing, however, refers not only to repeated understanding in specific situations, but also to repeated attempts at behavioral change. Understanding of oneself and others is arrived at gradually, through repeated and gradual approximations, and through an experience with oneself, in the presence and absence of significant others, and experiences with significant others that include being together and separated from them. To understand, an individual requires that the clinician attempt to know the patient through that person's internal, intrapsychic frame of reference, his or her personal language, imagery, and symbolism, personal history, tendencies to repeat traumatizing situations, tendencies to enter into disabling transferences, capacities or difficulties in taking charge of autonomous ego functions, tendencies toward self-evasion and protection. The clinician also attempts to know the patient in terms of the person's sense of self, ideal self as expressed in hopes, aspirations, and ambitions, as well as the nature of the character armor as expressed in the defense against entering into transference relationships. The clinician is prompted to know the patient in terms of the latter's inclinations toward attending to biopsychological functions, social connectedness, and interest in exploring novelty, and affecting the environment. Finally, the clinician strives to help the patient have a sense of personal balance between striving for autonomy and strivings for interdependence. Thus, understanding is achieved through a double process: the first engages a knowing on the part of the clinician, through the process of trial identification, and the second engages a knowing on the part of the patient. This latter takes place through a process of the clinician stepping away from the patient in order to regain a more objective perspective, thus disidentifying from the patient. This objectified perspective entails drawing on knowledge that derives from sources outside the internal purview of the clinician. It is hoped that eventually the patient too will master the capacity to know him- or herself from the inside out, as well as from the outside in within a more objectified frame of reference.[4]

---

[4]It is in this context that the meaning of Buber's words (1958) become clear: "As experience, the world belongs to the primary word I-It" (p. 5). He seems to refer here to the experience of the senses, perception, affects, and thoughts. "The primary word I-Thou establishes the world of relation (p. 6) . . . I do not experience the man to whom I

Practicing or working through is the process of continuously reinforcing associations that were illuminating when first encountered, but which require stabilization through facetization as well as generalization to a variety of situations so that new understandings become firmly encoded and structuralized within the individual's patterns of perceiving and thinking. The clinician, in order to get to know a patient, relies on the principle of practice and working through (which entails an ongoing process of understanding through gradual approximation) as much as the patient does. But in the last analysis, if the patient is to free him- or herself from the therapeutic bond (absorb it, incorporate it, and internalize it), the task of practicing, working through, and consolidating is the patient's.

CASE ILLUSTRATION OF THE MULTIFACETED TREATMENT PROCESSES[5]

To return now to the case illustration presented in chapter 8 as a diagnostic profile. The following illustrates the multifaceted movements that highlight alternately, and very often simultaneously, the nature of the therapeutic work. The illustration focuses on the manner in which the patient's developmental difficulties are addressed, how the characterologic envelope and its core self-processes engage the entire gestalt of the process, and how manifestations of the transference and the compulsion to repeat can be distinguished from other facets in form, content, and clinical approach.

---

say Thou. But I take my stand in relation to him. . . . Only when I step out of it do I experience him. . . . In the act of experience Thou is far away" (p. 9). Here Buber seems to be grappling with the concept of identification as different from the concept of objectification, differences we have tried to define above and in the theory section, that defines the I, I/Me, and Me/I processes. "I become [I] through my relation to the Thou; as I become [I], I say Thou . . ." (p. 11). Here Buber seems to convey the shadowing and interplay between knowledge from within and knowledge from without, as in the processes of trial identification and disidentification, or objectification.

[5]In order to maintain anonymity of other clinicians associated with the treatment of this patient, and for the sake of didactic illustration of the multifaceted treatment, the senior author, CHR, claims sole responsibility for the treatment of this case.

The reader will recall that the patient, a 50-year-old man who had survived the Holocaust as a child, initially sought consultation which led to psychoanalytic treatment due to two major circumstances: the first, and most significant from his conscious perspective, was precipitated by his failure at work, a failure of the intellect, as he saw it, which led to the loss of a significant client for his corporation and loss of face among his colleagues. This precipitant evoked his earliest significant experience of defeat, associated with the trauma of the loss of his parents and the major upheaval in his living conditions, and concerned his inability to learn in school. The second precipitant, which was in fact very much connected with the first but of which he was less conscious, was associated with his children's departure from home. For him, their growing autonomy meant real, concrete abandonment. From the perspective of a less traumatized parent, the departure of one's children to college and the workplace could also represent an abandonment of sorts, but a more symbolic one. For this patient, however, his children's departure from home constituted a replay of his first double loss in real life, namely, the loss of both parents at once. In the diagnostic evaluation, it was surmised that his temporary cognitive arrest was associated with the trauma of this loss, together with the loss of his home, his familiar surroundings and his move to another country where he was expected to communicate in a totally foreign tongue. His children's departure was now seen as an abandonment, not as an achievement in which he, as a parent, had played a positive part. These double precipitants instilled feelings of bewilderment and depreciation in the core self-processes. Unable to absorb and understand what was happening to him, he was overcome with a mass of angry feelings, which led to his resorting to the coping strategies of externalizing and blaming. Hence the explosions of temper and rage at home which also had begun to invade the workplace. It can now be seen that underlying the externalizing furor lay the aggression turned inward, namely, a deep-seated and unacknowledged depression.

The first three years of analytic treatment, however, reestablished this man's self-confidence to the extent of enabling him to maintain his functioning both in the workplace and at home. In the early phase of treatment, his life's story unfolded with considerable excitement that bordered on euphoria, for he felt that he had found both mother and father in his therapist, and was getting the sought after appreciation, even admiration for his exploits and courage to live through the years of persecution in the manner he had. But with the deepening of the transference within the psychoanalytic relationship, the inner workings of his personality were now coming into view and his characterologic coping strategies of self-assurance, taking charge, and being in control when he felt threatened and vulnerable, were no longer functioning as smoothly as they had before. For example, he gradually allowed himself to experience the pains and fantasies associated with separations, weekends, holidays, and vacations that disrupted the ongoing treatment and threatened the relationship. Now that his character armor was more pregnable and flexible, he was less able to withstand the onslaught of these disruptions and began to suffer the pains of separation. As is inevitable in any analytic work, a single crisis, or a number of crises, introduces the beginning of the middle phase of treatment, when all the pains, hopes, longings, aspirations, and all the workings of the patient's inner experiences become associated to the person of the analyst.

In this case, the patient's analytic crisis and his work crisis occurred almost simultaneously, the second having been initiated by the patient almost immediately after the first. The events were the following: The analyst had to interrupt the treatment for a prolonged period due to a death in her own family. The patient, now bereft of what had become the most important figure in his psychic life, precipitously decided to seek a change in his position at work. (Recall that the primary conscious precipitant that prompted his seeking treatment was his most recent work failure.) He decided to campaign for an opening for the vice-presidency that had appeared in the corporate hierarchy of the firm. This position was on a different track from the investment consultancy which he occupied. He discovered very quickly that he would never be considered for that position. At best, he might become a senior investment advisor. For reasons unknown to him at that point in treatment, he found himself unable to assimilate this new facet and understood it to be a reflection of his lack of competency. Thus, he experienced this as a major setback and disappointment, felt defeated, humiliated, and degraded, and consequently became seriously depressed. Strong bouts of anxiety and suicidal thoughts accompanied the depression. He had sleepless nights and loss of appetite. This usually active man began to experience an unsurmountable lassitude that he described as a "systemic, physical brown-out." He felt as though he moved and thought in slow motion. He was unable to make any kind of investment decision. He who had always relied on his staff to help in the preparation of background materials when considering investments, turned to them in utter helplessness to analyze and discuss the market and make the appropriate recommendations. Members of his staff were not unhappy about his new turn of events because they found him more reachable, easier to work with, and less arrogant in this state. But he felt awful, almost traumatized by his dependence, lack of stamina and productivity. Despite this enormous setback, however, he was able to continue to relate to his now grown children, his friends and associates, who all found him more reachable in this state of self-depletion. As for his wife, she continued to be his source of stability for everything from providing him with emotional nurturance, to running the household, to maintaining their social life. Thus, he was able to maintain a semblance of relatedness with others. But his internal sense of self was lost. He felt broken up inside, without future or hope.

Meanwhile, the events of the psychoanalytic treatment, though rooted in his genetic family history and the course of his ongoing outside life, took on a power of their own. The treatment between him and his analyst was now understood as a replay of his earlier psychological patterns, and events happening outside the treatment were now understood in terms of the "psychic life" of the treatment itself.

Thus, the analytic crisis proper, while it began with a death in the analyst's own entourage and was followed by an interruption of treatment (thus an analytic abandonment), culminated in full-blown fashion, when the analyst returned to work. Though she felt ready to resume work with most of her patient clientele, she was perhaps not quite ready to respond to this patient's self-involved, emotionally laden concrete demands for attention. He had his first explosion of rage toward his analyst when she "accidentally" kept him waiting in the waiting room for what seemed to him a long period of time, about 20 minutes, without coming to see whether he had arrived for his session. Subsequently, because this incident had been improperly understood and handled, the patient accused his analyst of dishonesty, lying, stupidity, professional incompetence, of not knowing how to work with him, of fearing her own countertransference, and the like. He, the patient, offered her, the analyst, an interpretation for why she had made him wait, which she was unable to handle analytically and rejected out of hand, as if he were talking about external reality, rather than about his intrapsychic reality. The rages increased over the subsequent sessions as the material between them remained misunderstood. Patient and analyst came to an impasse. After a few weeks, the patient once again let go with the barrage of invectives against his analyst, accusing her of incompetence. She, by now sufficiently recovered from her own trauma, asked him to sit up, and addressing him as an equal, said that she would not be able to continue working with him unless he learned to curb his anger and attempted to investigate together with her the source of his rages. As a first step in that endeavor, she wondered how he understood her slip-up in making him wait for such a long time after her return from her abrupt leave.

Feeling that now he might be listened to, and sensing also by the analyst's sternness that he may finally have encountered the missing (superego) father who would teach him how to become a "civilized" man, the patient ventured that he understood his analyst's behavior in several ways, all of which were in the nature of countertransference responses to him. The first view of her "forgetting" was that overcome with her own grief, she had temporarily forgotten about him (i.e., abandoned him). This was certainly understandable and a plausible interpretation. Based on the principle of analytic countertransference, the patient through the mechanism of projective identification (namely, the patient feeling forgotten attributed the act of forgetting to the analyst), understandably thought that his analyst had forgotten him, just as he thought that his parents had forgotten him when they were taken away. The patient's second view was that the analyst had unconsciously "staged" this episode. Namely, he thought she had wanted to teach him a lesson in empathy. It was an "unconscious" staging because the patient knew that providing the patient with a corrective emotional experience was not part of his analyst's treatment philosophy.

While the patient's interpretations of the analyst's intentions were not correct (she did not think she forgot about his appointment, nor did she intentionally mean to teach him a lesson about empathy), it is nevertheless true that she provided the essential ingredients that recreated the trauma in the analysis. For just as Freud said, a propos of working with the transference (Freud, 1912a, p. 108), one cannot work with the effects of trauma in *absentia or in effigy.* For when all is said and done, the patient must have the opportunity to relive and reenact in symbolic fashion and, one hopes under less traumatizing circumstances, the traumatic events he or she endured earlier in life. The patient must *learn* to endure some of the accompanying pain and agony associated in the *here and now* of the treatment situation in relation to the experienced trauma with his analyst; the patient must also be encouraged to explore and understand and be prevented from resorting to the semiconscious characterologic coping strategies (such as avoidance, transformation of affect, blaming, disconnecting, submission, and the like) or the intrapsychic defense mechanisms (such as denial, disavowal, reaction formation, projection, projective identification, and so on). All this is necessary in order to help the patient integrate the earlier traumatic injuries and help him undo the resistance to experiencing the hidden feelings, images, fantasies, and thoughts associated with the trauma.

The analyst understood that with this patient, multiply traumatized in childhood, she must intervene step by step (the bids of intervention will be detailed in chapter 9), as she had learned to intervene in her work with infants and their parents, first by *mirroring*, *reflecting*, and *labeling* the affects, thereby putting the feelings into words. This is the first task which targets primarily the developmental and character facets and helps the patient to integrate cognition with affect and bring the affect under the control of the intellect. Second, she must help the patient to express his thoughts in a manner that can be understood by her. Thus she must *facilitate* that expression and indeed teach him, namely, *expand* on what he may not quite know, that in order to be understood, he must consider the other person who is listening. This process itself also helps clarify for the patient his own feelings and thoughts, and helps him in the task of self-regulation. Part of this second task consists also of insisting that the patient *contain* (delay, modulate, or inhibit) his urges, feelings, propensities toward action, or even toward using excessively strong language aimed to incite. This second task primarily targets the patient's interpersonal and character facets. Third, she must gently *probe* in order to help him elaborate on his fantasies, urges, and the like. Part of this third task consists of *developing hypotheses* and *interpretations*, in collaboration with the patient, in order to convey her understanding through interpretation. This third task primarily targets the patient's intrapsychic and character facets. Thus she could convey her understanding through interpreting how the danger of the war years required immediate adaptations which prevented him, given his young age, from understanding and experiencing the multiple traumas to which he was subjected. She could also begin to explain the characterologic coping strategies, the search for admiration, having their origins in the pretrauma years, the vulnerable sense of self originating pretraumatically, the strengths in the developmental domains together with the posttraumatic arrests, and the numerous scars these left in their tracks.

In addressing his character strategies, the analyst must be exquisitely sensitive to timing; for the patient may have need for his character armor in dealing with future analytic crises, be they disruptions or resumptions in treatment, or disillusionments and disappointments in fantasies, hopes, aspirations, or ambitions.

And while the character armor can become more permeable and adaptive, it is the most in need of repeated experience and working through in a favorable environment before substantial change can occur in that facet.

To return to the analytic events within which the crisis was experienced and subsequently worked through, the emotional impact of the analysis and the attachment this man felt toward his analyst were understood in two ways, first, through his response to the separation which he handled by taking action in the outside world. Namely, he attempted to gain mastery over the trauma of the unanticipated separation by attempting to succeed in the workplace. This constituted a compulsion to repeat aimed at avoiding the pain of the disastrous consequences of the earlier separation which led to his school failure, in the hopes that this time he will succeed in the workplace. This was not to be, however, for he seemed to have almost willfully miscalculated his chances for success and, therefore, recreated the failure.

Second, his response to the reunion with the analyst underscored even more significantly the impact of the analytic process, since the response took place not outside the treatment frame, but within it. (As regards the issue of separation and reunion, Ainsworth and associates [1974] have noted that a child's attachment to its mother is gauged not by the emotional reaction to the separation, but rather, by the emotional response to the reunion.)

The question then arises, how could the analyst have responded to the patient's misery of having been "forgotten" in the waiting room when treatment resumed. He still wanted to know whether she had kept him waiting deliberately or whether she had forgotten about him that day when he returned for treatment. The analyst's answer came now as a simple yes; she had forgotten about him. The analyst whose practice it was to ask her patients not to ring the doorbell when they arrived, but to wait to be ushered into the consulting room after the preceding patient left, had, in fact, stepped out of her usual routine and stood by her desk sorting her mail all the while waiting for her patient to ring the bell. She had lost track of time, as it were, until suddenly, noticing how late it was, she began wondering what had happened

147

to her patient. When she opened the door to the waiting room, she found a concerned and irate man. His rage, however, did not come to the fore until later during the session when she was unable or unwilling to own up to the initial part of the incident, namely, that she had indeed stepped out of her habitual routine and kept her patient waiting. From then on, things went from bad to worse. Sensing the analyst's dishonesty, the patient felt that the interpersonal relationship was now disordered; gone were joint interest and reciprocity. All he experienced now was the analyst's attempt at overriding his experience: "Why didn't you ring the bell when you didn't see me coming?" she asked, which was a reasonable question, but hardly the point. The patient in the throes of a painful transference and the force of the compulsion to repeat was feeling abandoned and forgotten and expected his analyst to understand that. Instead, he felt disregarded for his judgment and observations, and belittled for his feelings. He then flew into the first of his rages, accusing her of stupidity and gross professional incompetence, of closed-mindedness, and of being unwilling to learn from her patient. (As regards the patient's perspective of the analyst's experience, see Hoffman [1983].)

This episode stung the analyst, for she had not the slightest intention, at least not consciously, of hurting this man for whom she had a basic and genuine liking. Had she indeed been "incompetent" with this particular patient? She knew that this incident almost broke their working alliance; the patient admitted to almost walking out on her, were it not for his commitment to better his condition. In a very real sense he felt that this treatment was necessary for his psychological survival. Also, prompted by his positive maternal and oedipal transference and (pre)conscious wish and fantasy for making a "decisive impression" on her, he hoped that he could be instrumental in some way in teaching her something about his condition and that of others like him.

What were the analyst's mistakes in the treatment up to that point? As alluded to earlier, they were mistakes in understanding, prompted by lack of knowledge and by the fear of coming into

conflict with her professional mentors of the past, her identification with and internalization of the analytic method. Her only
source of new knowledge, outside her work with this patient, was,
in fact, her work with parents and infants. It was through working
with them, paying minute attention to what babies and adults
were responding to from within and between them, together with
her determination to attempt to transmit to patients and trainees
a more useful way of looking at clinical theory, diagnosis, and
treatment, that she was able to see her survivor patient in a new
light. That patient of hers, being characterologically and interpersonally deficient, developmentally delayed, and intrapsychically
arrested required all the therapeutic bids that work with infancy
issues had taught her. Then, this analyst who now thought of
herself as a therapist, using the analytic method of free association
and transference as necessary and useful, began to relate to her
patient somewhat differently from the way she had in the past.
Particularly, when working with character issues, knowing how
each observation singes and hurts in direct proportion to the
magnitude of the injury to the self processes, she tactfully and
almost lovingly began reflecting and labeling for the patient his
lack of empathy for her predicament after her experience with
death. She did not have to be self-revealing about her own life,
all she needed to do was to be minutely attentive to the patient's
responses and probe into them. She coaxed him to share his pain
with her and she interpreted how her pain must have triggered
his own in relation to her. To experience pain in relation to the
therapist meant also to be able to withstand the abstinence of the
analytic situation. After all the patient does not remake his life
with his newly found object even though he may try to do so.
Instead he relives his unassuaged urges and feelings, and reframes
the story of his life many times over (Schafer, 1992). But if actions
are not the purview of psychological treatment, feelings in the
moment are, and they can be responded to, even reciprocated,
namely, the wish for gratification and its necessary limitations in
the therapeutic setting can be openly acknowledged.

Thus began the slow work of the dissolution for the tenacious
defense mechanisms of reaction formation, projective identification, and rationalization. More difficult still was working with the

coping strategies of blaming, provoking, reversal of affect, and withholding. Many occasions arose when the patient relived and practiced, together with the therapist, his mortifications, insults, injury, panics, yearnings, passions, disappointments, helplessness, and subsequent devitalizing depressions. These were serious clinical depressions that tended to undo the patient, putting him into a state of depletion. When asked what kept him going when he was in the grips of these depressions, neither he nor his therapist had answers to offer. Silence and an occasional inquiry if his pain were tolerable was all she had to offer. Occasionally, however, she acknowledged how much he was teaching her about treatment, in general, and Holocaust survivors, in particular. This proved to be a meaningful and healing acknowledgment on her part, because it had also been his earliest wish in relation to his parents that they recognize him not as the baby in the family, but as someone significant to contend with; and now it had become the most significant wish in his transference to her.

Powerful homosexual longings emerged as he attempted to balance interpersonal masculine strivings of autonomy with needs and fears of the many interdependencies that their relationship necessarily engendered. Finally, he was able to come face-to-face with his erotic heterosexual desires in relation to his woman analyst, behold them and look them plainly in the face, all the desires and resultant envy, hatred, and jealousy they engendered. Yet he stayed his course while doing so. He maintained solid reins on his emotions and integrated his emotions with thoughts, and allowed himself to feel his sense of self (the self processes) run down his spine as though they were fueling his entire being. When he ended the analytic treatment, he walked away from it having acquired the skills to face himself, with the facts such as they were, aware that the work of mourning this relationship would only be possible when he actually was no longer together with her. He had also acquired an ability to treat himself internally "as an equal" through introspection and self-observation (without being self-demeaning, self-punishing or self-aggrandizing). He had acquired the ability to maintain a sense of existential meaning, by attempting to transmit something of his own acquired knowledge to those he cared to affect.

In conclusion, it was not despite but because of the many upheavals in their work together, and because this work gave rise to the negative transferences, which mostly resulted from narcissistic injuries to the self-processes, and because these were then addressed and tackled in honesty on both parts that the treatment progressed and came to a successful conclusion. We hope this case illustration clarified for the reader how delay, deficit, arrest, and conflict interact, how the theory the clinician holds in his or her mind has to be sufficiently broad and complex to do justice to the complexity of the patient's mind, and how the therapeutic bids interact with the four psychological facets, their respective domains, and the numerous defense mechanisms and coping strategies.

9

Therapeutic Bids: A Coding Scheme of Interventions with Coded Therapy Sessions

The scheme we introduce here for analyzing and coding the psychotherapy process represents our best effort at describing the essential aspects of psychotherapeutic activity. The effort affords a better look at the nature of the process that occurs within the patient as well as between the patient and therapist.[1] Anchored in the theoretical perspectives on psychological functioning and therapeutic transaction described in the previous chapters, the coding scheme takes full cognizance of the degree of psychological health and pathology of the patients treated, be they infants, children, adolescents or adults, parents, foster parents, or grandparents.

The present scheme and coding system represents the most elemental aspects of the scientific method. It operates at the level of classification (observation and definition of phenomena) and descriptive explanation (conceptually derived inference of relationships between phenomena) to define and to describe by reference to the patient's response what it is that can be viewed as a

---

[1]Our work joins the work of others in their attempts at analyzing and coding the psychotherapy process; for example, Truax and Carkhuff (1967), Parloff, Waskow, and Wolfe (1978), Kiesler (1982), Strupp and Binder (1984), Hoffman and Gill (1988), Hill, Helms, Spiegel, and Tichenor (1988), Luborsky (1990), Luborsky, Barber, Crits-Christoph (1990), Mahrer, Sterner, Lawson, and Dessaulles (1990). These schemes employ theoreti-

153

therapeutic bid within the moment-to-moment transactional process. We have already described the transactional influences of observation and theory in shaping our process of classifying the therapeutic bids and developing the psychological theory advanced here. The scheme and its coding system are based on the theory of the nature of human psychological functioning and of the nature of therapeutic action. Since our point of reference is a transactional one, we assume that therapeutic bids can fulfill a number of functions depending on the psychological dimensions they engage in the patient. Whereas, however, all of the psychological facets may be affected by a certain bid, some facets may be more immediately responsive to some bids than to others. At any particular moment, one or another of the psychological facets will be in the foreground of experience, and the patient's response to a bid helps the therapist identify that psychological facet in the here-and-now of the therapeutic transaction. The therapist's bid, or combination of bids, may well be directed toward one or another facet, but the therapist's bid cannot dictate the patient's response or the activation of the particular facet sought for engagement. Rather, it is the patient's immediate foreground response to a bid that signals which facet is active or has become engaged. The facets are identified as they are expressed in terms of their content; the content, in turn, is a manifestation of the aims, coping strategies, or defense mechanisms of the facets. Because psychological functioning is transactional, background dimensions are also influenced by the activities of facets operating in the foreground of experience, but what happens to the background facets may not be known either to therapist or patient for quite some time.

We believe that with ever more detailed definitions of the theoretical facet of psychological functioning and therapeutic action it should be possible to code and represent the essentials of the therapeutic processes taking place in any given session. The coding scheme presented here could then be used to track the

---

cally derived classifications, and are based on extensive clinical experience. Our scheme is grounded in theory yet focuses on the specificity of the therapeutic bids.

course of an entire treatment, or a specific phase of treatment, and would also show what sorts of therapeutic bids were used and with what sorts of results. The coding scheme could be put to use to study any number of processes or outcomes in the treatment of specific psychological disorders.

We have found, too, that the therapeutic bids and the coding scheme serve well in training student psychotherapists. Reliability in methodology increases to the extent that phenomena can be classified with agreement and thus consistency, hence enhancing transmission of the methodology, which in this case involves the psychotherapy method. As it is woven into the fabric of our philosophical tenets, the goal of treatment is to transmit to the patient what the therapist has come to know about the patient and how the therapist has come to know the patient (i.e., the methods used). This is not a question of labels or terminology, but rather the transmission of relationship functions contained and expressed in methods of communication (therapeutic bids) leading to what is commonly termed *learning* and *internalization*. The patient's acquisition and personal (and thus unique) adaptation of therapeutic skills into self-reflective and self-directive skills is no less significant as an enduring effect of treatment than the narrative content of the treatment. Indeed, the narrative content depends upon the therapeutic skills for expression and elaboration. The patient's continued construction of a personal narrative beyond treatment depends in large part on the acquisition of those skills that enhance interpersonal and intrapersonal communication.

To summarize for review and preview: Any segment of a therapy or analytic session can be analyzed in terms of patient and therapist utterances which are conveyed within either the inter- or intrapersonal context. These contexts are not independent; each influences the other, though in differing ways and to varying degrees. That is, the intrapersonal always informs the interpersonal; the interpersonal would be meaningless without the background context of the intrapersonal. But the influence of the interpersonal on the intrapersonal may be more a matter of stimulation than information. The delusional transference is an example of an extreme instance. In the delusional transference, the interpersonal present is equated with the past as organized and represented from the intrapersonal facets. As such, the patient lacks a sense of personal history in that the patient makes no meaningful distinction between past and present. Still, something in the interpersonal present must operate as a cue to elicit the patient's transference reaction. In Piagetian terms, the patient's perception of the cue in the interpersonal present reflects a modicum of accommodation in a predominantly assimilatory (transferential) process (Wachtel, 1980). Gill's (1982) emphasis on the therapeutic need for the clinician to acknowledge and to examine with the patient those aspects of the clinician's actual behavior that elicit transference reactions from the patient highlights the significance of the interpersonal for the intrapersonal.

Each context is informed by its specific facets: that of the interpersonal context is the system; that of the intrapersonal context includes the developmental, character, and intrapsychic. Each facet has specific domains: The system's domain is the relationship, mutual and nonmutual; the developmental dimension includes the domains of cognition, affect, neuromotor, social, language and speech, and play, fantasy, and creativity; the character dimension includes the domains of the self expressed in the I, I/Me, Me/I processes, the ideal self processes, and the constitutional and neurophysiological components of regulation as expressed in temperament aspects of rhythmicity and activity level in mood, thoughts, and affects. The intrapsychic facet includes the domains of ego, superego, and the unconscious needs, wishes, and related fantasies and motives.

Each facet has aims that become the broad treatment aims. The aim within the system facet is to achieve optimal balance between autonomy and interdependence. The aims within the developmental facet seek to achieve balance between fulfillment of biopsychological requisites, social connectedness, and novelty-exploration and effectance. The aims within the character facet strive to elaborate the self processes, the ideal self, and of central importance to character—the facet within which inside and outside phenomena intersect—is the aim to achieve regulation between internally and externally impinging stimuli. The aims of the intrapsychic facet attempt to transform unconscious motives and fantasies into conscious understandings, to resolve the compulsions to repeat, to resolve disabling transferences, and to consolidate and strengthen the synthesizing functions of the ego. (The reader may wish to review Table 2.1 at this point.)

Each patient and therapist utterance reflects content expressing issues associated with the domains and their aims at any particular moment. The manner in which these contents are communicated assumes different forms. Thus, content can be communicated within the form of *dynamically* unconscious ego defense mechanisms (denial, disavowal, projection, introjection, projective identification, identification, reaction formation, rationalization, and sublimation). Content can also be communicated as conscious or *descriptively* unconscious coping strategies, which we have classified and defined as realistic appraisal/engagement, agreement, compliance, opposition/defiance, blaming, rejection, avoidance/disengagement, freezing/immobilization, and transformation of affect. (The second coping strategy in each instance is not a synonym, but rather more intense than the first.) Every utterance by a therapist and a patient is associated and conveyed with affect.

We classify the manner or form in which the therapist's utterances is conveyed as therapeutic bids, which include the following: receptive observation (which includes respect, empathy, tact), mirroring/imitating, reflecting/labeling, praising, probing, coaxing/encouraging, facilitating, expanding didactically, interpretation, containing (includes inhibiting, postponing and renouncing), disengaging, and self-observation. (The second therapeutic bid in each case is not a synonym, but rather more intensive than the first.) These individual bids can be grouped according to their functions and are clustered under the following terms: basically humane, supportive of the self, insight orienting, containing, internally orienting.

Not all utterances or bids are therapeutic, of course. We have identified and classified nontherapeutic bids, which we have taken from our observations of growth-inhibiting parental bids.

We classify these negative bids as follows: overriding, uninvolvement, verbal seductiveness, verbal abuse, physical seductiveness and seduction, and physical abuse. (In this work, however, we will focus our efforts on coding the therapeutic or positive bids only, postponing the full coding of the therapy sessions, including coding of the negative bids, for a future publication.)

DEFINITIONS OF THERAPEUTIC BIDS

The following are definitions of positive therapeutic bids organized according to their shared functions:

Receptive Observation, Respect, Empathy, Tact

Receptive observation represents the initial gambits of the dyadic engagement. The patient, whether parent or child, in order to overcome the initial anxiety of relating to the therapist, requires an invitation, or a type of coaxing, that is embracing without being stifling, that is neither too stimulating nor too tepid. Parent or therapist conveys through facial expression, posture, and vocal inflection a coaxing interest and acceptance of the child's or patient's intentions.

The actual behaviors associated with inviting receptivity are an inviting rounded upper torso body posture, facial features that include brows arched upward, open or closed-mouthed smile, and for infants, at least, a high-pitched vocal inflection. The therapeutic posture with the adult is actually quite similar. The receptive body posture and the interested open facial features are the same as with the infant. Attenuated but present is the vocal inflection which now becomes an echoing "hm-hm," and the smile is much attenuated though responsive to the patient's need to be accepted.

Receptive observation entails respect, empathy, and tact. Respect includes courtesy and esteem of what is personal to the individual, and keeps in sight that any intervention must be oriented toward enhancing the patient's psychological development. In our view, empathy refers, essentially, to the therapist's capacity to be receptively open to allowing his or her human alikeness with the patient to resonate with the patient's experience (Schwaber, 1981). As such, empathy implies that the therapist uses receptive observation on his or her own experience as it resonates with the patient's. Tact is closely related to respect and empathy in that it conveys respectful understandings through sensitive handling and communication of those understandings to avoid needless offensiveness or abuse of the patient's self-esteem.

Mirroring and Imitating

Mirroring is a two-step process which includes imitating. The first step requires the act of actual imitation (Meltzoff and Moore, 1977), and the second step requires that the mirroring person understand that the imitating itself entails and conveys an interpretation of the infant's or patient's expressed state. The interpreting aspect of mirroring represents how the parent or therapist reads the infant's or patient's expressed state of sensations, feelings, or thoughts. Whereas imitation involves repetition or echoing, Stern (1983) notes that mirroring is never exact and typically intensifies or mutes a perceived condition. A simple example of behaviors associated with imitating would be the parent or therapist who echoes the laughter of an infant or patient. An example of mirroring would be a parent's or clinician's more muted echoing of a child's or patient's overly excited laughter.

Reflecting and Labeling

Reflection and labeling involves the verbalization of what has been imitated behaviorally and mirrored affectively. The bid puts into words what the therapist reads, as it were, from the patient's state, sensations, facial expressions, feelings, wishes, thoughts, and behaviors. Reflection and labeling involves some intuition on the part of the therapist of the patient's condition, and labeling involves putting these thoughts into words. All bids are associated, to some extent, with how the therapist senses the patient's utterances, and therefore conveys positive or negative appreciation. Reflecting and labeling also represent the therapist's realistic appraisal of the patient's state, behavior, feelings, or thoughts. As such, reflecting and labeling can also provide background for the therapeutic bid of praise, together functioning as a "beacon of orientation" (Mahler, Pine, and Bergman, 1975) that can impart the therapist's sense that the patient is doing well or that the patient is perhaps on the wrong track. When the clinician reflects and labels a patient's resistance the bid also assumes that function of a confrontation (Bibring, 1954).

Praising

Praising functions to amplify mirroring as well as reflection and labeling. It expresses supportive approval of the patient's efforts in pursuing, expanding, or elaborating on the aims of psychological facets and respective domains within the inter- and intrapersonal contexts. As a therapeutic bid, praise must be used judiciously; it serves to the patient's benefit when it responds to behavior emerging developmentally or to behavior that largely by omission, hesitation, or fragmentation had shown indications of delay or deficiency. Parents, of course, use praise frequently to encourage and reinforce their child's development of positively valued behaviors. As such, praise may be viewed as representing an affective aspect of what we believe Loewald (1960) referred to when he wrote about parents responding to their children with an eye toward the future, seeing the child as he or she is about to become. It also may be viewed as representing an aspect of the parent–therapist's function as a "beacon of orientation" (Mahler, et al., 1975), providing supportive reassurance in the midst of uncertainty (see also Emde [1990]). Therapists, we submit, must operate with a similar kind of vision and implicit expectation. A parent's view is oriented by unconscious and conscious needs, desires, values, and beliefs, which provide an orienting frame of reference for the child. The therapist's vision is oriented largely by theory that channels his or her personal desires and expectations in the direction of seeking "understanding" as a means of promoting the unfolding of the patient's potentialities of growth. It should be emphasized that praise is not so much an act of celebration as it is an act of affect attunement to the child-patient's need for an affirmative response signaling safety in and encouragement of continued and further exploration.

Probing

Probing is defined as the therapist's wondering aloud to facilitate exploration with the patient about how and why the patient came to think about or do one thing or another, and about what the meaning of a thought or action might be. This bid is not expressed as a direct question, such as, "What are you thinking about?" but rather, "I wonder what you could be thinking, or how you got there." In other words the question is posed by the therapist to the therapist—"I am wondering"—and not directly to the patient. The bid functions as a probe inasmuch as it points to something that warrants exploration. Why be indirect? Direct questions are often perceived as implicitly accusatory or even persecutory regarding some deficit in understanding or wrongdoing in action. Moreover, probing in this fashion works in the direction of facilitating the development of self observation; developing an awareness of the other's view and need for objective or object-making perspective (what is the thing or object of the idea, feeling, or action) helps develop a perspective-taking self-observing orientation in the patient.

Coaxing and Encouraging

Coaxing and encouraging involves an intensification of probing: the therapist senses that the patient needs some encouragement to express a thought aloud. This requires courage on the part of the patient, and as such requires the therapist's respect and positive appreciation for the patient's effort. Encouragement not only reinforces the patient's pursuit of psychological aims within any of the facets, but also supports the patient's exploratory activity within the therapeutic engagement.

Facilitating

Facilitating is defined as helping another carry out a task, thought, feeling, that has been begun but that the person needs assistance in carrying through to completion. For example, the infant reaches for an object beyond his or her grasp and the parent-therapist facilitates by bringing the object to a position that enables the infant to conclude the initiated action. Or the patient tries to find a word that might describe his or her feeling or thought and the clinician offers a word that seems to fit. Facilitating, along with the following bid, didactic expansion, functions to promote exploration and learning in the patient by providing him or her with what has been described in psychoanalytic theory as an "auxiliary" ego. Vygotsky's (1986; and see Bruner, 1985) views on learning highlight the importance of the facilitating function as we think of it: the learning process is facilitated when a more competent individual (tutoring peer/caregiver) helps a less competent individual (tutored peer/child) by first allowing the latter to do on his or her own whatever can be done. Then, whatever the child (patient) cannot do spontaneously is completed by the caregiver (therapist). By this means, the patient makes vicarious use of the therapist until the patient acquires the competency or function supplied by the therapist. In this connection, Modell (1990) finds Vygotsky's investigations of learning to be significant for psychoanalysis in describing a stage of learning prior to internalization (although Modell is pointing to the psychoanalyst's interpretive actions as including this function). Facilitation entails the therapist sharing a view or task with the patient, but with a higher level organizational capacity, and thus facilitating a higher level integrative activity and functioning in the patient. Loewald's (1960) formulation from use of the parent–child relationship as a model for therapeutic action is relevant in this regard:

> The organization of the psychic apparatus . . . proceeds by way of mediation of higher organization on the part of the environment to the infantile organism. . . . The higher organizational stage of the environment is indispensable for the development of the psychic apparatus and, in early stages, has to be brought to it actively. Without such a differential between organism and environment no development takes place [p. 24].

Didactic Expansion

The act of elaborating on another's intentions or productions is called didactic expansion. This type of intervention has been described by Vygotsky (1978) as addressing the "zone of proximal development," helping exercise those embryonic and emergent functions that have not yet matured but are in the process of maturing (see also Emde, 1990). These functions require the assistance of a parent or therapist to bring the environment to the infant or patient while also providing incentive for the individual to stretch his or her reach, as it were. Parent or therapist enlarges, elaborates on, and provides a larger context for the infant's or patient's experience, thereby stretching the latter's emerging abilities. Even well-timed advice comes under this rubric, as well as some types of therapeutic training. Gedo (1988) speaks about teaching a patient when the latter shows .apraxias (developmental deficiencies in normally autonomous skills) in certain domains. The didactic expansion bid is instrumental when there is a lag, deficit, or emerging function in any of the psychological facets.

The behaviors associated with this bid include, for example, a parent's or therapist's introduction of a novel stimulus (e.g., toy, book, idea) that further engages the infant's or patient's interest. Another example would be when the therapist introduces a new idea that provides a larger or alternative perspective on the patient's habitual manner of coping with or understanding experience.

Interpretation

Interpretation is the sine qua non of the psychoanalytic therapeutic intervention aimed at explaining to the patient how the therapist understands the patient's preconscious or manifest intrapsychic or characterologic issues in the here-and-now transference with the therapist, and genetically, transference of the patient's past familial environment as it impacts on his or her intrapsychic and character formation. In our framework, interpretation refers to explaining to the patient how the therapist understands not only the interplay of intrapsychic and characterologic issues of self, regulation, coping strategies, and defenses in the here-and-now transference and in the internalized dynamics of family history. Interpretation also involves explaining to the patient how the therapist understands the interplay and transactions of the other two facets: the interpersonal with regard to the patient–therapist relationship and the patient's relations in the external world; the developmental with regard to its domains of cognition, language, physical patterning, affect, social connectedness, as well as the patient's proclivities for play and creativity.

Interpretation is a bid that verbally defines the patient's struggle in striving to attain certain aims within the interpersonal context and systems' facet, or within the intrapersonal developmental, characterologic, or intrapsychic facets. The patient's struggle may involve past or current family history, or past or current relationship to the therapist. Interpretation overlaps functionally with didactic expansion. The interpretive act constitutes an expansion insofar as it brings to light preconscious or conscious information from a number of diverse facets of the patient's experience. But interpretation is not didactic because the information is not new for the patient. Indeed, it is information gathered and accumulated bit by bit within the communications between patient and therapist.

Inhibiting

Inhibiting includes modulation of behavior, affect, verbal expression and the like, postponement, or renunciation, involves a two- or three-step process. Inhibiting functions to attenuate an unacceptable expression of emotion or behavior, or to postpone a wish or behavior in the short run (one need not run out of the room at the very moment one feels anxiety). In the long run one cannot, for example, do what one wishes until one is ready and capable of going it. Educationally and maturationally, one must learn to postpone, "No, you cannot marry your 4-year-old girl friend today"; or "You cannot buy the million dollar building until you have the money to cover the acquisition." Containment may involve renouncing something altogether; for example, "No you cannot put your hand in the electric outlet ever"; or "No you cannot kill your mother-in-law just because you profoundly dislike or even hate her!"

Inhibiting, however, also involves two other bids, namely refection/labeling and probing. Reflection/labeling acknowledges the patient's wish even if it is inadmissible to behavioral expression. Probing and coaxing inquire into the meaning of the wish or intention behind the inadmissible behavioral expression. Sometimes containing must precede any other bid for the sake of maintaining safety. Where safety is not an issue, reflection/ labeling and probing should be employed before inhibiting. Sometimes, and optimally, after an inadmissible wish is verbalized or reflected or looked into, the patient can do the self-observation necessary for self-containment. For example, the infant or patient may suddenly have an appetite for an unacceptable, sensually gratifying activity or a destructive desire that would be harmful to self or other. The parent or therapist would acknowledge the wish, inquire into its meaning or reason for its presentation, and then state that the realization of the wish is unacceptable while at the same time prohibiting the behavior or postponing or negating it altogether, as appropriate.

Disengagement and Silence

Disengagement and silence are associated with the therapist's employment of moments of benign disinterest and noninvolvement with the infant, child, or (adult) patient. The therapist's (or parent's) use of disengagement/silence enables the infant, child, or patient to be self-directed, to look inward, to be self-regulating and self-generating (see Winnicott's [1958] concept of the development of the infant's capacity to be alone in the presence of the mother). Also, disengagement is based on Ashby's concept of disjoin (Ashby, 1958; see chapter 3 for discussion of this concept). Our observations and clinical experience with this bid showed that noninvolvement provides the patient, regardless of age, with a space within the enveloping therapeutic matrix that enables a looking inward for the purpose of self-regulating, self-directing, and self-reorganizing. Parents sometimes disengage to pursue their own activities, but tend to do so most comfortably when their child is in a self-containing, self-regulated state (e.g., sleeping, looking around, playing alone). The parent who allows an infant to regroup with a moment of gaze aversion is providing a disengaging bid. The therapist's silence, when it is not vindictive or retributive, provides the patient with a space for wondering, exploring, inventing, organizing, and reorganizing ideas. Sometimes, the therapist's mind wanders too, and this also is significant clinical information as to what may be going on within the clinician, the dyad, or the patient alone.

Promoting Self-Observation

Self-observation is promoted through the activity of the therapist with the patient, which the patient internalizes through imitation, introjection, and identification as his or her own self-directing and self-observing activities (in this regard see also Schafer's [1968] and Meissner's [1980] theses on internalization). Essentially, self-observation consists of the patient pursuing the activity of exploring, learning, understanding, and practicing or working through by using the progressive therapeutic bids on him- or herself.

The therapist's self-observation is a bid used much more frequently than might appear at first sight. Self-observation does not necessarily mean that the therapist shares his or her countertransference reactions or feelings, such as, "Now you are really making me sad, mad, or the like," or "I can understand how your child or parent may feel, since I feel this way too." We suggest that self-observation, in the nature of countertransference reactions, be used sparingly, as they all too often serve only to confront and pit the patient against the therapist, or a significant other, rather than to enlighten and heal. Instead we recommend that self-observation be used as an introduction to another therapeutic bid, for example, the therapist says, "This is what I see, hear, feel or sense (self-observation) . . . that you are feeling upset, angry, needy, etc" (reflection and labeling). Why is it important to do it this way? Because, as one of our younger patients once said: "You don't know what I feel, you can only know what *you think* about it; also, if you tell me what you see or think about me, then I can tell you if I see the same thing or something else!" As stated in our basic philosophical tenets, transmission of therapeutic bids is one of the aims of treatment, together with accountability and equality. The therapist's self-observation in relation to the patient, and sometimes in relation to the therapist, must be explicit. Thus, self-observation is used frequently to introduce to or support the bids of reflection/labeling, facilitation, didactic expansion, interpretation, containment, and even disengagement/silence, as in, "I think I see that you need some space to think and for me to be quiet," or, "It feels to me that you are angry because of what I hear in your voice, some harshness perhaps; also, inside of me I was feeling pushed aside a bit" (the last self-observation *is* a countertransference response in the here-and-now).

CATEGORIES OF THERAPEUTIC BIDS

Our clinical working hypotheses include our observations that the therapeutic bids can be grouped according to the functions they perform and the psychological facets they engage. The bids in each grouping engage the therapeutic process with hierarchically greater degrees of intensity.

Heuristically, we have clustered the therapeutic bids into six groupings in terms of how they seem to function in relation to any or all the psychological facets they may engage: the humane therapeutic grouping, the supportive of the self grouping, the didactic-expanding, the containing, the insight-orienting, and the internally orienting grouping (see Table 9.1).

Receptive observation, empathy, tact, and respect form the *basically humane grouping* that provides the underpinnings in creating a basic set orientation for all the therapeutic bids. Receptive observation can be more easily taught to therapists than empathy, tact, and respect. Tact and respect are part of the therapist's characterologic adaptation, and while they too can be modified, much personal psychological work and life experience may be required to bring about change in this characterologic dimension. Empathy, such as transient identification—the capacity to remain both within a two-person system as well as to momentarily attempt to fuse with the patient—generative or intuitive empathy (Schafer, 1959), the capacity to see another's point of view or frame of reference (e.g., Schwaber, 1981), and the like (see Emde [1990], for discussion we have found particularly useful) can be acquired through personal psychological work on the part of the therapist. They can also be acquired through experiences in living and treating patients, and good didactic experiences with supervisors and teacher-clinicians.

TABLE 9.1
A Coding Schema for Therapeutic Bids and Their Functions

Therapeutic Bids	Categories of Bids
Receptive Observation	*Basically Humane grouping:* fosters primarily
Empathy	the therapeutic alliance, the interpersonal
Tact	facet, self-esteem of the character facet, as
Respect	well as the developmental facet.
Mirroring/Imitating	*Supportive of self grouping:* engages primarily
Reflecting/Labeling	the character and developmental facets.
Praising	
Probing	*Insight-Orienting grouping:* engages primarily
Coaxing/Encouraging	understanding intrapsychic and character
Interpretation	facets, also interpersonal and developmental.
Facilitation	*Learning grouping:* engages learning (zone
Didactic Expansion	of proximal development) within and across facets, primarily the developmental facet.
Inhibiting	*Containing grouping:* engages the character
Delaying (short- and long-term)	facet, in particular, the domain of temperament regulation.
Renouncing	
Disengaging/Silence	*Internally Orientating grouping:* engages any
Self-Observation	or all facets.

Mirroring/imitating, reflecting/labeling (putting into words), and praising are bids that feel supportive to the patient regardless of the facet engaged, but tend to enhance most the patient's sense of self (i.e., character facet). Hence, these bids constitute the *supportive-of-the-self grouping*.

Not all supportive bids are appreciated by all patients at all times, however. For example, depending on the degree of mental health and psychopathology, patients may feel underrated when a self-supportive bid is used instead of one that elicits more self-reflection and exploration through the challenge of a probe, an interpretation, or a necessary containment. But regardless of developmental age or degree of pathology, a patient will recognize a self-supportive bid for what it is, namely, an attempt on the therapist's part to recognize the validity of the patient's sense of self. By definition, then, the self-supportive grouping fosters development within and across all facets as well as the therapeutic alliance.

The manifestly *learning grouping* is made up of facilitation and didactic expansion. Any therapeutic bid, however, may teach the patient something she or he did not know, or was trying to know with help from the therapist, particularly if the patient has had little life experience with the positive effects of the kinds of communications represented in the bids. This grouping, then, fosters new learning and broadening of knowledge.

The *containing grouping* entails the therapist's promotion of necessary inhibition, self-regulation, self-discipline, short-term or long-term postponement, and renunciation of unacceptable behavioral expressions and pursuits of needs and desires. Other bids, such as disengagement and silence, probing, or reflection and labeling, may also function as containing bids, but these are not defined as containment proper. The containing group engages the character facet leading to enhanced self-regulation within and across all facets of the inter- and intrapersonal contexts.

The *insight-orienting grouping* includes the bids of probing, coaxing/encouragement, disengagement, and interpretation. This group engages particularly the intrapsychic and characterologic facets and transactionally fosters understanding within and across all facets.

The *internally orienting grouping* includes the bids of self-observation and disengaging/silence. This group engages the intrapersonal context and its respective developmental, characterologic, and intrapsychic aims, and by association with and internalizing of the significant other, this group also engages the interpersonal context and its aim.

A caution at this point is required. Much has been written in the clinical literature about the timing of an intervention, specifically about the timing of interpretations. Earlier we spoke of the supportive grouping being conducive to misunderstanding by patients. Here we want to generalize and restate that any therapeutic bid, regardless of supposed function, does not always function as the clinician anticipates. A number of reasons suggest themselves; for example, the timing of a bid or misunderstandings on the part of the therapist or the patient. Both timing and misunderstandings may feel invasive (as in overriding; see negative bids), seductive, abusive, or may reflect uninvolvement. Much self-observation on the part of the therapist in combination with probing and reflection may be necessary before understanding and communication are reestablished.

As a general rule, the therapist's use of the bids should proceed from the simple to the complex, from the concrete to the abstract. That is, the therapist begins with a bid that makes direct reference to behavior that the patient may observe along with the therapist. Only then would the therapist move to bids that draw upon and foster higher level inferential and representational processes. This may strike the reader as so obvious as hardly to warrant mention, but we have found that it is not at all uncommon for therapists to make rapid and broad inferential leaps from behavior to interpretation, or to make comments based on inference that sound more as though they are based on mere observation of behavior readily apparent to therapist and patient alike. In response, patients may nod their heads as if to indicate understanding or agreement when there really isn't any. The patient may assume, perhaps, that what seems so apparent to the therapist should be just as apparent to them. Or patients may assume that the therapist "knows" because of their expertise, or worse, patients may feel the therapist is reading their minds or becoming intrusive or stealing the show, as it were, in their "knowing."

An example of what is meant by proceeding from the simple to the complex, or from the behavioral to the inferential may be clarifying (see example of session, "Miranda," pp.180–188, chapter 9): A therapist (T) working with a young child (M) suffering from developmental expressive language disorder and autistic-like symptoms, comments as follows (the child has colored her hand and the therapist's hand): "M and T are the same." "M and T both have hands with colors." "M likes to have hands that are the same." The therapist's first bid is didactic/expansion; the second bid is reflection/expansion leaning toward an interpretation insofar as it states an inference of intentionality and of a cause–effect sequence of action on the child's part. The bids would have been better presented with the second preceding the first. That is, the didactic/expansion that draws attention to the patient–therapist similarity would have been better if it had followed the more simple, concrete observation of "M and T both have hands with colors." One might argue, too, that it might be better to state the didactic-expansion in more specific terms, "M and T's *hands* are the same," which would enhance the stepwise progression of observation and inference in the sequence of the content of the bids.

Another example from the same treatment session (earlier) may serve to highlight the importance of using the bids to proceed in small steps: "M is drawing on T's hand." M smiles. "M likes to draw on T's hand." "It makes M happy." The therapist's first utterance in this sequence is a reflection/labeling bid. M reacts with a smile, to which the therapist responds with what appears to be another reflection/labeling bid, but one that makes an inference on a behavior (smile) not explicitly observed aloud. It is not prudent to assume that any patients, especially those with autistic-like symptoms, are aware of their nonverbal expressions and communications, no matter how obvious they may seem to an observer. Indeed, developmental immaturity, delays, or deficiencies in verbal/nonverbal integrative functioning yielding phenomena sometimes classified in psychoanalytic terms as denial, dissociation, and splitting, or the defense mechanisms of disavowal and repression, often show their effects in apparent disconnections between words, meanings, and affects (Basch, 1983; F. Levin, 1991). In any case, it might have been better had the therapist voiced the reflection/labeling to observe aloud that "M is smiling." Were this followed by "*I think* M likes to draw on T's hand; *I think* it makes M happy," the comments would now be voiced as self-observation bids that point to the therapist's own inferential process in making meaning of the patient's nonverbal communication. Whereas previously those comments appeared to be reflection/labeling bids that perhaps contained too much inference to be mere reflection/labeling. "It makes M happy" is akin to stating a fact.

As such, the therapist's detailing of the steps of his or her observing and thinking provides the patient not only with the information necessary to know how the therapist got from point A to point B but also a model of how one might get from point A to point B in self-understanding and communication. This again emphasizes our conviction that the therapist should transmit to the patient not only *what* the therapist has come to know about the patient but also *how* the therapist has come to know the patient. And in this regard, what is good for the patient is good for the therapist. The therapist, too, necessarily becomes more aware of the steps of his or her own observing and thinking. The discipline provides the therapist with a means to discern distinctions between, for example, what is really observed from what is felt, what is observed concretely in sensation from what is inferred abstractly in representational elaboration at higher levels of conceptualization. The discipline should help the therapist sort out transactional phenomena related to issues of countertransference and projective identification, for example. Moreover, using the bids in this manner tends to reduce the hasty speed with which many therapists operate in their communication with patients of understanding which can occur even with experienced therapists who have become too sure of themselves and perhaps a bit careless of technique. As noted before, therapists typically find it difficult to resist making inferential leaps to explanations or interpretations that too often function to foreclose on exploration in order to quell the therapist's tensions about "not knowing" or pressures felt to provide immediate relief to a suffering patient. As Bion (1962, 1963) emphasized, psychological growth depends upon a tolerance for uncertainties, discontinuities, and ambiguities that signal the potential breakup of static integrations and provide the opportunity for fresh and higher level integrations (Eigen, 1985; Ogden, 1988). A therapist who has difficulty sustaining the tension necessary to tolerate the ambiguities of experience is in no position to help, and to provide a model for, the patient to develop an attitude and means to tolerate ambiguities and uncertainties necessary to forge refined integrations. Still, the appropriate use of the bids provides the therapist with a means to remain active in promoting receptivity to the patient's expressions, in exploring ambiguities, and in fostering therapeutic movement without resorting to what amount to negative bids (defined below), expressed, for example, in overriding the patient or becoming uninvolved even transiently with the patient.

We might add, too, that though we have not set ourselves the goal of defining commonly held psychoanalytic techniques or therapy metaphors by reference to the bids, the latter nevertheless may be viewed as offering a means of detailing the attributes of these techniques and providing a beginning measure of operational definition to the metaphors. For example, the bids of the basically humane and supportive-of-the-self groupings might constitute what has been conceptualized as a "holding environment" (Winnicott, 1971; Modell, 1976, 1990). The empathy bid of the basically common denominator group, combined with the therapist's use of the self-observation bid from the internally orienting group, may represent the fundamental attributes of the form of empathy Kohut (1984) defined as "vicarious introspection" (see also Wolf, 1988). The bids of the insight-orienting group in some combination with bids of the didactic/expanding group would comprise elements of clarification, confrontation, as well as interpretation (see, for example, definitions by Kernberg, Seltzer, Loenigsberg, Carr, and Applebaum, 1989).

DEFINITIONS OF NEGATIVE THERAPEUTIC AND PARENTING BIDS

There are also negative bids that affect the patient's psychological functioning and these bids may be prevented or remedied through didactic supervision and the individual treatment of the therapist.

Negative therapeutic bids may be engendered as part of the countertransference in the therapeutic relationship, or they may be a manifestation of the characterologic patterns of the therapist. If countertransferential, the negative bids will have to be understood and eliminated from or minimized in the therapeutic repartee. If part of the characterologic repertoire of the therapist, these bids will color the entire therapeutic relationship and will have be to reckoned with as affecting the patient's productions. (The reader may recognize some of these bids as stemming from the child development literature as regards negative parenting. We are referring particularly to the work done by Clark and Seifer [1985]; Clark, Musick, Stott, and Klehr [1980].)

The negative bids classified include the following: overriding, uninvolvement, verbal seductiveness, verbal abuse, physical seductiveness or seduction, and physical abuse. We have defined them as follows:

Overriding

To override someone means to impose one's own agenda on the other person (Clark and Seifer, 1985). The therapist tries to interrupt, intrude, or forcefully redirect the productions, thoughts, or utterances of the patient. Overriding may be expressed behaviorally or verbally.

Uninvolvement

Uninvolvement is defined as one member of a dyad being withdrawn from the other who is seeking a response (Clark and Seifer, 1985). The therapist remains unresponsive to the patient even though the patient seeks to be engaged. Uninvolvement differs from disengagement precisely because one member of the dyad seeks the engagement and the other withholds it. A simple behavioral example of uninvolvement would be a therapist who avoids the patient's gaze. Generally, uninvolvement is expressed in any manner in which the therapist tunes out the patient.

Verbal Seductiveness

Verbal seductiveness on the part of the therapist is defined as positively exaggerating certain qualities in the patient for ulterior motives. The therapist may compliment the patient for the sake of getting a positive response that feeds the therapist's narcissism.

Verbal Abuse

Verbal abuse is defined as negatively exaggerating certain qualities in the patient for ulterior motives. The therapist may criticize or heap abuse on the patient for qualities the former finds personally intolerable. Thus, harsh criticism, shaming, and threats are directed at the patient in order to hurt. The behavior may not necessarily be a response to the patient, but rather may be a form of projective identification with the patient.

Physical Seductiveness or Seduction

Physical seductiveness or seduction is defined as sensual or sexual exploitation. The therapist may arouse or sexually stimulate the patient and take advantage of the patient. Therapists have been reported to touch, hug, "play around and banter" with patients in overstimulating ways, presumably "to loosen them up" but also to sexually engage them for similar rationalizations.

Physical Abuse

Physical abuse is the injuring of another in an unequal position with the intention and purpose of hurting. The therapist may hit, pinch, push, or use a tool to intentionally injure the patient. This is not in response to the patient's behavior, but rather once again represents projective identification with the patient's unconscious or conscious defenses or coping strategies.

The negative bids of overriding, being uninvolved, and to a lesser extent, verbal seductiveness are, of course, more common in treatment than verbal abuse, physical seduction, and physical abuse. The latter more typically reflect disturbed functioning in the therapist or entirely derailed functioning in the character of the patient–therapist dyadic relationship. To repeat what was stated before, these negative therapeutic bids must be identified and understood if they are to be minimized (overriding, uninvolvement, verbal seductiveness) or eliminated (e.g., verbal abuse). Physical abuse and physical seduction almost certainly necessitate termination of "therapy" in that dyad since they represent a breach of professional ethics. Insofar as the negative therapeutic bids can be identified and understood, their occurrence provides the therapist with information about his or her personal sensitivities and proclivities to respond in certain negative ways under certain conditions. Whether the therapist's use of negative therapeutic bids reflects something about the character of the particular patient–therapist dyad, the effect of the particular patient's affect on the therapist, or the therapist's disposition to respond in a certain way to any patient under certain conditions, would be determined over time in examination of the particular treatment relationship and other treatment relationships.

As noted before, we focus our efforts in this work on coding only the positive therapeutic bids. It should be mentioned, however, that the negative therapeutic bids would be coded only for overtly expressed behavior. As such, however, a patient's identification of a negative bid (e.g., the therapist's "derogatory" tone of voice, averted glance, apparent interruption, or seeming dismissal of the patient's expressed view) would be coded parenthetically; therapists, like patients, may be unaware of nonverbal expressions and communications, and at any rate, the patient's observations or inference is meaningful in its own right. Moreover, the therapist may find it useful to note nonexpressed therapeutically antagonistic inclinations that can be coded in brackets as negative therapeutic bids. This may help the therapist sort out transference and countertransference issues in the dynamic interplay of the dyadic relationship. None of us is free of the subjective sensitivities and proclivities that engender vulnerability to committing negative bids. Indeed, were such sensitivities and proclivities not in play (in ideal terms more silently than actively), a therapist would have no real experiential basis from which to discern transference and countertransference expressions that convey significant information about the influence of the past on the present. Much, then, can be learned to the benefit of the patient and the therapist through attention to and identification of negative bids.

Case Illustrations of Bids and Coding Scheme

The sessions, as presented, are process notes written up shortly after each therapy session by trainees in the Parent–Infant Development Service (all advanced in their training, Ph.D.'s or Psychology Interns and C.H.R., the senior author), and some were taken verbatim during the session. The trainees were only asked to follow one requirement; namely, to record the session in two columns, the left being reserved for the patient's utterances and the right for the therapist's interventions.[2] These sessions were discussed both in individual supervision with C.H.R., as well as in an ongoing therapy process seminar where the therapist's interventions were analyzed in group fashion, and anchored by the definitions provided. No attempt was made at this time to establish interrater reliability. Our attempt, however, was to explore the feasibility of establishing reliability in coding and construct validity. First, we asked ourselves whether the bids were distinguishable from one another. The consensus was that they were.

---

[2]The reason for this requirement was to provide a set framework in the mind of the trainee to think about the transactional therapeutic process. Such a framework also tends to foster greater accuracy in remembering the sequence of events in any given session. Moreover, by having a column for the therapist's interventions, we were able to focus our attention on analyzing the nature of the therapeutic bids. Finally, by having a clear representation of the patient's utterances, we were able to focus our attention on the nature of the psychological facet and domains engaged. For training purposes this setup provided a discipline for the therapist to enlarge the scope of his thinking in the here-and-now, to develop the ability, while listening to the patient's utterances, to be both involved and engaged with the patient while at the same time also being able to think more easily holding a number of theoretical dimensions in mind.

Next we asked whether the patient's utterances reflected in a distinguishable manner the four psychological facets and aspects of their respective domains. It appeared that too was possible, but required considerable training in personality theory—this was done through reading, teaching, and discussion.

Encouraged by our progress in defining therapeutic bids and psychological constructs, we grew more ambitious and developed a nomenclature for the coping strategies (see chapter 5); the established defense mechanism needed no further elaborating. Further we identified all the known and defined affects. The psychological content issues derived from the psychological facets and their respective domains are summarized in Table 2.1 and detailed in chapter 8, Table 8.1.

Next, we asked ourselves, could we code domains, affects, defense mechanisms, coping strategies, content issues, as well? Yes, it would be possible to code in this manner, we concluded, but only if the therapy process recordings were to be more reliably gathered. Thus, we understood that while the current manner of recording the sessions was perfectly acceptable for didactic purposes as well as for advancing our conceptual work, it did not meet the necessary standards for collecting unskewed therapy data.

The sessions we present here, therefore, are to be regarded as illustrative samples, suggesting the possibilities for further systematic research. The significance of being able to define a typology of bids and different facets of psychological functioning is that this represents our first effort at bringing the transactional therapeutic process into the arena of the scientific, based on our multifaceted theoretical constructs and the therapeutic bids we have defined over the years. But for the purpose of clinical training and the conduct of our daily clinical work, our efforts in developing the multifaceted theories of psychological functioning and therapeutic transaction, the therapeutic bids and the new coding scheme have already proven their value.

Readers will have the opportunity to read fully coded and partially coded therapy sessions and decide for themselves whether they can recognize the internal structure of our thinking

TABLE 9.2
Key of Therapeutic Bids

Therapeutic Bids	Abbreviations
Receptive Observation	R/O
Empathy	EMP
Tact	TCT
Respect	RSPCT
Mirroring/Imitating	MIR/IMIT
Reflecting/Labeling	REFL/LABL
Praising	PRSE
Probing	PROB
Coaxing/Encouraging	CX/ENCRG
Interpretation	INTRP
Facilitation	FACIL
Didactic Expansion	DID/EXP
Inhibiting	INHIB
Delaying (short- and long-term)	DELAY
Renouncing	RENCE
Disengaging/Silence	DIS/SIL
Self-Observation	S/O

and our therapeutic techniques (Table 9.2 provides a key to abbreviations of therapeutic bids).

INDIVIDUAL PSYCHOTHERAPY

Emphasis: Developmental and Interpersonal Facets

Miranda

Miranda is a 4-year-old girl presenting with developmental expressive and receptive language disorder and autistic-like features of social unrelatedness and severe cognitive delay. This is one of the early sessions (session 8). The following process notes were recreated by the therapist to the best of her recall. The therapist had become familiar with the therapeutic bids as part of her training, but did not know the theory on which they were based. As such she was not working toward engaging any kind of facet or domain. The session was coded by consensus by three psychologists.[4]

Patient	Therapist
1. Walking down the hall, M makes whooshing sounds with her mouth as if she has been running.	2. Imitates M's sounds

Coding: 1-2

Bid: Mir/Imit
Facet: Developmental
Domain: Language
      Neuromotor
Affect: Interest
Coping Strategy: Cooperation

3. M looks at TH and smiles.

Coding: 3

Bid: Receptive Observation (R/O)
Facet: Interpersonal
Domain: Mutuality (joint)
Affect: Pleasure, Excitement
Coping Strategy: Cooperation

4. When in office, M sits at child's table, picks up a marker and taps on a piece of paper, making dots.	5. "Bang, bang. M is banging with the marker."

Coding: 4-5

Bid: Mir/Imit
     Refl/Labl
Facet: Developmental
Domain: Neuromotor
      Cognition
Affect: Interest, Excitement

---

[4]The therapist in this case was Dr. Tracy Karnatz. The three clinicians involved in the coding were Drs. Steven D. Kulb, Thomas Rizzo, and Chaya H. Roth.

Coping Strategy: Realistic appraisal

6. After several minutes of dots, M begins to draw circles with the marker.

7. "M goes round and round. Round and round with the marker."

Coding: 6-7

Bid: Refl/Labl
Facet: Developmental
Domain: Neuromotor
Cognition
Affect: Serious
Coping Strategy: Realistic Appraisal

8. M takes the marker, lifts up TH's hand and begins to draw lines down TH's fingers.

9. "M is drawing on T's hand."

Coding: 8-9

Bid: Refl/Labl
Facet: Developmental
Domain: Social
Cognition
Affect: Interest
Coping Strategy: Cooperation

10. M smiles.

11. "M likes to draw on T's hand. It makes M happy. TH takes a marker, reaches for M's hand to draw on her fingers."

Coding: 10-11
Bid: Refl/Labl
Facet: Interpersonal
Developmental
Domain: Mutuality (Joint)
Neuromotor
Affect: Pleasure, sensual arousal

Coping Strategy: Agreement

Coding: 12-13
Bid: Mir/Imit
Facet: Interpersonal
Domain: Mutuality (Reciprocity
Affect: Pleasure, sensual arousa
Coping Strategy: Agreement

12. M allows TH to draw on her hand and smiles. [This is the first time she has allowed TH to draw on her hand. She has pulled away in the past.]

13. M is quietly receptive and smiles.

14. M begins to tap the paper with the marker again, making dots.

15. "Bang, bang with the marker."

Coding: 14-15

Bid: Mir/Imit
Facet: Developmental
Domain: Neuromotor
Affect: Interest, excitement
Coping Strategy: Realistic appraisal

16. M picks up the trucks from the floor and brings them to the table. She begins putting the crayons in the back of the trucks.

17. "M is putting the crayons in the truck. Crayons go in."

Coding: 16-17

Bid: Refl/Labl
Facet: Developmental
Domain: Cognition
      Play

CHAPTER NINE

Affect: Interest, pleasure
Coping Strategy: Realistic appraisal

18. M uses the crayons to make dots on paper.

19. "Bang, bang. M goes bang, bang with crayons too."

Coding: 18-19
Bid: Mir/Imit; Refl/Labl
Facet: Developmental
Domain: Neuromotor
      Cognition
Affect: Interest, arousal
Coping Strategy: Realistic Appraisal

20. M vocalizes "Yo-eee."

21. "Yo-eee. What does that mean, M?"

Coding: 20-21

Bid: Mir/Imit; Prob
Facet: Developmental
Domain: Language
Affect: Pleasure, excitement
Coping Strategy: Cooperation

22. M draws more circles on her paper with the marker.

23. "Round and round and round."

Coding: 22-23
Bid: Refl/Labl
Facet: Developmental
Domain: Language
      Cognition
      Play
Affect: Pleasure, interest
Coping Strategy: Realistic Appraisal

24. M puts the crayons back in the truck.

25. "M wants the crayons in the truck."

Coding: 24-25

Bid: Refl/Labl
Facet: Developmental
Domain: Play
Affect: Interest
Coping Strategy: Realistic Appraisal

26. M taps the crayons and the markers lightly on the trucks.

27. "Click, click, click. M likes to play with sounds.

Coding: 26-27

Bid: Mir/Imit; Refl/Labl
Facet: Developmental
Domain: Play
Affect: Interest, arousal
Coping Strategy: Realistic Appraisal

28. M makes more dots and circles with her markers.

29. "Bang, bang. Round and round with the markers.

Coding: 28-29

Bid: Mir/Imit; Refl/Labl
Facet: Developmental
Domain: Neuromotor
    Play
Affect: Interest, excitement
Coping Strategy: Realistic Appraisal

30. M takes a marker and colors her own fingers.

31. "M wants to color her hand. I wonder why M is coloring her hand?"

Coding: 30-31

Bid: Refl/Labl; Prob
Facet: Developmental
Domain: Play
Affect: Interest, Sensual Arousal
Coping Strategy: Realistic Appraisal

32. M claps her hand with mine.

33. "M and TH are the same. M and TH both have hands with colors. M likes to have hands that are the same."

Coding: 32-33

Bid: Did/Exp
Facet: Developmental
Domain: Social
      Cognition
Affect: Pleasure, excitement
Coping Strategy: Cooperation

34. M puts markers in the truck.

35. "Back in the truck."

Coding: 34-35

Bid: Refl/Labl
Facet: Developmental
Domain: Play
Affect: Interest
Coping Strategy: Realistic Appraisal

36. M makes different breathing sounds for the next several minutes.

37. [TH imitates M's sounds], occasionally asking, "What does that mean? What does M want to say?"

Coding: 36-37

Bid: Mir/Imit; Prob

Facet: Developmental
Domain: Language, Play
Affect: Serious, interest
Coping Strategy: Realistic Appraisal

38. M clicks the markers and the trucks together.

39. "Click, click."

Coding: 38-39

Bid: Mir/Imit
Facet: Developmental
Domain: Play
          Language
Affect: Serious, Interest
Coping Strategy: Realistic Appraisal

40. M vocalizes "Aa-thoo."

41. [TH imitates M's sound.] Asks "What does M want to say? Tell me more."

Coding: 40-41

Bid: Mir/Imit; Prob
Facet: Developmental
Domain: Language
          Social
Affect: Serious, Interest
Coping Strategy: Cooperation

42. M gets up from table, goes over to play phones and picks one up. M babbles into the receiver.

43. "Hello. Is M saying hello? Who is M talking to?"

Coding: 42-43

Bid: Mir/Imit; Did/Exp; Prob
Facet: Developmental
Domain: Language
          Social

Facet: Interpersonal
Domain: Mutuality (Reciprocity)
Affect: Affection, Interest
Coping Strategy: Cooperation

44. M babbles "Yo-yo-yo" into the phone several times.

45. "Hello. Hello, M."

Coding: 44-45

Bid: Did/Exp
Facet: Developmental
Domain: Language
    Social
Facet: Interpersonal
Domain: Mutuality (Reciprocity)
Affect: Affection, Interest
Coping Strategy: Cooperation

46. M spends the rest of the session engaged in babbling and sound play.

47. [TH imitates M's sounds.] Occasionally says, "What does that mean? Tell me more. What is M saying?'

Coding: 46-47

Bid: Mir/Imit; Prob; Coax
Facet: Developmental
Domain: Language
    Social

M's mother knocks on the door to end the session.

Facet: Interpersonal
Domain: Mutual (Reciprocity)
Affect: Pleasure, affection, serious
Coping Strategy: Cooperation

Analysis of Therapeutic Transactions

Analysis of the coding schema reveals the following:

Total number of transactions (as recorded after the session): 47

Therapeutic Bids:	35
Mir/Imit	12
Refl/Labl	12
Prob	6
Did/Exp	3
Coax	1
R/O (Sil)	1
Facets engaged:	
Developmental:	22
Interpersonal:	6
Domains engaged:	
Language:	9
Neuromotor:	7
Mutuality:	
Joint:	2
Reciprocity:	2
Cognition:	7
Social:	4
Play:	9
Affects:	
Interest:	16
Serious:	5
Pleasure:	7
Affection:	3
Excitement:	1
Coping Strategies:	
Realistic Appraisal	13
Cooperation:	8
Agreement:	2

A total of 35 bids were recorded within 47 transactions. The preponderance of bids were supportive and engaged the developmental facet. However, as can be seen, by the time patient and

189

therapist arrived at transaction number 21, the range of bids expanded to probes, didactic expansions and coaxing. If this trend persisted over the course of a number of sessions, it could lead to engaging other facets, such as those of the character and the intrapsychic. Of note, however, is that the interpersonal facet was engaged from the onset. This child may have pervasive developmental delays in the domains of language and cognition, but in the interpersonal facet, she shows early in the session an interest in relating to the therapist with positive affect.

Most of the therapeutic bids engaged the developmental facet. As such 22 transactions engaged the developmental facet and 6 the interpersonal facet. Naturally, we have no way of knowing what other facets were beginning to become engaged "in the zone of proximal development," but in theory we surmise that, in time and with continued work, other facets could become engaged as well.

Looking at the domains engaged, we note that, in the beginning of the session, the neuromotor and cognition domains were observed to be active. With the progression of the sessions, the language and play domains came to the fore as well. We did not plan for this to occur in the manner it did, in truth, we did not know what would occur, but we certainly were surprised when we began coding the material as it evolved, that the expansion into the developmental domains was as it was. We do not think that this was a chance occurrence, for our aim was to help this child to learn to speak, think, and relate to her therapist with a sense of pleasure and self-satisfaction, but we were genuinely surprised by the moment-to-moment evolution of the events in the session as shown by the coding schema. (Of course, we do understand that independent, interrater reliability needs to be established before further quantification of the coding can take place, but as a conceptual phenomenon and a clinically structuralizing system we believe there is reason to move forward along these lines.)

Further, focusing on the interpersonal facet we note that from the very beginning, this child showed interest in her therapist. This was not only an expression of her own developmental need to connect socially (this would be scored developmental facet/social), but a response to her therapist's positive response to her attempt at social engagement. Thus, we felt justified in coding certain of the early transactions as engaging the interpersonal facet, within the domain of mutuality, characterized by joint interest and reciprocity.

We coded the affects either when they were specifically mentioned by the therapist, the child, or when they coincided with a specific serial of cognitive behavior. In this session, affects were labeled by the therapist, and pleasure was the only affect she noted. Our view of this was that the therapist wished to emphasize to the child that pleasure and good feelings are associated in her experience with human connectedness, with exploration and novelty-seeking, with learning to speak, play, and create, and with discovering a sense of herself as reflected through the eyes of her therapist. However, where we deduced interest, seriousness, affection, excitement, and arousal through behaviors, we labeled them as such. We also labeled the coping strategies and noted that Miranda showed an interest in appraising her environment (realistic appraisal) a wish to cooperate with her therapist (cooperation) and to go along with her in the course of the session (agreement).

The work in this session, then, emphasized the child's developmental[5] and interpersonal facets and their respective domains.

A CASE ILLUSTRATION OF A CODED INDIVIDUAL PSYCHOANALYTIC TREATMENT SESSION

Emphasis: Character and Intrapsychic Facets

Ernestine

Ernestine, a 32-year-old married woman, came to treatment to seek relief from intermittent but severe obsessive thoughts, and

---

[5]D. S. Levin (1985) would have termed this session a developmental experience. While we agree with the general meaning of the term as it relates to this child, we believe

feelings of guilt that impaired her capacity to live and work comfortably. The recurring thoughts told her that she must become a missionary and join Mother Teresa in India; the feelings of guilt were associated with having married outside of her church. Inhibited sexually, emotionally, and professionally, she made considerable progress in twice weekly psychotherapy, in which she was productively involved for a period of seven years, at which point she and her therapist decided to end treatment. The patient functioned well and made considerable progress in her professional career during the three years that followed the termination. She returned for eight additional years of intensive (three sessions-a-week) analytic work, when the obsessions returned and a medical consultation suggested she resume treatment with her former therapist for Obsessive-Compulsive Disorder (OCD). Medication was not prescribed. The excerpt below derives from an analytic session (in year 13) and will be discussed briefly according to the bids used and the patient's initiations.[3]

Patient	Therapist
1. "I'm too nervous to be here today . . . I think something really happened last session . . ."	2. "Yes, tell me . . ."
	Coding: 1-2
	Bid: R/O
	Probe
	Facet: Interpersonal
	Domain: Mutuality
	Affect: Anxiety
3. "I hated the way I left here on Friday; I was so defensive, unyielding. I feel absolutely terrible. . . I hate what I said. The worst is I	4. [TH is silent]
	Coding: 3–4

---

that our broader theoretical perspective enables us to focus more sharply on the specifics of the nature of the child's experience and any other psychological facets that become engaged as a result of defining the therapeutic interventions into more finely tuned therapeutic bids.

[3] C.H.R. was the therapist. These are verbatim notes taken during the session, with the patient on the couch.

don't know what to say; I still rely on you to coax me on . . . but I know I can't count on you to get started." [Patient is anxious and is reacting to a stormy transaction in the previous session where TH labeled and reflected, in a confronting manner, her characteristic mode of holding back and pretending she does not want to talk and to be in session, even though the material is filled with feelings of longing to be special and with erotic desire.]

Bid:Dis/Sil
Facet: Character
Domain: Self-I/Me
Coping Strategy: Realistic/
    Appraisal
Defense Mechanism: Reaction
    Formation
Affect: Anger
    Shame

6. "Yeah, I know but it's different. All I know is the way you were talking on Friday was really different. I have a feeling I did something wrong. I had been so careful and then suddenly I felt I lost control of you."

5. "Until now you felt you were hiding, but then you revealed yourself. But to me it felt that you were helping me get to know you." [TH affirms patient's self-observations (reflects and repeats) but also shares a self-observation of her own, namely that she, TH, felt that patient had joined the analytic/therapeutic alliance, thus encouraging her positive developmental interpersonal movement.]

Coding: 5-6

Bid: Refl/Labl
    S/O
    Intrp
Facet: Character
    Intrapsychic
    Interpersonal
Domain: Self-Me/I
    Character Armor
    Ucs Fantasy

Mutuality-Reciprocity
Defense Mechanism: Proj/Identification
Affect: Anxiety
Guilt

8. "I can't even remember that step. All I know is I came here with my rebellion and then I collapsed. I didn't realize what the consequences would be. Everything has changed." [In the previous session, TH interpreted to the patient that they were each enacting roles: the one in which the patient was the unwilling victim and the other in which the TH was the willing coercer. TH said that for the sake of the patient's treatment they would both have to stop this dance.]
Bid: cont

7. "You mean, from being 'forced' to talk to being a willing partner?"

Coding: 7-8

Bid: Did/Exp
Facet: Interpersonal
Domain: Non-Mutual:
Clash
Facet: Character
Domain: I/Me & Me/I
Coping: Compliance/Submission
Defy/Fight
Realistic/Appraisal

9. "It feels like being abandoned . . . I don't know exactly what's happening . . . "

10. "It looks to me like you're giving up a kind of control over me and over yourself."

Bid: Intrp
Facet: Interpersonal
Domain: Mutual; Reciprocity
Facet: Character
Domain: I/Me & Me/I
Affect: Anxiety
Sadness

11. "Not willingly. If I can't get you to coax me and cajole me then I'm on my own."

[Pause . . .]

12. "I must have hurt your feelings bad on Friday when I suggested that you could do things for yourself, but wanted me to be in charge of you."

"You also said I was making progress and I wanted to say 'Write it down!'"

[Pause . . .]

Bid: Intrp
Facet: Character
Domain: I/Me & Me/I
Affect: Anger

13. "I have a little inkling about what it's like to make things happen outside of here . . . like at work . . . or at home . . . or about initiating sex . . . I felt rebellious and wanted to say who cares! But I care. I noticed how I am holding back. I don't want to have any pleasure outside of here, because then you'd have to reciprocate! This is what you'd call a fantasy!"

"It's the same thing as wanting to be central to my mother and finding out that I'm not!" **Patient Bid: Self-exploration and observation**

14. [TH is quiet]

Coding: 13-14

Bid: Dis/Sil
Facet: Character
    Intrapsychic
Domain: Character Armor
    Ucs Wishes &
    Fantasies
Defense Mechanism: Reaction
    Formation
Affect: Excitement

16. "But don't you get it, there is nothing there, when you go down there all you find is someone who lashes out! If you get close enough I'll lash out. Sometimes I think if you were to touch me I'd smack you, but that is so opposite to what I really want."

15. "And what do you want . . .?"

Coding: 15-16

Bid: Prob
Facet: Intrapsychic
Domain: Self-I/Me
Defense Mechanism: Reaction
    Formation
Coping Strategy: Provoke/
    Fight
Affect: Despair
    Anger
    Longing

17. "I wish I could accept things from people, just ordinary things, like kindness and affection."

18. "Yes."

Coding: 17–18

Bid: Emp
   R/O
Facet: Character
Domain: I/Me
Affect: Longing

19. "This feels so central and calming, and also . . . giddy. I feel excited now, pleased. I did it, I broke through my own barrier."
Patient Bid: S/O

20. "Yes."

Coding: 19–20

Bid: Emp
   R/O
Facet: Character
Domain: Self-I
Coping Strategy: Realistic/
   Appraisal
Affect: Longing
   Affection
   Excitement

This was but a fragment of a session in 15 years of therapeutic and analytic work. The segment was taken from year 13. This illustration highlights the characterologic facet. The unconscious defenses have become conscious or preconscious coping strategies. The interpersonal respect patient and therapist have for one another sustains the difficult position they are in. The patient discovers that she, in fact, can do the work and has a significant contribution to make to her own self-knowledge. This enhances her pride, self-esteem, and enables her to join the therapist in the arduous task of intrapsychic self-exploration. By joining the working alliance the patient now can look at her impulses of badness, and her erotic longings in the transference and out.

Analysis of Therapeutic Transactions

An analysis of the coding schema reveals the following:

Total number of therapeutic transactions: 19

Therapeutic Bids: 13

    R/O, Emp: 3
    Prob: 2
    Dis/Sil: 2
    Refl/Labl: 1
    S/O: 1
    Intrp: 3
    Did/Exp: 1

Facets engaged:
    Character 9
    Interpersonal 4
    Intrapsychic 3

Domains engaged:
    Self—I/Me 3
        Me/I 1
        I/Me, Me/I 3
        I 1
        Character Armor
    Nonmutual—Clash 1
            Avoidance 1
    Mutual—Reciprocity 2
    UCS Wishes & Fantasies 3

Affects:
    Anxiety 3
    Anger 3
    Shame 1
    Guilt 1

Sadness   1
Excitement   2
Despair   1
Longing   1
Affection   1

Coping Strategies:
   Realistic Appraisal   4
   Submission/Compliance   1
   Defiance/Fight   2
   Cooperation   1

Defense Mechanisms:
   Reaction Formation   3
   Projective Identification   1

As can be seen from the layout of the coding schema, the therapeutic bids fall into the groupings that foster the alliance (the basically humane grouping—Empathy and Receptive Observation), that engage the character facet (through Praise, Reflection-Labeling), and that engage the intrapsychic and the character facets; they are Insight-Orienting (through the bids of Probing and Interpretation). There is one occasion for a Didactic/Expansion which engages the developmental facet, and one for self-observation on the part of the therapist which actually serves as a guide to the patient to also become self-observing. Finally, there are two occasions of Disengagement/Silence where the patient is left to figure things out, to explore by herself, and to become self-orienting.

Looking at the distribution of the facets engaged, character is engaged nine times (i.e., three times as often as the interpersonal and the intrapsychic facets respectively).

The domains indicate what aspects of the self are engaged. As such, the sense of I appears only at the end of the session after a considerable struggle has taken place between the therapist and the patient, and within the patient herself. The issues that preoccupy her at this time are I/Me processes, which represent how the patient wants to project herself onto and into the therapist; and the Me/I processes, which represent how she wants the therapist to reflect back to her, her own projected self-image.

The affects she expresses connote pain, anxiety, shame, guilt, sadness, despair. Only toward the end of the session, after much solid struggle on her part, is she able to experience the excitement of her inner self (the I) and a feeling of affection neither she nor the therapist had seen until then. In her own words, she had broken through some sort of barrier.

The defense mechanisms, as contrasted to the coping strategies, are relatively few, they are reaction formation and projective identification, in contrast to the more conscious and preconscious coping strategies of realistic appraisal, submission-compliance, defiance-fight, and cooperation.

Discussion

We have shown here that it is possible to develop a coding scheme for analyzing a therapy session. However, the analysis of these codes must remain a mere example of what can be done with such a conceptualization until further validation of the scheme. Yet as a way of organizing therapeutic data and therapeutic transactions, it can be seen that a common language for speaking about treatment with children and adults can be developed, without adultomorphizing the child, or infantilizing the adult. This can be ascertained by comparing the type of coding that applied to the pervasively developmentally delayed child, Miranda, as compared to the coding that applied to the complex and mature, characterologically disordered, and intrapsychically conflicted woman, Ernestine.

The next therapy session excerpts will not be fully coded. Only the therapeutic bids will follow the therapists' interventions. Nevertheless, we will leave it to the reader to conclude whether the conceptual framework we have presented provides something useful and transmittable to the complicated work of psycho-therapy.

ADDITIONAL CASE ILLUSTRATIONS AND CODING OF BIDS: INDIVIDUAL PSYCHOTHERAPY

Emphasis: Character, Intrapsychic and Interpersonal Facets

Mark

Mark is a 5-year-old foster child who had been seen weekly for an extended diagnostic evaluation. This is his fifth therapy session and tenth contact. He was removed from his home at age $1^1/_2$ due to extreme neglect and abuse. He was 5 at the time of this writeup, in his third foster home, and doing well there. Reason for referral included aggressive behavior, lying, and threatening to kill people.

Mark is early for his appointment and sees his therapist[6] walking into the waiting room with a little girl she sees before him. He wants to go with the therapist, but she tells him he has to wait because she has to set up the room for him. When she returns to the waiting room, Mark is lying in the hallway. When he sees her, he starts to run. Mark's lying on the floor may be seen as a reaction to seeing his therapist with another child (maybe he is anxious, or angry and jealous). Stress dysregulates him, and thus unable to contain himself, he runs down the hall. This is against the established rules of the clinic and also the frame of the thera-peutic work. However, his running may also be seen as his impa-tient anticipation to be with his therapist whom he already has

---

[6]The session was reconstructed shortly after the session by Lauren Wakschlag, Ph.D., currently the Director of the PIDS. Her work with this child and in directing the PIDS are gratefully acknowledged.

come to "love," understandably so, given his need to please, but prematurely so, given the relative brevity of their relationship.

Patient	Therapist
1. [Mark starts to run down the hallway, TH catches up with him and holds his hand.]	2. "I know you've been waiting for me, and it's hard to wait, but the rules of the hall are we cannot run."
	Coding 1-2: Emp **Bids: Inhib** **Facet: Character, Development**
3. [Still in the hallway] "You got any candy for me today? Got any candy?" [Perhaps he needs something special for his hurt feelings, due to seeing the little girl and having to wait.]	4. [TH is silent.]
	Coding 3-4 **Bid: R/O, Dis/Sil** **Facet: Character**
5. "I got to wash my hands, and go to the bathroom." [He stays in the bathroom for several minutes.] "I turned the lights on and off!" [As they turn the corner to enter the office, Mark slows down and drags his feet.]	
6. [Enters the room] "Where is my stuff? Where's my stuff? Where's my toys?"	7. "Sounds like you're worried that your stuff is not here."
	Coding 5-6-7: Emp **Bid: Refl/Labl** **Facet: Character, Intrapsychic**
	8. "We didn't see each other last time, and it sounds like you think something may have happened to your toys."

9. [Rummages in his toy bin.] "That girl made a mess here."

10. "You're thinking maybe she has been using your stuff when she was here with me."

Coding 8-9-10
Bid: Intrp
Facet: Interpersonal, Intrapsychic

11. "Can I take these cars home? I don't have enough cars. Do you got any candy? Hey, where's your candy? What's in your purse?"

12. "Seems like you think I got candy, but I just don't want to give it to you."

Coding 11-12
Bid: Refl/Labl
Facet: Interpersonal, Intrapsychic

13. "Yaa . . ."

14. "How come?"

Coding 13-14
Bid: Prob
Facet: Interpersonal, Intrapsychic

15. "Cause I want the candy to put in my box, and I don't want to share. Did that girl sit in this chair?"

16. "Wondering what I did with her, if she got any candy?"

Coding 15-16
Bid: Intrp
Facet: Interpersonal, Intrapsychic

17. "She didn't get no candy neither? I'm changing chairs. Did she sit here? Something smells—who farted? Huh? Did you? It's that girl, she must have. She smelled it up in here. I'm taking my soldiers out [sets them up with a wide stream of conversation]. How come you aren't saying nothin?"

18. "I need to watch and listen so we can figure out together what's going on inside you."

Coding 17-18
Bid: S/O
   Did/Exp
   Dis/Sil
   R/O
Facet: Interpersonal, Intrapsychic,
   Character

19. "But you don't have to be quiet. You say what you say, and I say what I say. C'mon, talk!"

20. "It's hard to listen to what's inside. You want me to talk a lot, so we don't have to listen."

Coding 19-20
Bid: Emp
   Intrp
Facet: Intrapsychic, Character

21. "OK, you be quiet. I'm setting up my men to shoot and fight."

[Mark is able to transform his transferential anger at TH into symbolic play. Also, he accommodates and complies, because he does not want to antagonize her for fear that she will then turn away from him. Nevertheless, this capacity to comply to her wishes while feeling sufficiently free to develop his own play fantasy augurs well for his capacity to change both in character and psychic structure.]

Coding 21-22
Bid: Sil
Facet: Character, Intrapsychic

Analysis of Therapeutic Bids

This therapy session includes 21 transactions between Mark and his therapist and 17 therapeutic bids. They are the following:

Empathy: 3
Reflecting/Labeling: 1
Inhibiting: 1
Receptive/Observation: 2
Probing: 1

Didactic/Expansion: 1
Self/Observation: 1
Interps: 5
Disengaging/Silence: 2

Six of the bids are insight-orienting, three are internally-orienting, five are in the basically humane grouping, and of the bids that are supportive, inhibiting, and promote learning, each occurs only once. Based on the content of the communications between Mark and his therapist, we believe that the facets engaged by the specific bids occurred with the following frequency:

Character   6
Intrapsychic   8
Developmental   1
Interpersonal   5

Discussion

Our initial estimate about the nature of our work was that it focused primarily on the characterologic and the intrapsychic. But our subsequent coding, albeit subjective, indicated that the primary emphasis was characterologic, followed by the intrapsychic, the interpersonal, and last the developmental.

What is clear from this brief segment is that Mark was an extremely anxious boy as fearful of abandonment as of his angry feelings. Also, he was highly excited in this session and manifested the excitement in dysregulation. He clamored for concrete nurturance (candy) but accommodated and submitted to his therapist's rules for the sake of maintaining her symbolic nurturance and caring attentiveness. This augured well for his treatment, because character work in an empathic and supportive relationship fosters also developmental growth and expansion as well as intrapsychic exploration and structuralization.

Unfortunately, Mark's treatment lasted less than one full year. He was removed from the foster parents who brought him to treatment (his third placement), and was transferred to another foster family that opted to discontinue therapy.

INDIVIDUAL PSYCHOTHERAPY

Emphasis: Character, Intrapsychic and Developmental Facets

Matt

Matt, a 7-year-old boy who was severely sexually and physically abused at age 2, presented at our clinic with severe speech delay, hyperactivity, posttraumatic stress disorder (PTSD), and the question of attention deficit hyperactivity disorder (ADHD). He was seen in individual psychotherapy once weekly. The notes of the session used for illustration represent a fragment of the entire session. He is in constant motion. He takes a toy, seemingly at random, touches it, tries to take it apart, throws it up in the air. The throwing escalates. The therapist[7] labels and reflects in words the child's throwing and his driven quality:

Patient	Therapist
1. [Matt jumps up and down.]	2. "I think you are as jumpy on the inside as this ball is on the outside. Neither you nor the ball want to take a moment to rest."

Coding 1-2
Bids: Mir/Imit
Refl/Labl
Did/Exp

---

[7]The therapist in this case was Dr. Carole Emerson. Her work and reconstruction of this therapy session are gratefully acknowledged.

Facet: Character, Developmental

3. "These are all little balls; they are like rats, and they are going all over you."

4. "Rats? How come?"

Coding 3-4
Bids: Prob
Facets: Intrapsychic

5. "Because they are bad and they will hurt you."

6. "They will hurt me like you've been hurt?"

Coding 5-6
Bids: Intrp
Facet: Intrapsychic

7. "No, I want to hurt you."

8. "I wonder why."

Coding 7-8
Bids: S/O
    Prob
Facet: Intrapsychic

9. "Because it's dark and I'm afraid of rats and I'm going to hide under your desk."

10. "Now you can rest a bit and no harm will come to you here, because you can talk of fears and hurts, of wanting to be little and hide and hoping to be safe."

Coding 9-10
Bids: Intrp
    Did/Exp
Facet: Character, Intrapsychic, Interpersonal

Analysis of Therapeutic Bids

This fragment of a therapy session includes ten transactions between Matt and his therapist and includes eight therapeutic bids. They are the following:

Mir/Imit: 1
Refl/Labl: 1
Prob: 2
Did/Exp: 1
Intrp: 2
S/O: 1

Four of the bids are insight-orienting, two are supportive, one promotes learning and one is internally orienting. Based on the content of the communications between Matt and his therapist, we believe that the facets engaged by the specific bids occurred with the following frequency:

Intrapsychic: 4
Character: 2
Developmental: 1
Interpersonal: 1

Discussion

Our initial estimate about the nature of our work was that it aimed primarily at engaging the characterologic and intrapsychic facets in order to address the issues of PTSD and ADHD, followed by work on the developmental and interpersonal facets and their respective domains, so as to help the child with his learning difficulties as well as with his behavioral problems with teachers and peers.

Our subsequent coding of this segment, to the extent that it accurately represents the work within this specific phase of his treatment, suggests that the primary emphasis was intrapsychic (in order to help him with the PTSD and its psychological sequelae), followed by emphasis on character (in order to help remedy his dysregulation associated with the trauma caused by the abuse, as well as with the possible sequelae of ADHD).

In this example, we witness a multifaceted emission of dysregulated movement and affect. The therapeutic responses the therapist chooses to use are put in symbolic language. For example, in the beginning of the session she compares the child to a bouncing ball, telling him that he is acting on the outside the way he is feeling on the inside. This reflection and labeling is aimed at engaging the character facet, to help the child identify his internal state and thereby to also help him become better regulated and calmer. The first intervention "neither you nor the ball want to take a moment to rest" and the last "now you can rest a bit . . . " are didactic expansions providing the child with new options (resting rather than being in constant motion). In the first instance the expansion leads to symbolic expansion in the child. He now compares the small protrusions on the bouncing ball to rats which are going all over the therapist. The meaning of rats is not totally clear but, given his environment and the aggression and disgust displayed in the session toward the therapist, one surmises that the rats are an unconscious fantasy of aggression and disgust emanating from the intrapsychic facet, and the defense mechanism is projective identification. In the second instance the child has taken in the therapist's suggestion that he rest a bit and he is now able to own up to his own feelings (not needing to externalize them) and can state, ". . . I'm afraid of rats. . . ."

Finally, aware of his anxiety, the repetition of trauma under a less frightening condition leads Matt to an enactment in the room; namely he resorts to the coping strategy of avoidance and flight in the face of fright; this is manifested by his telling her, "and I'm going to hide under your desk."

The principle of multiple function leads us to the following thoughts as regards these very complicated if few transactions between Matt and his therapist. True, he now feels safe under her desk, at least sufficiently so to stop his incessant activity. But under her desk he is also hiding from her (from himself) so as to disavow or suppress the feelings and thoughts associated with trauma. And most importantly, he also has come to fear his therapist, the positive trustworthy person in his life, as a potentially harmful transference figure. Thus, much work lies ahead first in developing and then in working through the multiple threads of this patient–therapist relationship.

The treatment of the child with this therapist ended after one year. He did resume treatment with another therapist, is now receiving medication (Ritalin) for his hyperactivity, but continues to replay scenes of sexual aggression in his psychotherapy sessions.

10

Parent–Infant/Child Interaction Treatment: Principles and Guidelines with Coded Therapy Sessions

In this chapter we draw on the parent–infant paradigm to describe modes of parent–infant/child interaction treatment that highlight the significance of the transactional influences in shaping the psychological functioning of the individual within a relationship. Parent–infant/child interaction treatments entail a cluster of psychotherapeutic interventions that pursue the overarching aim of remedying disordered parent–child relationships by engaging the interpersonal, developmental, characterologic, and intrapsychic facets and their respective domains in the parent as well as in the child. More specifically, parent–child interaction treatments aim at remedying disorders in the character of the parent–child relationship, focusing on the dyad's moment-to-moment behavioral interactions compromised by dysfunction in the developmental, characterologic, and intrapsychic facets of either or both parent and child. Whenever possible, treatment focuses on the dyadic context to address difficulties in the parent–child relationship. When treatment cannot be focused on the dyadic context, due to severe pathology in either parent or child, individual as well as concurrent adjunctive treatments may be required.

A number of factors contribute to disordered parent–child relationships: (1) difficulties in the parents' capacities to parent, namely to provide for the basic growth-promoting needs of the child; (2) disturbed patterns in the parent–infant/child behavioral interactions and transactions; (3) significant delays, deficits, arrests, and conflicts in the parents or child; and (4) extreme stressors in living conditions.

With regard to growth-promoting parenting tasks, while the empirical research has been spotty, there has been commonsense consensus that children fare best in their psychological growth when the parenting they experience over time includes a number of elements provided on a more or less consistent basis by either one or both parents or by adequate substitute caregivers. The necessary elements include the provision of: (1) safety, security, and physical nourishment; (2) love expressed in pleasure and emotional nurturance; (3) an environment that appeals to and interests the child's exploratory inclinations; (4) a consistent framework in which certain rules of "civil" behavior are maintained; (5) an expectation of a modicum of self-regulation leading to eventual self-discipline; (6) opportunities for learning and meeting new challenges; (7) respect for the child's unique individuality, giftedness, and limitations; (8) the parents' or caregivers' heritage and values. (Appendix D lists the parental growth-promoting tasks and their aims.)

Parents who show few caregiving capacities, as defined by the elements cited above, clearly need help. Still, it must be noted that research has not identified the necessary and sufficient conditions for adequate parenting (and probably cannot identify such conditions given the unique configuration of every parent–child relationship). Some factors, of course, are reasonably well established: providing for the physical survival of the child is of the essence; human emotional contact is necessary for growth in the emotional as well as all other developmental domains; the child contributes his or her own genetic, biophysical, and temperamental characteristics which significantly affect the particular caregiving environment. But how much parental interest, discipline, stimulation, expectation, support, and personal/cultural transmission are required as necessary and sufficient for any particular child to balance between innate and experiential transactional processes, remains largely a matter of conjecture (Burlingham and Freud, 1942; Spitz, 1945; Provence and Lipton, 1962; Murphy and Moriarty, 1976; Rutter, 1981, 1985, 1987; Garmezy, 1983, 1985; Garmezy, Masten, and Tellegen, 1984; Cohler and Anthony, 1987; Greenbaum and Auerbach, 1992).

Extensive research and clinical literature over the past decade have addressed the issue of what is considered to be a disordered parent–child relationship. The discussion of diagnostic issues that defines the character of a dyadic system is relevant here. To repeat, disordered dyadic patterns are characterized by nonmutuality manifested by asynchrony, unilateralness (one-sidedness), parallel behaviors (little or no interaction between the pair), dyadic avoidance (avoidant behaviors expressed in some form of turning away from each other), and dyadic clash (expression of opposing intentions and/or subsequent avoidance of coming to terms with the conflict). Positive parent–infant/child dyadic patterns are characterized by mutuality manifested by reciprocity and joint attentiveness to shared interests and concerns. The negative parenting bids identified and defined the nefarious parent–child transactions in the moment-to-moment interchange. To repeat, the negative bids include overriding (i.e., invasiveness), uninvolvement (i.e., lack of responsiveness), verbal seduction (i.e., saying pleasing but untrue or inappropriate things to the child or parent to derive only personal-narcissistic benefit), verbal abuse (i.e., hurling insults at the child or parent with the intention of hurting or depreciating as expression of, for example, sadistic or projected masochistic inclinations), or physical seduction or abuse (i.e., child or parent playing with the other in an inappropriately sensual or sexual manner).

Pathology in developmental, character, or intrapsychic functioning within either or both parent and child can contribute significantly to derailing a parent–child relationship. We will defer discussion of the influence of these individual disturbances on the parent–child relationship to the description of the three types of interaction treatment presented later.

Finally, severe life stressors can also negatively affect the parent–child relationship. Parents function as stimulus barriers for the infant as well as buffers and titrators of reality for the infant and child. Parents severely pressed by environmental stressors are vulnerable to being distracted from, and functionally if not actually unavailable for, appropriately attuned synchronous and reciprocal responsiveness to their infants or children. Lack of appropriate parental responsiveness manifesting, for example, in under- or overstimulation of the infant can transmit the parent's preoccupying worries and anxieties to the child through emotional cues.[1] The infant or child's adjustment to the stressed parent—the beacon of orientation to reality—is an adaptation to external reality, and this adjustment if perpetuated by the parent's stress-laden behavior, may crystallize into later adaptations that function as a constitutional disposition, as it were, in relating to the outside world.

In thinking about how changes in disordered parent-child relationships take place in the moment and over time, we believe that it is the immediate adjustments to interactional perturbations and behaviors in the moment that lead to changes in the character of the dyad over time. From our perspective, being able to differentiate between behaviors in the moment and the character of the dyad over time is important because the interplay between the therapeutic bids and the psychological facets they engage is also associated with an interplay between the different functions over time. Namely, therapeutic bids in the moment-to-moment interaction by the therapist or the parent essentially break up the habitual dyadic patterns of transaction and help foster new ones, thereby altering the character of the relationship in the long run, albeit to a small degree.

---

[1]Daniel Stern's (1977) discussion of "missteps in the dance" well describes the negative influence of the parent's under- or overstimulation of the infant on the infant's development of self-regulating and dyadically (or mutually) regulating capacities.

PARENT–INFANT AND PARENT–CHILD
INTERACTION PSYCHOTHERAPIES

General Issues

As mentioned in the beginning of the chapter, parent–infant/ child treatments form a cluster of interventions built on the same framework as all other interventions that encompass our treatment model. Given that interaction treatments involve both adults (as parents) and infants or children, that is, two distinctly different populations with developmentally, characterologically, and intrapsychically different capacities to behave, think, self-regulate, and the like, the task is not only to decide what type of treatment might work best for a particular dyad (though that in itself can be a complicated task), but also what is best for both individuals, the child and the parent. The general challenge of parent–child treatments involves creating conceptual guidelines from which one can generalize from individuals' cases to others with similar psychological profiles. Interaction treatments, as we think about them, incorporate all the subtleties of the back-and-forth interplay between the individuals' diagnostic profiles, the character of the dyad and their transactions in the moment, and the therapist's repertoire of therapeutic bids. Therefore while we have developed treatment guidelines which aim to remedy the character of the parent–child relationship and the moment-to-moment interplay between them, each dyad necessarily requires a treatment strategy tailored to fit its unique needs.

A considerable body of literature has evolved since Selma Fraiberg and her associates developed that form of intervention with babies and their mothers, and fathers, in the mid-1970s and early 1980s (see Fraiberg, Adelson, and Shapiro, 1975; Fraiberg, Shapiro, and Adelson, 1976; Fraiberg and Adelson, 1977). Much of the emphasis in this form of treatment, however, lay on the shoulders of the parent, primarily the mother. The infant, while seen as essential in bringing to life the parental conflict and transference of the parent to the child, was not seen as the active interactive partner he or she would become from the mid-1980s on. Cramer and Stern (1988), working from a similar frame of reference as Fraiberg, have attempted to document via a single-case design methodology the efficacy of brief mother–infant psychotherapy. Still, their model, despite their theoretical adherence to acknowledging the impact of the infant on the parent, primarily emphasized the significance of the parent's fantasies and projections onto the baby, and the effect of these on the baby and on the parent–infant relationship. With the influence of research by Beebe and Lachmann (1988) and Cohn and Tronick (1988) among others, on the one hand, and the influence of the clinical work of Beebe and Sloate (1982), Greenspan, Wieder, Lieberman, Nover, Lourie, and Robinson (1987), Lieberman and Pawl (1993), and Pawl (1993), on the other, the balance began to shift from focusing the primary work of intervention on the parent to focusing the work of intervention on the parent and the child together.

Our efforts at defining infant–parent and child–parent interaction treatments is still different from those of the clinicians noted above. While based on the work of the clinicians cited above, we recognize the seminal contribution of Mahler (1976) who (together with Furer) coined the parent-child treatment as the *tripartite design* (p. 234). In the years of training in this form of intervention we have discovered that we distinguished among a number of types and subtypes of interaction treatments, primarily as a result of the distinctions we have made in interpersonal, developmental, character, and intrapsychic disorders. We found that it was possible to distinguish and define with what therapeutic bids to begin intervention, and what to emphasize if the clinician hopes to address a certain facet of functioning with both parent and infant or child. But to do this successfully, the clinician needed a clear grasp of the diagnostic perturbances within each of the individuals' (baby's and parents') psychological facets and their respective domains.

Interaction treatments, then, cluster in three types: in type 1, the parent is treated by the therapist in the presence of the infant; in type 2, the child is treated in the presence of the parent;

in type 3, the parent and child are treated by the therapist as a veritable dyad, the therapist emphasizing and facilitating communication between the two. As can be readily surmised, interaction treatment need not involve only one parent; it can and sometimes does involve both caregivers. When both parents or more than one caregiver is involved in treatment, it becomes infant–family psychotherapy as described by Roth and Morrison (1993). Usually, however, one parent elects to work in treatment with the child, either due to necessity (many families are single-parent households), or because problems in the relationship manifest themselves most with one or another of the parents. (Usually it is the mother who elects to come for treatment owing to the still prevalent trend for mothers to spend more time in the moment-to-moment and day-to-day attention and attendance to the child's instrumental and social-emotional needs.) Common to all three types of interaction treatment is the child's participation with the goal of fostering his or her biopsychosocial development, thereby also improving the parent's general sense of well-being and parenting efficacy.

Diagnostic decisions determine the choice of interaction treatment type. Diagnostic decisions involve assessment of the following: (1) the severity of the disorder in the parent–child relationship; (2) the parent's capacity to parent; (3) the parent's and child's respective developmental problems; (4) the parent's and child's respective characterologic difficulties and their incapacitating conscious and unconscious coping strategies; (5) intrapsychic conflicts and defense mechanisms that contribute to transference distortions, usually from parent to child, but sometimes, and especially under conditions of trauma, from child to parent or foster parent. Finally, if one decides to use interaction treatment, one must decide if this form of treatment should be the only intervention or one among other concurrent interventions. Possible concurrent interventions could include individual psychotherapy for parent or child, marital or family treatment, or if required by developmental delays or deficits in specific domains in the functional capacities of the young infant, child, or parent, adjunctive treatments such as speech, occupational, or sensorimotor integration therapies may be needed to complete the treatment protocol. When difficulties or impoverishment exist within the environment, consultation with schools and social agencies are also a necessary component of the treatment plan.

Parent–infant interaction treatments are not always appropriate, however. It is important to remain cognizant of problems that indicate that interaction treatments should *not* be initiated at a particular time. Most salient in this regard is evidence of parental psychopathology too severe to make interaction treatment viable. This is especially a concern when the parent in question is the child's only caregiver. If, however, there are two caregivers (mother, father, grandparents, foster parent, or the like), interaction treatment can still be initiated, if appropriate, with the substituting caregiver.

Finally, if interaction treatment is deemed to be the treatment of choice for any given phase or for the entire course of the child's and parent's treatment, then it is important to select the type of interaction treatment best suited for a particular dyad at a particular phase of treatment. Issues related to the selection of type of interaction treatment are included in the discussion that follows. (A summary of the issues associated with the different types of interaction treatment is included in Table 10.1.)

INTERACTION TREATMENT TYPE 1: TREATING THE PARENT IN THE PRESENCE OF THE INFANT

We recommend treating the parent in the presence of the infant when the parent's essential difficulties center on their doubts and insecurities about parenting itself, and their baby does not present with significant delays or deficits and is still too young to talk or walk. In such cases, the parents' complaints refer to their perceived inabilities to appropriately respond to their infants; in a general sense, they feel inadequate. Postpartum affects, anxiety, or depression may be troubling the parent. The parent may tend to interpret the baby's gastric discomfort, gaze avoidance, crying, and the like, as reflecting her own inadequacies as a parent. If the baby presents with moderate feeding, sleeping, or other regulatory difficulties, the child's difficulties may be experienced by the parent as much more severe than they are when compared to others, and they may see their baby as the figure incarnate of a hated, disliked, despised family member; the child then has become a transference figure for the parent. It is under these conditions that interaction treatment with the parent in the presence of the infant is most appropriate.

In the prototypical session of this form of treatment, the main transactions are between parent and therapist, although both parent and therapist think and talk about the infant, and the therapist, in particular, may "speak" for the infant, using empathically resonating intuition, as it were, to translate the infant's needs, apprehensions, discomfort, and the like. The therapist wonders and probes to engage the parent's capacity to perceive and understand the infant's dilemma, to see to what extent the parent can attend to the infant and can separate his or her own needs from those of the infant. The therapist also coaxes-encourages the parent to develop solutions to immediate problems and challenges. When and if the parent's solution fails to meet the infant's needs, the therapist may offer suggestions to the parent about what might work. Such an intervention on the part of the therapist may well be in the form of a didactic bid (i.e., providing information about parenting that is new to the parent and vital that he or she learn). Or the intervention may be in the form of a facilitating bid, namely, helping the parent to do something that he or she could not quite manage alone. Alternately, the parent who entirely misperceives the needs of the child and thus sees the child as evil, greedy, rapacious, assaultive, crazy, and so forth, is manifesting a transference reaction to the infant carried over from the past and possibly overloaded as well with current stresses—marital, familial, and environmental. In response, the therapist probes into the parent's history to discover who in the parent's past is intruding on his or her own realistic

TABLE 10.1
Forms of Parent–Infant and Child Interaction Treatment

Overarching aim: To remedy disorders in parent–child relationships due to primary disorders in the child, the parent, the dyadic or family fit.

	Type 1: Treating the Parent in the Presence of the Infant	Type 2: Treating the Infant or Child in the Presence of the Parent	Type 3: Treating the Parent and Child as a Veritable Dyad
Parent	Mild to severe anxiety or depression (postpartum) associated with parenting. Infant is seen as a significant figure in the parent's past and not for his or her actual self.	*Condition (a)*: Parent cannot understand, cope with, or handle the severe condition manifested by the infant or child and requires guidance, empathy, understanding, and the acquisition of specific skills. Parent mourns the healthy child she/he did not bear.	Parent and child relationship are characterized by lack of reciprocity and joint interest. Asynchrony, unilateralness, invasiveness, avoidance, clash and each going their own way (parallel) are characteristic of their relationship. The source of the dyadic disorder is manifest in each member of dyad.
Infant/Child	Preambulatory and prespeech. Manifests moderate distress in sleep, eating, digestion patterns. Temperament ill-suited for parent (either too placid or too active).	Infant, child presents with severe developmental delays or deficits in cognition, neuromotor, language, social, affect, play or creativity domains. Diagnoses can be PDD, Autism, CDD, ADHD, ODD, or PTSD.	
Parent		*Condition (b)*: Parent is intimidated or inhibited in dealing with the child especially as regards her participation in interaction treatment. (Parent may be much older than average, or of a different culture.)	
Infant/Child		Infant or child may present with moderate delays or deficits, symptoms of anxiety, depression, impulsivity or aggression.	

TABLE 10.1 (continued)
Forms of Parent–Infant and Child Interaction Treatment

	Type 1: Treating the Parent in the Presence of the Infant	Type 2: Treating the Infant or Child in the Presence of the Parent	Type 3: Treating the Parent and Child as a Veritable Dyad
Parent		*Condition(c)*: Parent's psychological condition is such that she cannot attend to the child. He/she may present as a severe narcissistic or borderline character disorder, or affective disorder, schizophrenia, or psychosis. Under milder forms of the pathology parent may be able to stay in the room with child. When pathology is severe, parent may be accompanied by another caregiver. Sometimes the parent in spite of pathology may be able to work with the child (this is rare). Sometimes the parent is misdiagnosed and draws on resources that enable the dyadic work.	
Child		Child may present with severe anxiety, self-mutilating behavior, biopsychosocial dysregulation, or more moderate manifestations of stress, delays and deficits.	

perception of this infant. The therapist, then, listens to the parent's narration of past and present concerns as they are engaged and intensified by the presence of this infant. Often in the process of listening to the parent's painful concerns, the infant shows positive changes in behavior. As if by magic, the baby might become quieter, begin to gurgle, and look at parent or therapist. With some encouragement, the parent may now pick up the baby, hug and otherwise comfort it and the parent, seeing and experiencing something never before beheld, may begin to cry tears of relief. (This type of treatment has been described most evocatively in the works of Fraiberg and her associates.)

The criteria for type 1 interaction treatment include an infant who is at risk, even at high risk, for developmental, characterologic, and interpersonal dysfunction, but one who as yet shows no manifest signs of delay or deficit functioning. The criteria also include a parent who sees the infant as a transference figure and therefore tends to respond to the infant with manifest signs of disturbance in the relationship, such as asynchrony, onesidedness, avoidance, and clashing. The parent may express negative bids in the forms of parental overriding, intrusiveness, uninvolvement, and verbal abuse in his or her moment-to-moment behavior toward the infant. Manifest signs in the infant of severe delays, deficits, or developmental and characterologically disordered coping strategies such as disconnecting, freezing, or transformation of affect, however, indicate that a type 1 treatment strategy is not appropriate and that both parent and infant require a different type of intervention.

INTERACTION TREATMENT TYPE 2: TREATING THE INFANT OR CHILD IN THE PRESENCE OF THE PARENT

A baby or toddler is treated in the presence of the parent under three conditions: (1) the child presents with severe developmental or characterologic deficits (e.g., Autism, PDD, Conduct/

Disruptive Disorder); (2) the parent experiences disturbing degrees of stress due to any number of infant or child dysfunctions (not only the most severe) but for the moment lacks the capacity to work with the child in interactive treatment type 3 (i.e., parent and child work together with therapist); (3) the parent presents with a diagnostic profile that raises questions as to whether he or she suffers from psychopathology that would undermine interaction treatment type 3. Type 2 treatment, then, is used in cases where the child shows problems that require greater parental capacities than would appear to be immediately available. Under the first condition, the child's difficulties exceed the average caregiver's functions and capacities to work with the child. Under the second condition, the child's difficulties are not so grave, but the parent is truly too inhibited, frightened, or worried to feel at all competent as a caregiver, or too inhibited to do anything in the presence of or together with the therapist. In regard to the latter situation, parents sometimes experience "inhibitions" stemming from values and attitudes influenced by cultural background that are different from that of the therapist (see Sue, 1981; McGoldrick, Pearce, and Giorao, 1982). Under the third condition, the initial diagnostic assessment indicates further evaluation of the parent's stability in psychological functioning with respect to his or her capacity to become a working ally in the treatment strategy and process. Type 2 treatment is initiated as a means of beginning treatment of the child while also evaluating further the parent's ability to become beneficially involved with the treatment.

In type 2 treatment, the parent is encouraged to sit back, and watch the therapist at work with the child, while the therapist observes, imitates, reflects-labels, and probes in working with the child and translates to the parent as the work proceeds.

Under the first condition, the therapist works with the child in the presence of the parent and translates to the parent how the therapist and child are working together, how they are relating to each other, and what therapeutic bids the therapist is using with the child. When the therapist and child have found a way of working together, and when the child shows responses that indicate progress in one area or another (i.e., when therapy seems to be getting off the ground), the therapist enlists the parent as a cotherapist to work with the therapist and the child. (This approach is similar to Reichler and Schopler's [1973] earlier model for working with parents and their autistic children.) The child presenting with these kinds of deficits typically requires concurrent interventions as well. In our framework, we maintain that parent–infant or child therapy cannot provide specialized interventions, such as sensorivestibular input, speech therapy, and other forms of specialized developmental and educational training. The interaction treatment remains a psychological treatment, not an educational or rehabilitation program aimed at remedying focal deficiencies or deficits of neurocognitive development. Thus, the therapist focuses on the child's affects, social connectedness, self-regulation, sense of self, wishes and needs, and fantasy and play. Even a child suffering from deficiencies in neurocognitive development is presumed by definition to have these capacities. But the therapist may have to reach down to the child's most basic and elemental levels of experience to engage the rudiments of these potentialities.

Under the second condition, the child is treated in the presence of the parent, not because the child is so profoundly defective or delayed, but because he or she shows moderate developmental difficulties, characterologic perturbation, or intrapsychic conflict. The *parent* may show a moderate impairment of caregiving capacity because of fear, inhibition, or a feeling that working with the child is beyond his or her capacity, or that working together with the professional is not culturally sanctioned and therefore unacceptable (i.e., shyness). For example, the parent may be too frightened to work with a failure-to-thrive baby and may want to watch what the therapist is doing; or the parent may be too inhibited to "play" with an inhibited, shy toddler. An initial invitation to the parent to sit back and watch the therapist work with the child can help the parent become familiar with his or her child's distress and how that distress impacts on the relationship with the therapist. While working with the child, the therapist will comment to the parent not only about his or her understanding of what goes on inside the child but also about his or her own self-observations on the experience of working with the child. At the same time, the therapist will repeat to the child what he or she had just told the parent. Note that in this case, it is important to assuage the parent's anxiety and to engage the parent's alliance. A parent may show timidity, inhibition, shyness, and an unwillingness to get down on the floor with his or her child, so a period of sitting back and not having to perform, but rather watching the therapist work with the child, makes the parent feel that the therapist values the parent's presence. This therefore decreases the effect of the parent's timidity and enhances his or her self-esteem. These parents may in time become exceptionally adroit therapeutic partners, and eventually take over the treatment of their children and then the daily tasks of parenting.

Under the third condition, the diagnostic evaluation may not make clear whether the parent possesses the capacity to work with the child and to share beneficially in interaction treatment. Parents who absolutely cannot participate in interaction treatment most often suffer from psychoses, major affective disorders, or from the self-regulating deficiencies and self-esteem vulnerabilities of severely borderline or narcissistic personality organizations. When these diagnoses are relatively easy to make, the parent may be excluded from the interaction therapy, or another co-parent may be added to the interaction treatment. But sometimes a parent presents with a diagnostic profile that seems to fall in a gray area, which leaves the therapist with the question as to whether the parent can participate with the child in interaction treatment type 3. As such, type 2 treatment is initiated that will eventually move to type 3 interaction treatment with the parent and child together, or individual treatment for the parent, as well as for the child, if another co-parent cannot be added to make type 3 treatment possible. For these parents, the initial invitation to sit back and watch the therapist work with the child can give further indication of the therapeutic viability of the parent's presence. A parent showing respect, empathy, and tact regarding the therapeutic process and the child's engagement in the process will gradually become involved as the treatment progresses, at which point it has become type 3 treatment. A parent showing extreme self-involvement with an abrupt and incessant invasiveness of the process, outright hostility toward it and even assault on the child, or an excessive distance or withdrawal from the proceedings during the initial therapist–child interaction work, is probably signaling a need for their own individual treatment.

INTERACTION TREATMENT TYPE 3: PARENT AND CHILD WORK TOGETHER WITH THE THERAPIST

Type 3 treatment is based on the same principles as family or group treatment. This treatment is appropriate for parent–child relationships in which both the child and parent exhibit problems that interfere with the relationship, and in turn, the troubled relationship perpetuates the disordered functioning of both individuals. As such, the child is developmentally ready to use language, is able to walk and presents problems that may range the gamut of anxiety, depression, inhibition, aggression, self-mutilation, enuresis, encopresis, excessive masturbation, night fears, terrors, nightmares, all below the age of 3. The parent feels inadequate, frightened, or enraged with the child, or overburdened with other stresses to an extent that he or she does not want to attend to the child. Disordered functioning is evident in many domains in both child and parent, but both show a capacity to attend for at least an hour at a time to what goes on in a treatment session that involves the parent, child, and therapist.

Therapists typically find the work of this form of interaction treatment to be quite taxing. The treatment process requires the therapist to translate the utterances of one member of the dyad to the other, with varying degrees of emphasis and focus on the parent and child as individuals, and as dyads. (In this regard see also Dahl's work [1983] where she identifies the therapist's function as one of decoder.) Addressing both parent and child in turn, the therapist reflects-labels, probes, or facilitates the concerns or interests of the one to the other as parent and child address each other and the therapist.

As in all triangular situations, dyads form, so the therapist must be attuned to the needs of the "left-out" individual who clamors to be heard, or who retreats into isolation. In this connection, the therapist will find it challenging to keep the action and the concerns of the parent and child contained within the room, the framework of the treatment setup, and the central issues of the interaction treatment. All too often, for example, a parent seizes the opportunity of the interaction session to discuss stressful life events that indirectly rather than directly affect the child and the parent–child relationship. Bringing the parent's concerns back "to the room" and to the most salient issues of the relationship treatment is as difficult or no more difficult (depending on the clinical situation) than redirecting a member of a therapy group who begins discussing personal difficulties that exist entirely outside the group session. That is, the therapist tries to find a common basis for the particular patient's expressed concern among the other group members; so too with the child. When the parent discusses concerns external to the relationship, the therapist tries to find the common base that will bring those concerns or the effects of those concerns back to the child and to the issues of the parent–child relationship. But bringing the parent or child back to the psychological affairs in the here-and-now is also as complicated in a parent–child therapy session as it is in a family therapy session, because here we find the tensions of the interpersonal and intrapersonal dynamics extremely forceful. As such, a mere "translation" reflecting and labeling may be insufficient. Rather, a didactic expansion (an explanation as regards the aims of the treatment), containing (suggesting a separate session or telephone call but redirecting the action to the room), or an intrapsychic interpretation (such as, how difficult it is to share the session given the parent's past experiences), may be necessary to bring the action back to the immediate therapeutic process.

SUMMARY

In the parent–child interaction treatment, the therapist strives to maintain equidistance from and equal closeness to both parent and child. The therapist translates the parent's and child's intentions, expression, wishes, and so on, from one individual to the other as appropriate. As such, the therapist repeats in the language of the parent what the therapist under-stands about the child's intentions, offerings, or utterances. Similarly, the therapist translates to the child what the therapist understands about the parent's intentions, offerings, or utter-ances. At first, this way of intervening may seem strange to the therapist, but soon it becomes part of the ordinary parlance and it conveys as nothing else can that the set and orientation in the interaction treatment is the three-way communication between all participants. The parent and older child very soon, usually, begin to imitate the therapist and to incorporate the set and orientation for interaction treatment. The therapist maintains the set and orientation of the form of treatment throughout, pulling back gradually from the active interaction as indicated by the parent's and child's developing capacities to negotiate successfully between each other. As has been de-scribed, in the triangular interaction of parent–child treatments, the therapist typically mirrors, reflects-labels, coaxes-encourages, facilitates, probes, didactically expands, and interprets (geneti-cally according to parental or child history, or in the here-and-now transaction) according to the transactions between the participants' positive and negative patterns of functioning and relating. The therapist may also contain either child or parent in affective or physical outburst by inhibiting, delaying, or denying (i.e., containment category), or by helping to create a mental space by encouraging a quiet space (disengaging/ silence) for all to reflect on experience (promoting self-observation) that might later be verbalized in an acceptable and more communicable and enlightening manner of expression.

PARENT-INFANT INTERACTION TREATMENT: TYPE 1:[3] JIMMY AND MRS. L

This is a brief diagnostic treatment segment to illustrate parent–infant interaction treatment, type 1, treating the parent in the presence of the child. The session involves a 10-month-old, failure-to-thrive, African-American, infant boy and his 32-year-old, moderately depressed, moderately retarded, alone and economically deprived mother. It is early in the diagnostic treatment, the sixth contact, and the purpose of the videotaped sequence is to ascertain the psychological strengths and weaknesses in this dyad.

Patient	Therapist[4]
1. MO: [Bottle feeds the baby; he sits on her lap, facing outward, his back against her chest. Mother looks away toward a far corner of the room, her face is expressionless, seemingly despondent.]	
2. INFT: [Holds bottle with both hands, sounds phlegmy, but he drinks.]	

---

[3]Type 1 Interaction Treatment is one in which the main verbal therapeutic communications take place between the parent and the therapist in the presence of the child although the therapist does speak for the child and helps the mother to act on the child's behalf.

[4]This segment was taken from a videotaped interaction sequence. The diagnostician-therapist was Ms. Margie Morrison, LCSW; her help in this work is gratefully acknowledged.

3. MO: [Pulls bottle abruptly out of his mouth, sets bottle down, takes a cracker from the table, puts it in his hand, and helps bring the cracker to his mouth.] "Eat, eat."

4. INFT: [Cries for his bottle, tries the cracker, coughs, cries some more. Mother takes the crackers abruptly out of his hands, and gives him the bottle. Infant grabs onto the bottle and ravenously tries to drink. Mother appears desolate and looks in the direction of the far end of the room then once again, with a jerk and a tug, pulls the bottle out of his mouth. And the baby cries, coughs up phlegm and cries.]

5. "Ms. Light, it looks like you are tired and not feeling too well, and Jimmy here wants his bottle, but you want him to have both, the bottle and the crackers, is that so?"

Coding 1-5
Bid: Refl/Labl, Emp (for mother and child)
Facet: Developmental, Interpersonal

[Here therapist addresses mother, first, then reflects the infant's wishes, then once again therapist reflects her understanding of mother's behavior in relation to baby.]

6. MO: [Nods in agreement.]

7. [Speaking for and to the baby.] "It looks like you only want to drink

right now and not eat a cracker, and maybe also, you would like to see your mommy's face and she yours, so she'll know what you want, because you can't talk yet, right? Ms. Light, would you like to see Jimmy's face while he drinks so you'll know what he wants?''

Coding 6-7
Bid: Refl/Labl (for mother and child)
Did/Exp (for mother)
Facet: Developmental (child; mother)
Interpersonal (mother; child)

[Now, therapist reflects/labels the baby's feelings first, labeling and putting into words his actions and facial expressions. Next therapist encourages mother to expand on her repertory, by changing the baby's position, looking at him so she'll be able to better read his expressions. When the developmental facet is limited or defective, much"stretching" of limits (expansion) needs to take place, but that requires the utmost sensitivity and knowledge or guesswork, as to what the baby may be able to take in at this time and what the mother is capable of offering. Generally speaking, a good expansion follows on the heels of careful observation of the previous utterance or gesture, to capture what the patient had already mastered; and with this observation, the therapist can take the patient one step further. In this case, the mother had pushed crackers into Jimmy's hands and mouth. This act implied that she was intent on feeding him, but did not know what was appropriate to feed him or how to go about it. Therefore, the therapist's suggestion that she look at him was a didactic expansion built on mother's intent that he ingest other food beside milk from the bottle.]

In a free play sequence, the mother is asked to play a game with her child that she played when she was a little girl.

Patient	Therapist
8. MO: [Tries to get her baby to sit up to play pat-a-cake.]	
9. INFT: [Jimmy does not have the muscle tone to remain in the sitting up position. He falls over.]	
10. MO: "Oh, no, no, no. Don't do that!" [She steadies him with her shoulder and with her hands she plays pat-a-cake with him . . . and sings to him.]	
11. INFT: [Jimmy cries, he coughs.]	
12. MO: "Oh, No! No! Don't cry, let's play pat-a-cake." [She pats him on the back and tries to console him. Jimmy stops crying.]	
	13. "Yes, you're so right, Jimmy has a hard time sitting up."

Coding 8-13
**Bid: Refl/Labl (for mother and
      child)**
**Facet: Developmental, Interper-
      sonal, Character**

[Therapist reflects and labels Jimmy's conditions to confirm that it
isn't mother's incompetence that
makes the baby cry, but his own
developmental difficulties.]

14. MO: "Ok, what do you want
to do?" [MO looks at her baby, trying to read from his cues. He nes-
tles into her shoulder, and she
rocks him, soothes him, chest to
chest.]

15. "Ms. Light, you want to get to
know your child. So you are looking at him and giving him what he
needs right now, even though I
asked you to play a game with him,
you are thinking for yourself and
deciding what is best for him."

Coding 14-15
**Bid: Refl/Labl (for mother and
      child)**
Encrge/Prse (for mother)
Facet: Character, Developmental

[The therapist affirms mother's
judgment as well as her move to
look at him, to follow his lead—
something the therapist suggested
during the feeding—and to respond to his wish to being held
and rocked. Ms. L also showed her

233

independent judgment by not complying with the request to play a game with her son, but rather to attend to a more basic biopsychological requisite on his part.]

Analysis of Therapeutic Bids

These brief episodes taken from a videotaped diagnostic treatment session include 15 transactions between the mother, her baby and the therapist, and 13 therapeutic bids. They were the following:

Bids	From Therapist to Mother	From Therapist to Child
Reflecting/labeling:	5	4
Empathy:	1	
Didactic Expansion:	1	
Praise:	2	
Facets engaged		
Developmental:	4	2
Character:	2	
Interpersonal:	3	1

It is clear from these brief segments that the therapist's bids were directed primarily toward the mother, engaging, we believe, the developmental, character, and interpersonal facets. The bids are supportive of mother's development, attempt to expand on her knowledge and encourage further growth, including the essence of her autonomy in her parenting role.

The therapist also speaks for the child and to the child—thereby engaging the child's social and language domains (developmental facet), and also translating to the mother her infant's needs—thereby teaching the mother to be a more sensitive "reader" of her baby's cues.

Discussion

It is evident in this step-by-step analysis of transactions between the therapist, mother, and child that the focus of communications is primarily from the therapist to the mother. This is treatment of the mother in the presence of the child focusing on helping the mother to become more comfortable and adept in her parenting role, with this particular child; to read his cues more accurately and foster her sense of autonomy about her observations and the decisions she makes.

Our observations of Ms. Light and her baby confirmed our diagnosis that while the child was indeed at high-risk (since he manifested all the signs of failure-to-thrive), and Ms. Light presented with dysthymia as well as with deficits in cognitive functioning, her character structure was wholesome; that is, she did not present with a major character deficit. Thus, she could work in interaction treatment, individual treatment, and participate in a mother's group on her own and her child's behalf.

The treatment of this dyad lasted seven years. Mother was seen in individual treatment where she learned to express herself, to read her own internal cues, to talk about her condition, her past, her present, and even her future. The interaction treatment lasted three years. In time, as the child and mother developed their respective developmental skills, the treatment emphasis changes from type 1 to type 2, and then to type 3. Now mother and Jimmy learned to play, to share, to imitate, to make all sorts of sounds—car sounds, siren sounds—reading picture books together to her child, play-acting and making faces together (such as pointing to each other's noses and laughing together). Jimmy's cognitive delay required a special education program. Mother, with ongoing once-a-week individual psychotherapy, became more active and less depressed. The treatment bids, we discovered, in this early treatment case (1981), remained the same regardless of treatment modality: receptive observation, imitating and mirroring, reflection and labeling, probing, encouraging and facilitating, expanding and some interpreting, some containing when Jimmy became enlivened and overly active, and disengagement, the latter only to replace the others when the nature of the disengagement could be discussed, such as when mother's attention was not focused on Jimmy, or when Jimmy turned away from mother in order to play by himself.

A significant bid fairly early in the treatment was that of probing. For someone who never was asked her opinion, and for a child whose mother did not think that opinions mattered, to probe was both incomprehensible and frightening. Ms. L once told her therapist: "When you ask what I think it is like going into a deep, black cave." In the beginning the cave looked black; there was nothing to say or think about. With encouragement, reflections, and labeling of feelings and behavior, words began to come, ever so slowly, but they did come. Work on self, character, feelings, wishes, needs, even aspirations began to bud. Intrapsychic conflicts appeared, in the mother as well as in the child. Interpretation in the transference in individual treatment with the mother took place. But in interaction treatment the interpretations were at an interpersonal level, reality-based, in the here-and-now, aimed at the goings-on between mother and child, or between the child and his therapist. For example, the therapist said to Jimmy on one occasion, "It looks to me like you would rather throw this stuff around and not think about what you're doing. I can believe you are mad at me or at mom, but you still can't throw." Or when the therapist said to the mother in an interaction session, "I think you would rather talk about the things that worry you, rather than be here, the three of us, thinking about what we are doing together with Jimmy."

The treatment was lengthy. Development takes time and has to take its course. Also, there were setbacks. Jimmy developed a cancerous tumor and required an operation and chemotherapy. But the suffering brought everyone that much closer to one another and cemented the treatment relationship. All discovered that they could count on the therapist and the support staff. There were other developments, too. With Jimmy's improvement, mother married her boyfriend. Ms. L's therapist left the clinic and mother left treatment. She had another baby girl, and she named her after her therapist. But 18 months after termination that baby girl became failure to thrive. This time, Ms. L returned for treatment with a positive alliance which had generalized from the individual relationship with her previous therapist to the PIDS service in general. Ms. L and her new baby girl picked up very quickly where she, Ms. L, seemed to have stopped. Adaptive functioning on both sides was reestablished within six months. At the end of treatment both children, Jimmy and the new baby girl, were doing well, the one at school, the other at home. And Ms. L enrolled in a training course to become a beautician.

Is this a happy ending? We don't really know what the future holds for this family. But we do know that there is no panacea for the treatment of the psyche. What there are, are little steps that can lead toward righting something in the here-and-now; these little steps can be defined and transmitted. They can be understood, and are relatively simple to execute. But where they land, on which of the multiple facets of the human psyche, can never be determined in advance. We stayed in contact with Ms. L and her family for three years posttermination; namely, we were in touch with the L family for a total of ten years. Today, however, fifteen years after the beginning of treatment, we do not know how the L family is faring.

PARENT–INFANT INTERACTION TREATMENT: TYPE 2:[5] CHERYL AND MS. CAS

Cheryl was a 9-month-old, Caucasian baby girl born with an intractable, irritable temperament. She shunned her parents' touch and gaze. She was physically well developed, but temperamentally highly irritable, not easily consolable, and physically very active, but unpredictable in her sleep cycles and feeding patterns. Toys

---

[5]Parent–infant interaction treatment, type 2, is defined as treatment done in the presence of the parent, when the child's developmental or characterologic functioning is so disordered that the therapist has to find his or her way into the child before communication can be fostered between the parent and the child (see pp. 222–224).

and novelty items captured her attention, but people did not. Her language development included vocalizations, but babbling for pleasure was not in her repertoire.

Diagnostic evaluation sought to rule out early infantile autism, and the sequelae of Sturge-Weber syndrome due to a discoloration on the upper left corner of her face.

Both parents were involved in the diagnostic evaluation, but the work of parent–infant interaction was left to the mother. Both were well functioning psychologically but considerably stressed by the child's temperament and their fears regarding possible neurophysiological deterioration. Because Cheryl was a difficult baby, the clinician[6] decided to work with her in the presence of her mother, type 2 interaction treatment, explaining that one way of getting to know what Ms. Cas was up against was to deal with Cheryl in her presence. The clinician would then share with her what she did, discovered, and thought about the child so that Ms. Cas could then work together with the therapist with the aim of eventually taking over.

Patient	Therapist
1. MO: [Entering the therapy room]"She has been pretty difficult this morning."	
	2. "How so?"
	Coding 1-2 **Bid: Prob (to mother)** **Facet: Interpersonal**
3. "Crying, not wanting to eat, turning her head away from me."	
	4. "That's pretty tough to take. I wonder what is bothering Cheryl."
	Coding 3-4 **Bid: Emp (for mother)** **Prob (for child)**

---

[6]The therapist-diagnostician was C.H.R., then Director of the PIDS.

Facet: Interpersonal

5. "How would you like to just sit back and see what she and I can do together. Then when we find a way to deal with Cheryl, we'll do it together, Ok?"

Coding 5
Bid: Did/Exp (for mother)
Facet: Developmental

[Therapist is saying to mother, let's explore. I don't know the answer to Cheryl's behavior either.]

6. [MO and TH install the baby on the floor with some of her own toys.]

7. [MO sits on the couch.]

8. [Therapist is on the floor. She does not approach Cheryl.]

Coding 6-8
Bid: R/O, Dis/Sil (for child)
Facet: Interpersonal, Character

9. [INFT looks on the floor after own toys; she does not touch them.]

10. [Therapist is silent; watches baby.]

Coding 9-10
Bid: R/O (for child)
  Dis/Sil (for child)
Facet: Interpersonal

11. [Therapist introduces a see-through rattle with many-colored

shapes and trinkets inside; she shakes the rattle.]

Coding 11
Bid: Did/Exp
Facet: Developmental

12. [INFT glances toward rattle.]

13. "What pretty colors and noises. I see you are looking at the rattle."

Coding 12-13
Bids: Mir/Init (toward child)
      Refl/Labl (toward child)
Facet: Developmental

14. [INFT reaches for the rattle from her sitting up position, but the rattle is not within reach. She looks at TH.]

15. "I see you are looking at me, and you want the rattle."

Coding 14-15
Bids: Refl/Labl (toward child)
      Mir/Imit (toward child)
Facet: Developmental

16. [INFT looks away from TH and rattle.]

17. [Therapist shakes rattle, but does not bring it closer to Cheryl.]

Coding 16-17
Bids: R/O (toward child)
      Did/Exp [Therapist hopes child will reach out.]
Facet: Developmental

18. [INFT reaches for rattle, without looking at TH; the rattle is out of reach and Cheryl falls over. She

cries, and the crying becomes louder; but it is hard to distinguish whether the cry is a loud wail of misery or of protest.]

19. "You really fell there trying to get the rattle all by yourself."

Coding 18-19
Bid: Emp (toward child)
Refl/Labl (toward child)
Facet: Developmental

20. "I'm sorry you are hurt!"

Coding 20
Bid: Emp (toward child)
Refl/Labl (toward child)
Facet: Character, Intrapersonal

21. "Would you like me to help you?" [Therapist picks baby up and replaces her in sitting position.]

Coding 21
Bid: Facil (for child)
Facet: Developmental, Interpersonal

22. [INFT is quiet; she looks at the toy; she looks at the TH.]

23. "I will push the rattle towards you so it will be easier for you to reach."

Coding 22-23
Bid: Facil (for child)
Facet: Developmental, Interpersonal

24. [INFT is now able to take the toy. She looks at it, explores it visually and orally. Then she looks at

the TH. She looks toward her MO who is sitting behind the TH. Then she smiles.]

25. "That was wonderful, Cheryl. You got to hold the pretty rattle."

Coding 24-25
Bid: Prse (for child)
Facet: Developmental, Interpersonal

26. "You were also looking at me and smiling at your mommie."

Coding 26
Bid: Prse (for child)
      Did/Exp (for mother)
Facet: Developmental, Interpersonal

27. [Therapist translates to mother what just happened.] "At first Cheryl was not interested in any toys. Then she became curious about the *new* rattle (she likes novelty), but couldn't reach it." But she was not making contact with the therapist. Therapist also wanted to see whether Cheryl would stretch her limits in reaching for the toy. She did not. So, the therapist let her fend for herself. Then she fell. Now she needed the therapist for some sort of comfort and help and the therapist did that—she pushed the toy closer to Cheryl. Cheryl responded positively to the praise about her interest in novelty and exploration, and then she was able to make contact

with the human face, the therapist's and the mother's. She did
not smile at the therapist, but she
did smile at her mother.

Coding 27
Bid: Refl/Labl (for mother)
    Did/Exp (for mother)
**Facet: Interpersonal, Develop-
mental**

Analysis of Therapeutic Bids

This episode taken from the beginning of a parent–infant interaction session, type 2, includes 27 transactions between the therapist, the baby, and the mother, and 28 therapeutic bids. They
were the following:

Therapist to Mother:	7 bids	Therapist to baby:	21 bids
Probe:	1	Probe:	1
Empathy:	1	Empathy:	2
Didactic/Expansion:	4	Didactic/Expansion:	2
Reflecting/Labeling:	1	Receptive/Observation:	3
		Silent/Disengagement:	2
		Mirroring/Imitating:	2
		Reflecting/Labeling:	5
		Facilitating:	2
		Praising:	2

There were 19 bids directed toward the child which included
one probe, two empathic bids, two didactic expansions, three
receptive observations, two silent disengagements, two mirroring
imitating bids, five reflecting/labeling bids, two facilitating bids,
and two praises.

There were seven bids directed toward the mother which
included one probe, one empathic bid, two didactic expansions,
and one reflecting/labeling bid.

The facets these bids were assumed to have engaged based on the responses or new initiations of the child, or on the aim of the therapist were:

For the child:	Developmental facet	7	(curiosity, novelty, effectance)
	Character facet	2	(temperament, self-esteem)
	Interpersonal	6	(social attentiveness, i.e., connectedness)
For the mother:	Interpersonal	3	(mutuality: reciprocity and joint interest)
	Developmental	2	(helping the parent help)
For the therapist:	Developmental	1	(trying to understand the child and her mother)
	Interpersonal	1	

Discussion

The interactions between the mother, child, and therapist indicate that in this treatment episode the primary focus was on the child, with an introduction to the mother regarding the framework and aim of the session.

From this first episode of the interaction section, the therapist and Cheryl moved to another episode. This time it concerned a wooden dog with a red-pegged tail. The interaction was similar except this time the therapist did not allow the child to fall, this in order to develop a positive alliance with the child. And Cheryl once again looked at her mother when she was able to reach the dog.

During the third episode, the therapist showed Cheryl a squeaky doll, no bigger than an adult's hand. This time she asked the mother to join her on the floor. The therapist was still the conductor of the actions, but mother and therapist sat close together, like a pair. Thus, several pairs had formed during the course of one session. The first was Cheryl and the therapist, shadowed by mother. The second was therapist and mother in the presence of Cheryl. The goal for the last one would be for

Cheryl and her mother to communicate and play directly—shadowed by the therapist. When this happened, as it did eventually, the interaction treatment was no longer a type 2, but had become a type 3 interaction treatment.

Cheryl was not autistic, neither did she have the Sturge-Weber syndrome. However, she was a willful, determined, intelligent child, interested in novelty and exploration. She tended to be more inner directed and tended to enjoy taking the initiative in her activities. She had to learn to curb her temper and to attend to other people as well. But as of our last contact, Cheryl and her mother and father were manifestly attached to one another, and relating to one another with greater mutuality.

PARENT–CHILD INTERACTION TREATMENT: TYPE 3:[7] MOLLY AND HER GRANDMOTHER

Molly, a lively $2^{1}/_{2}$ year-old, African-American girl, presented with "hyperness," difficulty in toilet training, and delayed speech. She lived with her grandmother because her own mother had lost custody due to neglect and possible abuse.

The child was diagnosed as having language delay in the developmental facet, character issues manifested by high activity level in the temperament domain, as well as anxieties deriving from intrapsychic conflict associated with unconscious needs, wishes, and fantasies. Interaction treatment type 3 seemed indicated as the first phase of treatment to help grandmother help the child in her development and to improve on their volatile relationship.

---

[7] Type 3 interaction treatment is one in which the therapist translates the child's communications to the parent and the parent's to the child with the intent of fostering direct reciprocal communication between the two (see p. 226.)

Molly and Her Grandmother

Therapist[8]

1. [Walking to the office, Mrs. T is talking about the weather and how she had to leave work early to get to the clinic on time.]

2. "I sympathize with the difficulties of Chicago's winters."

Coding 1-2
Bid: Emp (to GMO)
Facet: Interpersonal, Character

3. [Molly is quiet and smiling in response to my greeting but makes no eye contact.]

4. I say hello to Molly. "How are you doing? "It's good to see you."

Coding 3-4
Bids: Rspct (to child)
Tct (to child)
Facet: Interpersonal, Character

5. [Mrs. T tries to get her to respond.]

6. Molly is saying "no" and smiling.

7. [Therapist is silent.]

Coding 5-7
Bids: R/O (to child)
Dis/Sil (to child)
Facet: Interpersonal

8. [In the office, Molly wants to climb in my lap while she explores the toys on the table. Mrs. T explains that things have been going better this week than last week.]

9. "Momma says you did well this past week."

[8] This treatment was conducted by David Paul Smith. We gratefully acknowledge his contribution to this chapter. The treatment began as a type 3, but due to the grandmother's overriding and leading interventions, she was encouraged to sit back and let the

Coding 8-9
Bid: Prse (to child)
GMO's bid: Prse (to therapist about child)
Facet: Interpersonal (clash)

10. [Molly reaches for a bird toy on the table; she is having trouble reaching it.]

11. "Do you want help?"

Coding 10-11
Bid: Facil (to child)
Facet: Developmental

12. "Ya." [Shifts attention to the box with different shape blocks.] "Open up. . . box."

13. Mrs. T—"Op-En. Molly. O-pen."

14. "Molly, momma wants you to say 'open' . . . You're talking a lot today. Mama wants you to talk, and you are talking."

"Good talking. Momma seems happy." [I look over to Mrs. T.] "Right?"

Coding 12-14
Bids: Refl/Labl (to child)
          Prse (to child)
GMO's bid: Did/Exp (to child)
TH's bid: Mir/Imit (to GMO)
Facet: Developmental

15. [Mrs. T. nods.]

16. [Mrs. T. nods again.]

---

therapist work with the child. In this session, we still note the therapist trying to translate the grandmother's wishes to the child.

17. Mrs. T: "Molly bring me a cup of tea." [Molly is playing with blocks . . . then she is playing with a color spin toy. She is touching all the toys on the table and exploring.]

18. "Momma wants you to play the Tea game. What are you doing? What are you playing?"

[Mrs. T is taking the lead in play.]

Coding 15-18
Bids: R/O (to child)
GMO's bids: R/O (to child)
      R/O (to child)
      Overriding (to child)
TH's bids: Refl/Labl (to GMO)
      Prob (to child)
Facet: Interpersonal

19. Mrs. T: "The baby-sitter said Molly did not wet herself this week."

20. "Oh, Molly! Momma said that you stayed dry all day. Wow, like a big girl all by yourself."

Coding 19-20
Bids: Refl/Labl (to child)
      Prse (to child)
GMO's bid: Refl/Labl (to child)
      Prse (to child)
Facet: Developmental

22. Mrs. T: "Molly, don't do that. Get down, O.K.?"

23. [Sitting next to Molly ready to catch her.] "Molly, momma is worried that you might hurt yourself.

You're trying to get in the basket. Here, let me put the basket down."

Coding 21-23
Bid:Refl/Labl (to child)
    Refl/Labl (to GMO)
    Facil (to child)
GMO: Cont (to child)
Facet: Interpersonal, Developmental

24. [Molly gets down. She takes out blocks and plastic beads and sits on the floor. She is playing quietly.]

25. [Mrs. T gives up trying to get her attention and is playing with blocks in her chair by herself.]

26. "Molly, you're playing with blocks yourself and momma is playing with blocks over there by herself. You're playing your own game."

Coding 24-26
Bids: Refl/Labl (to child)
    Refl/Labl (to GMO)
Facet: Developmental

[Here we see the first attempt to separate the child's from the grandmother's intentions. By maintaining the alliance with the grandmother in the early transactions, the therapist was able to separate the grandmother's intense concerns from the child's without being critical or didactic, but merely by labeling and reflecting.]

27. Mrs. T: "I'm playing with blocks; that's O.K., you can play with those blocks yourself."

28. Molly hears a noise and says, "plane."

29. Mrs. T: "No, that's a door."

30. Molly: "Door."

31. A plane flies by, Molly says, "What dat?"

32. Mrs. T: "An airplane."

Coding 27-32
GMO's bid 27: Encrg (to child)
GMO's bid 29: Did/Exp (to child)
GMO's bid 32: Did/Exp (to child)
Facet: Developmental

33. [Molly covers her ears and grimaces in a playful fashion. . . Everyone is silent.]

34. "You have us both watching you playing there."

Coding 33-34
Bids: Refl/Labl (to child)
R/O (to child)
Facet: Developmental

35. [Mrs. T laughs.]

36. Molly: "Ya."

37. "It feels good to be the center of attention."

Coding 35-37
Bid: Refl/Labl (to child)
Facet: Interpersonal

38. Mrs. T: "Yeah, she went potty

by herself this week. I went through a lot of Pampers. Boy, she's almost 3, but she is finally coming along"

39. "Yes, I can imagine it was worrying you, and it is a relief now."

Coding 38-39
Bid 39: Emp (to GMO)
Refl/Labl (to GMO)
Facet: Interpersonal

40. "Yeah, she's almost 3."

41. "Molly, momma is happy that you can do things by yourself like a big girl. You did it all by yourself."

Coding 40-41
Bid: Emp (to child)
Refl/Labl (to child)
Facet: Developmental

42. Molly: "No."

43. "Oh ... sometimes it feels good to be a baby ... taken care of."

Coding 42-43
Bids: Emp (to child)
Refl/Labl (to child)
Facet: Developmental

44. [Molly is counting the pop-up boxes.]

45. "You're counting?"

Coding 44-45
Bid: Refl/Labl (for child)
Prob (for child)
Facet: Developmental

46. Molly: "Yup."

47. Mrs. T: "Molly, one. . . two. . . three. . . etc.

48. "Momma wants you to show me you can count. She knows you can and she wants you to show me."

Coding 46-48
Bid: Refl/Labl (for child)
Refl/Labl (for GMO)
Facet: Developmental

49. [Mrs. T nods proudly that I understand.] "She talks at home."

50. [Therapist is silent.]

Coding 49-50
Bid: Dis/Sil (for GMO)
Dis/Sil (for child)
Facet: Developmental

51. [Molly is taking beads apart and putting them together, finally in a circle.]

52. "You're putting the beads together, now in a circle."

Coding 51-52
Bid: Refl/Labl (for child)
Facet: Developmental

53. [She gets very quiet and slowly puts them on her head, but before she puts it on she laughs out loud and pulls the chain apart.]

54. "Now, we're getting quiet. Now, we're loud and you're pulling the beads apart, each one by one."

Coding 53-54
Bid: Refl/Labl (for child)
Facet: Developmental

55. Molly: "Put it back." [She is putting the beads together again.]

56. Mrs. T: "Why are you doing that, don't pull them apart. . . oh. . .OK. . .if you want to do that then, OK."

57. Therapist to Molly: "It's not easy but you're doing it any-way. . . tricky."

"It feels good to do it yourself, huh?"

Coding 55-57
Therapist Bid: Encrg (to child)
GMO Bid: Cont (to child)
Therapist Bid: Refl/Labl (to
            child)
Facet: Developmental, Interper-sonal

58. [Molly is having trouble completing the circle.]

59. "Maybe you want if off, Molly."

Coding 58-59
Bid: Refl/Labl (to child)
      Prob (to child)
Facet: Developmental

60. "Ya. . . It's a wheel mom-my. . .shoes off and pants myself, momma." [She tries taking her shoe off.]

61. Mrs. T: "No, leave it on." [Molly is kicking her heel against the ground.]

62. Molly: "Un, huh."

63. Mrs. T: "Leave it on. . .why do you want it off. . . OK."

64. "It feels good to be growing up. Sometimes it is frustrating."

Coding 60-64
Therapist Bid: Refl/Labl (to child)
Emp/Encrg (to child)
GMO's bid 63: Cont (to child)
Facet: Interpersonal

65. Molly: "Hurts momma." [She rubs her foot, the sock comes off and Mrs. T rubs her foot.]

66. "Maybe it does hurt."

67. Mrs. T: "Maybe it does."

68. Molly: "Hurt."

Coding 65-68
Therapist Bid: Emp (to child)
Refl/Labl (to child)
GMO's bid 67: Refl/Labl (to child)
Facet: Interpersonal

69. Mrs. T: "Now, I'll help you put it on."

70. "Momma wants to help you put it on."

Coding 69-70
Therapist Bid: Refl/Labl
GMO's bid 69: Facil
Facet: Developmental

71. Mrs. T: "Do *you* want to?" [Molly gives a big smile and laughs.]

72. "Oh, you want to show me how you can put it on yourself."

Coding 71-72
Therapist Bid: Refl/Labl (to child)
GMO's bid 71: Did/Exp (to child)
Facet: Interpersonal

73. [Molly turns away and hides her foot.]

74. "You're doing it yourself but you're hiding it from me maybe in case it does not work."

Coding 73-74
Bid: Refl/Labl (to child)
      Prse (to child)
Facet: Interpersonal

75. [Mrs. T is smiling and motions to TH to come over and see how Molly is doing.]

76. To Molly: "You're doing it yourself."

Coding 75-76
Bid: Refl/Labl (to child)
      Prse (to child)
GMO's Bid 75: R/O (to child and therapist)
Facet: Interpersonal

77. Molly: "Put it in hole."

78. "Do you want me to help you?"

79. [She gives up and Mrs. T helps her a little. Then Molly takes over again and tries to push the lace through the eye in her shoe. . . then she comes over to TH.]

Coding 77-79
Therapist Bid: Prob (to child)
GMO's Bid: Facil (to child)
Facet: Developmental

255

80. [When the lace is almost through she pulls away to finish it herself.]

81. "Good job." [A few moments of silence.]

82. "Well, it's time to start getting ready to leave."

Coding 80-82
Bid: Prse (to child)
    Cont (to child)
Facet: Interpersonal, Character

83. [Molly hides under the desk.]

84. [Mrs. T asks why she does that.]

85. "Well, it's hard to leave especially when you are doing things you enjoy. When you lose control pulling away helps keep your sense of 'being out of control' contained."

Coding 83-85
GMO's Bid: Prob (to therapist and child)
Therapist Bid 85: Did/Exp (to child)
    Intrp (to child)
Facet: Interpersonal, Character

86. [Finally, we get up and Molly decides to comply. She gets her stroller in the hall and pushes it ahead of us.]

87. [Therapist continues to talk about possible reasons why Molly does what she does and how it is a good thing to reflect about what

she might be thinking. Therapist
says good-bye to both of them.]

Coding 86-87
Bid: Refl/Labl
    Did/Exp
Facet: Interpersonal, Character

[Molly and Mrs. T smile and say-
good-bye.]

Analysis of Therapeutic Bids

This full treatment hour illustrates how the therapist begins to
work in type 3 interaction session with the child and her grandmother who is also her foster mother. The reader will be able to
follow how the grandmother gradually begins to understand the
aim of the treatment, which is to help her help the child achieve
a balance in the developmental aims of encouraging her curiosity
and exploration, her social connectedness, and meeting the biopsychological requisites appropriate for her age. Another aim is
the regulation of her temperamental high-activity level and impul-
sivity. And the final aim for this first phase of the treatment is to
help both grandmother and child improve their often difficult
and volatile relationship.

This hour consists of 87 transactions between the therapist,
grandmother and child, and a total of 80 bids from therapist
to child and grandmother, and from grandmother to child and
therapist. Below we summarize the number of bids from therapist
to child and grandmother, and from grandmother to child and
therapist.

As can be seen, the majority of the bids (52) are from the
therapist toward the child; however, a few are also directed toward
the grandmother (8). The bids in the basically humane grouping
aim to establish an alliance with both child and grandmother

Therapeutic Bids

From TH to child		To GMO	Bids from GMO	
			To Child	To TH
Emp	4	2		
Rspct	1			
Tct	1			
R/O	3	1	3	1
Dis/Sil	2	1		
Prse	6		1	
Facil	2		2	
Drd/Exp	2		4	
Mir/Imit	1			
Refl/Labl	21	5	2	
Prob	4		1	1
Energe	2		1	
Cont	1		2	
Intrp	1			
Overrid			1	
Total Bids	52	8	18	2

(9 to child; 3 to grandmother). Receptive observation, however, conveys an interest on the part of the therapist toward the dyad that engages the developmental, character, and interpersonal facets.

The early internally orienting bid of silence/disengagement is not accidental. Its aim is to create a space for the child and the grandmother to promote whatever facets the child needs to bring out. The praising, mirroring/imitating, and reflecting/labeling bids are all supportive bids (28) aimed at engaging the developmental and character facets. The facilitating and didactically expanding bids (4) which make up the teaching/learning grouping aim at engaging the developmental facet. The probing, interpreting, and encouraging bids (7) which form the insight-orienting grouping aim at this time to engage the child's developmental and character facets. Finally, the renouncing bid ("it's time to start getting ready to leave") which is part of the containing grouping, engages the character.

The grandmother's bids were interesting, few as they were, in that they progressed (as we will see in Figure 10.1 below) from praising (2) the child's progress during the week, didactically expanding (2), reflection/labeling (1), inhibiting (1), receptive observation (2), to overriding (1). She takes the lead in introducing a game to the child and tells her what to do and encouragement in the first part of the session (up to transaction 29), to didactically expanding (1) and inhibiting (1) in the second part of the session (up to transaction 58), to inhibiting (1), reflecting/labeling (1), facilitating (2), didactically expanding (1), receptively observing (1), and probing (1) in the third part of the session (up to transaction 87). We notice that the child, in order to pursue her developmental and interpersonal aims, turns away at times from both the therapist (3, 6, 73) and the grandmother (17, 24, 83).

In an attempt to examine the flow of the session the 87 transactions were divided into three segments: part 1 included transactions 1–29, part 2 transactions 3–58, and part 3 transactions 59–87 (see Figure 10.1).

The therapist's bids were fairly evenly distributed, with a preponderance of bids from the supportive grouping (Mir/Imit and Refl/Labl) in each time segment. Nevertheless, part 2, the middle part of the session, manifests the most supportive bids (9) and from the humane grouping (5). The child, for her part, shows the most activity in that segment, the developmental facet (13) and the domains activated are also elevated: 6 language, 3 cognition, 3 play, 1 physical motor. Nevertheless, she too shows a fairly even distribution of facets engaged in all 3 time segments: part 1 manifests interpersonal engagement (6) and developmental (9). Part 3 manifests interpersonal engagement (7), character (3), developmental (11).

What is most apparent is that during segment 2, when the therapist and child are most active, the grandmother is least active. She is most active in segment 1, least in segment 2, and regains a more focused engagement with her child in segment 3.

259

GROUPING	BIDS	THERAPIST	CHILD FACETS & DOMAINS	GRANDMOTHER	BIDS
		1 2 3 4 5 6 7 8 9	1 2 3 4 5 6 7 8 9	1 2 3 4 5 6 7 8	
Humane	Emp		INTERPERSONAL, CHARACTER:		Part 1 1-29 transactions
	Rspct	5	2 Alliance, Self-Esteem		
	Tct			2 Did/Exp	
	R/O		1 INTERPERSONAL:		
Internal	Dis/Sil	1	Clash		
			DEVELOPMENT:		
Supportive	Prse	1	3 Language	1 Prse	
			3 Cognition		
Learning	Facil	2	2 Play	2 R/O	
Supportive	Mir/Imit	1	1 Physical	1 Override	
Supportive	Refl/Labl	5	INTERPERSONAL:	2 Refl/Labl	
Insight	Probe	1	3 Unilateral, Avoidant, Parallel	1 Prse	
				1 Encrge	
				1 Inhi	
Supportive	Refl/Labl	9	DEVELOPMENT:	1 Did/Exp	Part 2 30-58 transactions
Humane	R/O	2	6 Language		
Humane	Emp	3	3 Cognition		
Insight	Prob	1	3 Play		
Internal	Dis/Sil	2	1 Physical	1 Prob	
Insight	Encrge	1	INTERPERSONAL:	1 Inhib	
			1 Unilateral		
			1 Mutual, Joint		
Supportive	Refl/labl	6	DEVELOPMENT:		Part 3 59-87 transactions
Insight	Prob	1	6 Language		
Humane	Emp	1	4 Physical	1 Inhib	
Insight	Energ	1	1 Play	1 Refl/labl	
Supportive	Prse	2	INTERPERSONAL:	1 Facil	
Cont	Inhib	1	2 Unilateral, Avoidant	1 Did/Exp	
Learning	Did/Exp	2	2 Mutual, Reciprocity, Joint	1 R/O	
			3 CHARACTER: Temperament		

Figure 10.1. Bids by Therapist and Grandmother and Child Facets in 3 Parts of Interaction Treatment Session: Type 3

Discussion

In this early session we see the grandmother's concern with raising her granddaughter. She worries that the child is developmentally delayed. The therapist observes the grandmother's overriding and need to take the lead, both to impress the therapist and to help the child. The therapist sees his first task as supporting his alliance with the grandmother. He reflects and labels her concerns to Molly and to herself. He also reflects and labels Molly's attempts to be more autonomous in her strivings for novelty/exploration and effectance.

As the session moves on, grandmother seems to understand what the therapist is trying to do; namely, to help Molly become more self-reliant for the biopsychological requisites (toilet training) of which she is now capable. Thus, grandmother is less overriding and, following the model of the therapist, more supportive of Molly's forays into autonomous exploration and play.

But Molly lets them know she is also still a little girl who requires help and discipline especially when it is time for separation.

This treatment phase, which lasted one year, has worked very well in supporting the child's developmental facet and the respective domains of cognition, language, physical patterning and play, and in promoting the grandmother's sense of and actual competence in parenting.

Due to the grandmother's earlier concerns she intruded on the child's developmental space, and as a result promoted a difficult unilateral and clashing relationship between herself and Molly. As can be seen in Figure 10.1, toward the end of session (end of part 2) the dyad manifests mutuality.

Currently, during the second year of treatment, in order to help Molly engage other psychological facets, she has begun to work in individual psychotherapy with her therapist to allow for the intrapsychic conflicts and characterologic issues to emerge in the transference and in the interpersonal relationship with her therapist. The grandmother continues to see the therapist for individual support and developmental guidance as Molly's treatment progresses.

CONCLUDING REMARKS

In this book, we have delineated the multiple theoretical perspectives that have influenced our thinking about the complexity of human psychological functioning. Taking the infant and parent as the basic paradigm for theory building, we hope that we have shown the universal applicability of our model to the human being, who develops and changes over time, and that the theory is applicable across age and psychopathology. We have discovered that much clinical suppleness is required in the back and forth movement from facet to facet, from foreground to background, in order to follow the psychic activity of any given individual, whether alone or in relation to another. We do believe, however, that we have begun to achieve a certain cohesion in theory building by clarifying facets, assumptions, principles, domains, and aims of the various facets that frame our psychic functioning.

Similarly, the task of developing an integrated theory of therapeutic transaction that logically derives from a theory of psychological functioning requires a different sort of clinical suppleness. When to support, bolster, encourage, teach, probe, disengage, interpret or contain depends on the clinician's understanding of which facet the patient has engaged at any given moment. We have but begun to articulate the specific issues of the various disordered domains that require detail and amplification, and we have yet to become more specific in elaborating what is involved in the processes of exploration, understanding, learning, and working through. Nevertheless, the therapeutic bids, which are relatively simple and concisely defined steps in intervention, have already proved effective as tools for training and for conveying to patients certain aspects of the therapeutic work that they can apply to themselves and to their children. However, much work needs to be done in moving forward toward operationalizing and standardizing their use. We will be gratified if our work prompts other clinicians and researchers to carry it further, or to develop alternate schemes for similar purposes.

Appendices

APPENDIX A
Affects

Sober/Serious	Grief
Interest	Sadness
Affection	Depression
Longing	Anxiety
Pleasure	Fear
Joy/Happiness	Panic/Terror
Excitement	Shock
Sensual Arousal	Anger
Erotic/Sexual Arousal	Rage
Displeasure	Outrage
Discomfort	Contempt
Pain	Disgust
Shame/Humiliation	Remorse
	Guilt

Sources: Based on & adapted from Tomkins (1962–1963), Izard (1971), Ekman and Oster (1979), Izard, Huebner, Risser, McGinnis, and Dougherty (1980), Tomkins (1980), Demos (1984, 1988).

APPENDIX B
Conscious or Descriptively Unconscious Coping Strategies

Realistic Appraisal
Agreement/Cooperation
Compliance/Submission
Avoidance/Disengagement
Externalization/Blame
Defiance/Fight
Freeze/Becoming Immobilized
Transformation of Affect

Sources: Based and adapted from Lazarus et al., 1974; Fraiberg, 1982.

APPENDIX C
Dynamically Unconscious Ego Defense Mechanisms based on Repression[a]

Denial
Undoing
Isolation
Projection
Reaction Formation/Reversal into the opposite
Projective Identification[b]
Splitting of the object[b]
Omnipotent control of the object[b]
Introjection
Identification
Internalization
Rationalization/Intellectualization
Sublimation

[a] The defense mechanisms are based on the works of Freud (1926) and A. Freud (1936).
[b] These defense mechanisms are based on M. Klein's 1921–1945 and 1946–1963 contributions.

APPENDIX D
Growth Promoting Parenting Tasks

AIMS of Psychological Facets

Autonomy & Interdependence (Interpersonal)
Novelty, Exploration, & Effectance (Development)
Self Processes & Regulation (Characterologic)
Ego Functions & Superego (Intrapsychic)

Are promoted by the following parenting tasks which provide for:
Safety, Security, and Physical Nurture
Love, Fun, and Emotional Nurture
An Appealing and Interesting Environment
A Framework for Rules of Civilized Behavior
Expectations of Self-Regulation and Self-Discipline
Opportunities for Learning
Respect for the Child's Individuality
Transmission of Parental Values and Heritage to the Child

Source: Based on Roth, Levin, Morrison and Leventhal, 1986.

References

Abraham, K. (1921), Contributions to the theory of the anal character. *Selected Papers.* New York: Basic Books, pp. 370–392.

—— (1924), The influence of oral eroticism on character formation. *Selected Papers.* New York: Basic Books, pp. 393–406.

Abrams, S. (1992), Confronting dilemmas in the study of character. *The Psychoanalytic Study of the Child,* 47:253–262. New Haven, CT: Yale University Press.

Ainsworth, M. D. S., & Bell, S. (1969), Some contemporary patterns of mother-infant interaction in the feeding situation. In: *Stimulation in Early Infancy,* ed. A. Ambrose. London: Academic Press, pp. 133–170.

—— Bell, S., & Stayton, D. (1974), Infant-mother attachment and social development: Socialization as a product of reciprocal responsiveness to signals. In: *The Integration of the Child into a Social World,* ed. M. Richards. Cambridge, U.K.: Cambridge University Press.

Altschul, S. (1988), Trauma, mourning, and adaptation: A dynamic point of view. In: *Childhood Bereavement and Its Aftermath,* ed. S. A. Altschul. Madison, CT: International Universities Press.

American Psychiatric Association (1980), *Diagnostic and Statistical Manual of Mental Disorders,* 3rd. ed. (DSM-III). Washington, DC: American Psychiatric Press.

—— (1987), *Diagnostic and Statistical Manual of Mental Disorders,* 3rd ed. rev. (DSM-III-R). Washington, DC: American Psychiatric Press.

——— (1994), *Diagnostic and Statistical Manual of Mental Disorders,* 4th ed. Washington, DC: American Psychiatric Press.

Anthony, E. J. (1987), Risk, vulnerability, and resilience: An overview. In: *The Invulnerable Child,* ed. E. J. Anthony & B. J. Cohler. New York: Guilford Press, pp. 3–48.

Arlow, J. A., & Brenner, C. (1964), *Psychoanalytic Concepts and the Structural Theory.* New York: International Universities Press.

Ashby, R. (1958), *An Introduction to Cybernetics.* London: Chapman & Hall.

Atwood, G., & Stolorow, R. (1984), *Structures of Subjectivity: Explorations in Psychoanalytic Phenomenology.* Hillsdale, NJ: Analytic Press.

Balint, M. (1968), *The Basic Fault.* London: Tavistock.

Basch, M. F. (1977), Developmental psychology and explanatory theory of psychoanalysis. *The Annual of Psychoanalysis,* 5:229–263. New York: International Universities Press.

——— (1983), The perception of reality and the disavowal of meaning. *The Annual of Psychoanalysis,* 11:125–154. New York: International Universities Press.

——— (1988), *Understanding Psychotherapy.* New York: Basic Books.

Bates, E., O'Connell, B., & Shore, C. (1987), Language and communication in infancy. In: *Handbook of Infant Development,* 2nd ed., ed. J. D. Osofsky. New York: John Wiley.

Beebe, B., & Lachmann, F. M. (1988), Mother-infant mutual influence and precursors of psychic structure. In: *Frontiers in Self-Psychology,* Vol. 3A, ed. A. Goldberg. Hillsdale, NJ: Analytic Press.

——— Sloate, P. (1982), Assessment and treatment of difficulties in mother-infant attunement in the first three years of life: A case history. *Psychoanal. Inqu.,* 1:601–623.

——— Stern, D. N. (1977), Engagement-disengagement and early object experiences. In: *Communicative Structures and Psychic Structures,* ed. N. Freedman & S. Grand. New York: Plenum, pp. 35–55.

Bennett, S. (1976), Infant-caretaker interactions. In: *Infant Psychiatry,* ed. E. Rexford, L. Sander, & A. Shapiro. New Haven, CT: Yale University Press, pp. 79–90.

REFERENCES

Bertalanffy, L. von (1968), *Organismic Psychology and Systems Theory,* Worcester, MA: Clark University Press.

Bibring, E. (1954), Psychoanalysis and the dynamic psychotherapies. *J. Amer. Psychoanal. Assn.,* 2:745–770.

Bion, W. R. (1962), *Learning from Experience.* New York: Basic Books.

—— (1963), *Elements of Psychoanalysis.* London: Heinemann.

—— (1970), *Attention and Interpretation.* New York: Basic Books.

Bollas, C. (1983), Expressive uses of the countertransference. *Contemp. Psychoanal.,*19:1–34.

Bowlby, J. (1951), Maternal care and mental health. Presentation at the World Health Organization, Geneva.

—— (1969), *Attachment and Loss,* Vol. 1. New York: Basic Books.

—— (1973), *Attachment and Loss,* Vol. 2. New York: Basic Books.

—— (1980), *Attachment and Loss,* Vol. 3. New York: Basic Books.

—— (1988), *A Secure Base.* New York: Basic Books.

Brazelton, T. B., Koslowski, B., & Main, M. (1974), The origins of reciprocity. In: *The Effect of the Infant on Its Caregiver,* ed. M. Lewis & L. Rosenblum. New York: Wiley-Interscience.

Breuer, J., & Freud, S. (1893–1895), Studies on Hysteria. *Standard Edition,* 2. London: Hogarth Press, 1955.

Bruner, J. (1985), Vygotsky: A historical and conceptual perspective. In: *Culture, Communication and Cognition,* ed. J. Wertsch. Cambridge, U.K.: Cambridge University Press.

Buber, M. (1958), *I and Thou.* New York: MacMillan/Collier.

Burlingham, D., & Freud, A. (1942), *Young Children in Wartime.* London: Allen & Unwin.

Carpenter, G. (1974), Mother's face and the newborn. *New Scientist,* 61:742.

Cassirer, E. (1955), *The Philosophy of Symbolic Forms,* Vol. 1. New Haven, CT: Yale University Press.

Chasseguet-Smirgel, J. (1976), Some thoughts on the ego ideal: A contribution to the study of the "illness of ideality." *Psychoanal. Quart.,* 45:345–373.

Chessick, R. D. (1989), *The Technique and Practice of Listening in Intensive Psychotherapy.* Northvale, NJ: Jason Aronson.

Clark, G., & Seifer, R. (1985), Assessment of parents' interactions with their developmentally delayed infants. *Infant Ment. Health J.,* 6:214–225.

Clark, R., Musick, J., Stott, F., & Klehr, K. (1980), *The Mother's Project Rating Scales of Mother-Child Interaction.* Unpublished manuscript.

Clark-Stewart, K. A. (1973), Interactions between mothers and their young children: Characteristics and consequences. *Monographs of the Society of Research in Child Development,* 37:153.

Cohler, B. J. (1987), Adversity, resilience, and the study of lives. In: *The Invulnerable Child,* ed. E. J. Anthony & B. J. Cohler. New York: Guilford Press, pp. 363–424.

────── Anthony, E. J., Eds. (1987), *The Invulnerable Child.* New York: Guilford Press.

Cohn, J., & Tronick, E. Z. (1987), Mother-infant face-to-face interaction: The sequence of dyadic states at 3, 6, and 9 months. *Develop. Psychol.,* 23:68–77.

────── ────── (1988), Mother-infant face-to-face interaction: Influence is bidirectional and unrelated to periodic cycles in either partner's behavior. *Develop. Psychol.,* 24:386–392.

Condon, W., & Sander, L. (1974), Synchronization of neonate movement with adult speech: Interactional participation and language acquisition. *Science,* 183:99–101.

Connell, J. P. (1990), Context, self and action: A motivational analysis of self-system processes across the life span. In: *The Self in Transition,* ed. D. Cicchetti & M. Beeghly. Chicago: University of Chicago Press, pp. 61–97.

Cramer, B., & Stern, D. (1988), Evaluation of changes in mother infant brief psychotherapy: A single case study. *Infant Mental Health J.,* 9:20–43.

Dahl, E. K. (1983), The therapist as decoder: Psychotherapy with toddlers. In: *Clinical Infant Reports 2: Infants and Parents: Clinical Case Reports,* ed. S. Provence. New York: International Universities Press.

Demos, V. E. (1984), Empathy and affect: Reflections on infant experience. In: *Empathy,* Vol. 2, ed. J. Lichtenberg, M. Bonnstein, & D. Silver. Hillsdale, NJ: Analytic Press, pp. 9–34.

REFERENCES

———— (1988), Affect and the development of the self: A new frontier. In: *Frontiers of Self Psychology*, ed. A. Goldberg. Hillsdale, NJ: Analytic Press, pp. 27–53.

Dobzhansky, T. (1967), *The Biology of Ultimate Concern*. New York: New American Library.

Edelman, G. (1987), *Neural Darwinism*. New York: Basic Books.

Eigen, M. (1985), Toward Bion's starting point: Between catastrophe and faith. *Internat J. Psycho-Anal.*, 66:321–330.

Ekman, P., & Oster, H. (1979), Facial expression of emotion. *Ann. Rev. Psychology*, 30:527–554.

Emde, R. N. (1983), The prerepresentational self and its affective core. *The Psychoanalytic Study of the Child*, 38:165–192. New Haven, CT: Yale University Press.

———— (1988a), Development terminable and interminable: I. Innate and motivational factors from infancy. *Internat. J. Psycho-Anal.*, 69:23–42.

———— (1988b), Development terminable and interminable: II. Recent psychoanalytic theory and therapeutic considerations. *Internat. J. Psycho-Anal.*, 69:283–296.

———— (1990), Mobilizing fundamental modes of development: Empathic availability and therapeutic action. *J. Amer. Psychoanal. Assn.*, 38:881–914.

———— Gaensbauer, T. G., & Harmon, R. J. (1976), Emotional Expressions in Infancy: A Biobehavioral Study. *Psychological Issues*, Monograph 37. New York: International Universities Press.

———— Harmon, R. J., Eds. (1984), *Continuities and Discontinuities in Development*. New York: Plenum.

———— Kligman, D. H., Reich, J. H., & Wade, T. D. (1978), Emotional expression in infancy: I. Initial studies of social signaling and an emergent model. In: *The Development of Affect*, ed. M. Lewis & L. Rosenblum. New York: Plenum.

Erikson, E. H. (1950), *Childhood and Society*. New York: W. W. Norton.

Escalona, S., & Heider, G. M. (1959), *Prediction and Outcome*. New York: Basic Books.

Fairbairn, W. R. D. (1954), *An Object Relations Theory of the Personality*. New York: Basic Books.

Fantz, R. (1961), The origin of form perception. *Sci. Amer.*, 204:66–84.

Fenichel, O. (1945), *The Psychoanalytic Theory of Neurosis*. New York: W. W. Norton.

Flavell, J. (1963), *The Developmental Psychology of Jean Piaget*. Princeton, NJ: Van Nostrand Reinhold.

Fogel, A. (1988), Cyclicity and stability in mother infant face to face interaction: A comment on Cohn and Tronick. *Develop. Psychol.*, 24:393–395.

Fraiberg, S. (1971), Intervention in infancy. *J. Amer. Acad. Child Psychiatry*, 5:285–309.

——— (1982), Pathological defenses in infancy. *Psychoanal. Quart.*, 51:612–635.

——— Adelson, E. (1977), An abandoned mother, an abandoned baby. *Bull. Menn. Clinic*, 41:162–180.

——— ——— Shapiro, V. (1975), Ghosts in the nursery: A psychoanalytic approach to the problems of impaired infant-mother relationships. *J. Amer. Acad. Child Psychiatry*, 14:387–421.

——— Shapiro, V., & Adelson, E. (1976), Infant parent psychotherapy on behalf of a child in a critical nutritional state. *The Psychoanalytic Study of the Child*, 31:461–491. New Haven, CT: Yale University Press.

Freud, A. (1936), *The Ego and the Mechanisms of Defense*. New York: International Universities Press, 1965.

Freud, S. (1905), Three essays on the theory of sexuality. *Standard Edition*, 7:123–243. London: Hogarth Press, 1953.

——— (1912a), The dynamics of transference. *Standard Edition*, 12:97–108. London: Hogarth Press, 1958.

——— (1912b), Recommendations to physicians practising psychoanalysis. *Standard Edition*, 12:111–120. London: Hogarth Press, 1958.

——— (1913), On beginning the treatment. (Further recommendations on the technique of psychoanalysis I). *Standard Edition*, 12:123–144. London: Hogarth Press, 1958.

——— (1914a), On narcissism: An introduction. *Standard Edition,* 14:67–102. London: Hogarth Press, 1957.

——— (1914b), Remembering, repeating, and working through. (Further recommendations on the technique of psychoanalysis II). *Standard Edition,* 12:145–156. London: Hogarth Press, 1958.

——— (1915), Observations on transference-love. (Further recommendations on the technique of psychoanalysis III). *Standard Edition,* 12:195–171. London: Hogarth Press, 1958.

——— (1916–1917), Introductory Lectures on Psychoanalysis. *Standard Edition,* 15/16. London: Hogarth Press, 1961.

——— (1920), Beyond the Pleasure Principle. *Standard Edition,* 18:1–64. London: Hogarth Press, 1955.

——— (1923), The Ego and the Id. *Standard Edition,* 19:1–59. London: Hogarth Press, 1961.

——— (1926), Inhibitions, symptoms and anxiety. *Standard Edition,* 20:87–172. London: Hogarth Press, 1959.

Friedman, L. (1978), Trends in the psychoanalytic theory of treatment. *Psychoanal. Quart.,* 47:524– 567.

Garmezy, N. (1983), Stressors of childhood. In: *Stress, Coping and Development in Children,* ed. N. Garmezy & M. Rutter. New York: McGraw-Hill.

——— (1985), Broadening research on developmental risk: Implications from studies on vulnerable and stress-resistant children. In: *Early Identification of Children at Risk,* ed. W. K. Frankenburg, R. N. Emde, & J. W. Sullivan. New York: Plenum Press, pp. 45–48.

——— Masten, A. S., & Tellegen, A. (1984), The study of stress and competence in children: A building block for developmental psychopathology. *Child Develop.,* 55:97–111.

Gedo, J. E. (1979), *Beyond Interpretation.* New York: International Universities Press.

——— (1981), *Advances in Clinical Psychoanalysis.* New York: International Universities Press.

——— (1986), *Conceptual Issues in Psychoanalysis.* Hillsdale, NJ: Analytic Press.

——— (1988), *The Mind in Disorder.* Hillsdale, NJ: Analytic Press.

———— Goldberg, A. (1973), *Models of the Mind.* Chicago: University of Chicago Press.

Gianino, A., & Tronick, E. Z. (1987), The mutual regulation model: The infant's self and interactive regulation and coping and defensive capacities. In: *Stress and Coping,* ed. T. Field, P. McCabe, & N. Schneiderman. Hillsdale, NJ: Erlbaum, pp. 47–68.

Gill, M. M. (1982), *Analysis of Transference,* Vol. 1. New York: International Universities Press.

Giovacchini, P. L. (1987), *A Narrative Textbook of Psychoanalysis.* Northvale, NJ: Jason Aronson.

Gray, P. (1994), *The Ego and Analysis of Defense.* Northvale, NJ: Jason Aronson.

Greenbaum, C. W., & Auerbach, J. G. (1992), The conceptualization of risk, vulnerability, and resilience in psychological development. In: *Longitudinal Studies of Children of Psychological Risk: Cross-National Perspectives,* ed. C. W. Greenbaum & J. G. Auerbach. Norwood, NJ: Ablex, pp. 9–28.

Greenberg, J. R., & Mitchell, S. (1983), *Object Relations in Psychoanalytic Theory.* Cambridge, MA: Harvard University Press.

Greenson, R. R. (1965), The working alliance and the transference neurosis. *Psychoanal. Quart.,* 34:155–181.

Greenspan, S. I. (1975), A Consideration of Some Learning Variables in the Context of Psychoanalytic Theory. *Psychological Issues,* Monograph No. 33. New York: International Universities Press.

———— (1979), Intelligence and Adaptation: An Integration of Psychoanalytic and Piagetian Developmental Psychology. *Psychological Issues,* Monograph No. 47/48. New York: International Universities Press.

———— (1981), *Psychopathology and Adaptation in Infancy and Early Childhood: Principles of Clinical Diagnosis and Preventive Intervention.* New York: International Universities Press.

———— (1982), Three levels of learning: A developmental approach to "awareness" and mind-body relations. *Psychoanal. Inqu.,* 1:659–694.

REFERENCES

———— (1989), *The Development of the Ego: Implications for Personality Theory, Psychopathology, and the Psychotherapeutic Process.* New York: International Universities Press.

———— Lieberman, A. F. (1980), Infants, mothers and their interaction: A quantitative clinical approach to developmental assessment. In: *The Course of Life: Psychoanalytic Contributions Toward Understanding Personality Development*, Vol. 1, ed. S. I. Greenspan & G. H. Pollock. Washington, DC: U.S. Government Printing Office, pp. 271–312.

———— Lourie, R. L. (1981), Developmental structuralist approach to classification of adaptive and pathologic personality organization: Application to infancy and early childhood. *Amer. J. Psychiatry,* 138:725–736.

———— Lourie, R. S., & Nover, R. A. (1979), A developmental approach to the classification of psychopathology in infancy and early childhood. In: *The Basic Handbook of Child Psychiatry*, Vol. 2, ed. J. Noshpitz. New York: Basic Books, pp. 157–164.

———— Polk, W. J. (1980), A developmental approach to the assessment of adult personality functioning and psychopathology. In: *The Course of Life: Psychoanalytic Contributions Toward Understanding Personality Development*, Vol. 3, ed. S. I. Greenspan & G. H. Pollock. Washington, D.C.: U.S. Government Printing Office, pp. 255–297.

———— Wieder, S., Lieberman, A. F., Nover, R., Lourie, R., & Robinson, M., Eds. (1987), Infants in multirisk families: Case studies in preventive intervention. *Clinical Infant Reports,* No. 3. New York: International Universities Press.

Grotstein, J. S. (1980), A proposed revision of the psychoanalytic concept of primitive mental states. Part I. Introduction to a newer psychoanalytic metapsychology. *Contemp. Psychoanal.,* 16:479–546.

———— (1983), A proposed revision of the psychoanalytic concept of primitive mental states. Part II. The borderline syndrome—section 1: Disorders of autistic safety and symbiotic relatedness. *Contemp. Psychoanal.,* 19:570–604.

—— (1984a), A proposed revision of the psychoanalytic concept of primitive mental states. Part II. The borderline syndrome—section 2: The phenomenology of the borderline syndrome. *Contemp. Psychoanal.*, 20:77–119.

—— (1984b), A proposed revision of the psychoanalytic concept of primitive mental states: Part II. The borderline syndrome—section 3: Disorder of autistic safety and symbiotic relatedness. *Contemp. Psychoanal.*, 20:266–343.

—— (1986), The psychology of powerlessness: Disorders of self-regulation and interactional regulation as a newer paradigm for psychopathology. *Psychoanal. Inqu.*, 6:93–118.

—— (1988), A critique of borderline patients: Psychoanalytic perspectives. *Psychoanal. Inqu.*, 8:422–437.

Group for the Advancement of Psychiatry (1966), *Psychopathological Disorders in Childhood: Theoretical Considerations and a Proposed Classification*, Vol. 6, Report No. 62. New York: Group for the Advancement of Psychiatry, Mental Health Materials Center.

Guntrip, H. (1961), *Personality Structure and Human Interaction: The Developing Synthesis of Psychodynamic Theory*. New York: International Universities Press.

—— (1969), *Schizoid Phenomena, Object Relations and the Self*. New York: Basic Books.

Hartmann, H. (1939), *Ego Psychology and the Problem of Adaptation*. New York: International Universities Press, 1958.

—— Kris, E., & Lowenstein, R. M. (1946), Comments on the formation of psychic structure. *The Psychoanalytic Study of the Child*, 2:11–38. New York: International Universities Press.

—— —— —— (1964), *Papers on Psychoanalytic Psychology*. New York: International Universities Press.

Hedges, L. E. (1983), *Listening Perspectives in Psychotherapy*. New York: Jason Aronson.

Hendrick, I. (1942), Instinct and the ego during infancy. *Psychoanal. Quart.*, 11:33–58.

Hill, C. E., Helms, J., Spiegel, S. B., & Tichenor, V. (1988), Development of a system for assessing client reactions to therapist interventions. *J. Counsel. Psychol.*, 34:27–36.

REFERENCES

Hoffer, W. (1949), Mouth, hand, and ego-integration. *The Psycho-analytic Study of the Child*, 3/4:49–56. New York: International Universities Press.

Hoffman, I. Z. (1983), The patient as interpreter of the analyst's experience. *Contemp. Psychoanal.*, 19:389–421.

—— (1991), Discussion: Toward a social-constructivist view of the psychoanalytic situation. *Psychoanal. Dialogues*, 1:74–105.

—— Gill, M. (1988), A scheme for coding the patient's experience of the relationship with the therapist (PERT): Some applications, extensions, and comparisons. In: *Psychoanalytic Process Research Strategies*, ed. H. Dahl, H. Kachele & H. Thoma. New York: Springer-Verlag.

Horner, T. (1986), Seeking the emergent self. In: *Readings*, 1:5–9.

Hunt, J. Mc V. (1979), Psychological development: Early experience. *Ann. Rev. Psychol.*, 30:103–143.

Huttenlocher, P. R. (1982), Synaptogenesis in the human visual cortex: Evidence for synapse elimination during normal development. *Neurosci. Letter*, 33:247–252.

Izard, C. E. (1971), *The Face of Emotion*. Meredith, NY: Appleton-Century-Crofts.

—— (1978), On the ontogenesis of emotions and emotion-cognition relationships in infancy. In: *The Development of Affect*, eds. M. Lewis & L. Rosenblum. New York: Plenum, pp. 389–413.

—— Huebner, R., Risser, D., McGinnis, G., & Dougherty, L. (1980), The young infant's ability to produce discrete emotional expressions. *Develop. Psychol.*, 16:132–140.

Jacobson, E. (1964), *The Self and the Object World*. New York: International Universities Press.

Joseph, B. (1989), *Psychic Equilibrium and Psychic Change: Selected Papers of Betty Joseph*, ed. M. Feldman, & E. B. Spillius. London: Tavistock/Routledge.

Kafka, E. (1984), Cognitive difficulties in psychoanalysis. *Psychoanal. Quart.*, 53:533–550.

Kernberg, O. F. (1974), Contrasting viewpoints regarding the nature and psychoanalytic treatment of narcissistic personalities: A preliminary communication. *J. Amer. Psychoanal. Assn.*, 22:255–267.

—— (1975), *Borderline Conditions and Pathological Narcissism.* New York: Jason Aronson.

—— (1976), *Object Relations Theory and Clinical Psychoanalysis.* New York: Jason Aronson.

—— (1984), *Severe Personality Disorders: Psychotherapeutic Strategies.* New Haven, CT: Yale University Press.

—— (1987), Projection and projective identification: Developmental and clinical aspects. *J. Amer. Psychoanal. Assn.,* 35: 795–819.

—— (1991), Transference regression and psychoanalytic technique with infantile personalities. *Internat. J. Psycho-Anal.,* 72:189–200.

—— (1992), Psychopathic, paranoid, and depressive transferences. *Internat. J. Psycho-Anal.,* 73:13–28.

—— Seltzer, M. A., Loenigsberg, H. W., Carr, A. C., & Appelbaum, A. H. (1989), *Psychodynamic Psychotherapy of Borderline Patients.* New York: Basic Books.

Kiesler, D. J. (1982), Interpersonal theory for personality and psychotherapy. In: *Handbook of Interpersonal Psychotherapy,* ed. J. C. Anchin & D. J. Kiesler. New York: Pergamon Press, pp. 3–24.

Klein, G. (1976), *Psychoanalytic Theory: An Exploration of Essentials.* New York: International Universities Press.

Klein, M. (1932), *The Psycho-Analysis of Children.* London: Hogarth Press.

—— (1935), A contribution to the psychogenesis of manic-depressive states. *Contributions to Psychoanalysis, 1921–1945.* London: Hogarth Press, pp. 282–310.

—— (1940), Mourning and its relations to manic-depressive states. *Contributions to Psychoanalysis, 1921–1945.* London: Hogarth Press, pp. 311–338.

—— (1946), Notes on some schizoid mechanisms. *Internat. J. Psycho-Anal.,* 27:99–110.

Knobloch, H., & Pasamanick, B., Eds. (1974), *Gesell and Amatruda's Developmental Diagnosis: The Evaluation and Management of Normal and Abnormal Neuropsychological Development in Infancy and Early Childhood,* 3rd ed. Hagerstown, MD: Harper & Row.

REFERENCES

Kohut, H. (1971), *The Analysis of the Self.* New York: International Universities Press.

———— (1977), *The Restoration of the Self.* New York: International Universities Press.

———— (1984), *How Does Analysis Cure?* Chicago: University of Chicago Press.

Korner, A., & Thoman, E. (1972), The relative efficacy of contact and vestibular proprioceptive stimulation in soothing neonates. *Child Develop.,* 43:443–453.

Kris, E. (1951), Ego psychology and interpretation in psychoanalytic theory. *Psychoanal. Quart.,* 20:15–30.

Lazarus, S. R., Averill, J. R., & Opton, E. M. Jr. (1974), The psychology of coping: Issues of research and assessment. In: *Coping and Adaptation,* ed. G. V. Coelho, D. A. Hamburg, & J. E. Adams. New York: Basic Books.

Levin, D. S. (1985), *Developmental Experiences: Treatment of Developmental Disorders in Children.* New York: Jason Aronson.

Levin, F. (1991), *Mapping the Mind: The Intersection of Psychoanalysis and Neuroscience.* Hillsdale, NJ: Analytic Press.

Lewis, M., & Brooks-Gunn, J. (1979), *Social Cognition and the Acquisition of Self.* New York: Plenum Press.

Lichtenberg, J. (1983), *Psychoanalysis and Infant Research.* New York: Analytic Press.

———— (1989), *Psychoanalysis and Motivation.* New York: Analytic Press.

Lieberman, A. F., & Pawl, J. H. (1993), Infant-parent psychotherapy. In: *Handbook of Infant Mental Health,* ed. C. Zeanah. New York: Guilford Press.

Loewald, H. (1960), On the therapeutic action of psychoanalysis. *Internat. J. Psycho-Anal.,* 41:16–33.

———— (1978), Instinct theory, object relations, and psychic structure formation. *J. Amer. Psychoanal. Assn.,* 26:493–506.

Luborsky, L. (1990), A review of theory-based process research. *J. Consult. & Clin. Psychol.,* 58:281–287.

———— Barber, J. P., & Crits-Christoph, P. (1990), Theory-based research for understanding the process of dynamic psychotherapy. *J. Consult. & Clin. Psychol.,* 58:281–287.

———— Crits-Christoph, P. (1990), *Understanding Transference: The CCRT Method (The Core Conflictual Relationship Theme)*. New York: Basic Books.

Mahler, M. S. (1976), Longitudinal study of the treatment of a psychotic child with the tripartite design. In: *The Selected Papers of Margaret S. Mahler*, Vol. 1, *Infantile Psychosis and Early Contributions*. New York & London: Jason Aronson, 1979.

———— Pine, F., & Bergman, A. (1975), *The Psychological Birth of the Human Infant*. New York: Basic Books.

Mahrer, A. R., Sterner, I., Lawson, K. C., & Dessaulles, A. (1986), Microstrategies: Distinctively patterned sequences of therapist statements. *Psychotherapy,* 23:50–56.

McGoldrick, M., Pearce, J. K., & Giorao, J., Eds. (1982), *Ethnicity and Family Therapy*. New York: Guilford Press.

McLaughlin, J. T. (1981), Transference, psychic reality, and countertransference. *Psychoanal. Quart.,* 50:639–664.

McLean, D. (1992), Maturational and experiential components of character formation. *The Psychoanalytic Study of the Child,* 47:235–252. New Haven, CT: Yale University Press.

McWilliams, N. (1994), *Psychoanalytic Diagnosis*. New York: Guilford Press.

Meissner, W. W. (1980), Internalization in Psychoanalysis. *Psychological Issues*, Monograph, No. 50. New York: International Universities Press.

Meltzoff, A. N. (1985), The roots of social and cognitive development: Models of man's original nature. In: *Social Perception in Infants*, ed. T. Field & N. Fox. Norwood, NJ: Ablex, pp. 1–30.

———— Moore, M. K. (1977), Imitation of facial and manual gestures by human neonates. *Science,* 198:75–78.

Miller, J. G. (1955), Toward a general theory for the behavioral sciences. *Amer. Psychologist,* 10:513–531.

Modell, A. H. (1976), The holding environment and the therapeutic action of psychoanalysis. *J. Amer. Psychoanal. Assn.,* 24:285–307.

———— (1984), *Psychoanalysis in a New Context*. New York: International Universities Press.

REFERENCES

———— (1990), *Other Times, Other Realities: Toward a Theory of Psychoanalytic Treatment*. Cambridge, MA: Harvard University Press.

Moore, B., & Fine, B. (1968), *A Glossary of Psychoanalytic Terms and Concepts*. New York: American Psychoanalytic Association.

Murphy, L., & Moriarty, A. (1976), *Vulnerability, Coping, and Growth*. New Haven, CT: Yale University Press.

Ogden, T. H. (1982), *Projective Identification and Psychotherapeutic Technique*. New York: Jason Aronson.

———— (1986), *The Matrix of the Mind: Object Relations and the Psychoanalytic Dialogue*. Northvale, NJ: Jason Aronson.

———— (1988), On the dialectical structure of experience: Some clinical and theoretical implications. *Contemp. Psychoanal.*, 24:17–45.

———— (1989), *The Primitive Edge of Experience*. Northvale, NJ: Jason Aronson.

Oster, H., & Ekman, P. (1977), Facial behavior in child development. In: *The Development of Affect*, ed. M. Lewis & L. Rosenblum. Hillsdale, NJ: Erlbaum, pp. 43–75.

Papoušek, H., & Papoušek, M. (1975), Cognitive aspects of preverbal social interaction between human infants and adults. In: *Parent-Infant Interaction* (Ciba Foundation Symposium). New York: Associated Scientific Publishers.

Parloff, M. B., Waskow, I. E., & Wolfe, B. E. (1978), Research on therapist variables in relation to process and outcome. In: *Handbook of Psychotherapy and Behavior Change*, 2nd ed., ed. S. L. Garfield & A. E. Bergin. New York: Wiley, pp. 233–283.

Pawl, J. H. (1993), A stitch in time: Using emotional support, developmental guidance, and infant-parent psychotherapy in a brief preventive intervention. In: Development in Jeopardy: Clinical Responses to Infants and Families *(Clinical Infant Reports 6)*, ed. E. Fenichel & S. Provence. New York: International Universities Press.

Piaget, J. (1952), *The Origins of Intelligence in Children*. New York: International Universities Press.

———— (1970), *Structuralism*. New York: Basic Books.

Pine, F. (1982), The experience of self: Aspects of its formation. *The Psychoanalytic Study of the Child,* 37:143–168. New Haven, CT: Yale University Press.

—— (1988), The four psychologies of psychoanalysis and their place in clinical work. *J. Amer. Psychoanal. Assn.,* 36:571–596.

—— (1990), *Drive, Ego, Object, Self: A Synthesis for Clinical Work.* New York: Basic Books.

Plomin, R. (1986), *Development, Genetics, and Psychology.* Hillsdale, NJ: Erlbaum.

Provence, S. T. (1972), Psychoanalysis and the treatment of psychological disorders in infancy. In: *Handbook of Child Psychoanalysis,* ed. B. B. Wolman. New York: Van Nostrand Reinhold, pp. 34–58.

—— Lipton, R. C. (1962), *Infants in Institutions.* New York: International Universities Press.

Racker, H. (1968), *Transference and Countertransference.* New York: International Universities Press.

Rapaport, D. (1960), The Structure of Psychoanalytic Theory: A Systematizing Attempt. *Psychological Issues,* Monograph 6. New York: International Universities Press.

—— (1967), *The Collected Papers of David Rapaport,* ed. M. M. Gill. New York: Basic Books.

Reich, W. (1949), *Character Analysis.* New York: Orgone Institute Press.

Reichler, R. J., & Schopler, E. (1973), Developmental therapy: A program for providing individualized services in the community. In: *Psychopathology and Child Development,* ed. E. Schopler & R. J. Reichler. New York/London: Plenum Press.

Rodgers, T. C. (1994), The clinical theories of John Gedo: A synopsis. *Psychoanal. Inqu.,* 14:235–242.

Roffwarg, H. P., Muzio, J. N., & Dement, W. C. (1966), Ontogenetic development of the human sleep-dream cycle. *Science,* 152:604–619.

Rogers, C. R. (1951), *Client-Centered Therapy.* Boston: Houghton-Mifflin.

Roth, C. H., Levin, D. S., Morrison, M., & Leventhal, B. L. L. (1986), Interventions for infants and their families: A systems perspective. Unpublished manuscript.

REFERENCES

——— Morrison, M. (1993), Infant-family psychotherapy: One approach to the treatment of infant and family disturbances. In: Development in Jeopardy: Clinical Responses to Infants and Families, eds. E. Fenichel & S. Provence. *Clinical Infant Reports*, 6. Zero to three/National Center for Clinical Infant Programs. Madison, CT: International Universities Press, pp. 231–301.

Rutter, M. (1981), Stress, coping and development: Some issues and some questions. *J. Psychol. & Psychiatry*, 22:323–356.

——— (1985), Resilience in the face of adversity: Protective factors and resistance to psychiatric disorders. *Brit. J. Psychiatry*, 147:598–611.

——— (1987), Psychosocial resilience and protective mechanisms. *Amer. J. Orthopsychiatry*, 57:316–329.

Sameroff, A. (1975), Transactional models in early social relations. *Human Develop.*, 13:65–79.

——— (1982), Development and the dialectic: The need for a systems approach. In: *The Concept of Development*. Minnesota Symposium on Child Development, Vol. 15W, ed. A. Collins. Hillsdale, NJ: Erlbaum.

——— Chandler, M. J. (1975), Reproductive risk and the continuum of caretaking causality. In: *Review of Child Development Research*, Vol. 4F, ed. D. Horowitz. Chicago: University of Chicago Press.

Sander, L. W. (1962), Issues in early mother-child interaction. *Amer. Acad. Child Psychiatry*, 1:141–166.

——— (1975), Infant and caretaking environment: Investigation and conceptualization of adaptive behavior in a system of increasing complexity. In: *Exploration in Child Psychiatry*, ed. E. J. Anthony. New York: Plenum Press.

——— (1982), Toward a logic of organization in the early infant-caretaker system. Paper presented at the 13th Margaret Mahler Symposium in Philadelphia.

——— (1983), Polarity, paradox, and the organizing process in development. In: *Frontiers of Infant Psychiatry*, Vol. 1, ed. J. D. Call, E. Galenson & R. L. Tyson. New York: Basic Books, pp. 333–346.

———— (1987), A 25-year follow-up: Some reflections on personality development over the long term. *Infant Ment. Health J.,* 8:210–220.

Sandler, J. (1987), *Projection, Identification, and Projective Identification.* Madison, CT: International Universities Press.

Sanville, J. (1991), *The Playground of Psychoanalytic Therapy.* Hillsdale, NJ: Analytic Press.

Schafer, R. (1959), Generative empathy in the treatment situation. *Psychoanal. Quart.,* 32:43–57.

———— (1968), *Aspects of Internalization.* New York: International Universities Press.

———— (1992), *Retelling a Life.* New York: Basic Books.

Scharff, J. S. (1992), *Projective and Introjective Identification and the Use of the Therapist's Self.* Northvale, NJ: Jason Aronson.

Schlesinger, H. (1992), What does psychoanalysis have to contribute to the understanding of character? *The Psychoanalytic Study of the Child,* 47:225–234. New Haven, CT: Yale University Press.

Schlessinger, N., & Robbins, F. (1983), *A Developmental View of the Psychoanalytic Process: Follow-Up Studies and Their Consequences.* New York: International Universities Press.

Schwaber, E. (1981), Empathy: A mode of analytic listening. *Psychoanal. Inqu.,* 1:357–392.

Schwartz, A. (1992), Not art, but science: Applications of neurobiology, experimental psychology, and ethology to psychoanalytic techniques. I. Neuroscientifically guided approaches to interpretive "whats" and "whens." *Psychoanal. Inqu.,* 12:445–474.

Skinner, B. F. (1938), *The Behavior of Organisms: An Experiential Analysis.* New York: Appleton-Century-Crofts.

Solnit, A. J. (1970), A study of object loss in infancy. *The Psychoanalytic Study of the Child,* 25:257–272. New York: International Universities Press.

Solomon, I. (1992), *The Encyclopedia of Evolving Techniques in Dynamic Psychotherapy.* Northvale, NJ: Jason Aronson.

Spitz, R. A. (1945), Hospitalism. An inquiry into the genesis of psychiatric conditions in childhood. *The Psychoanalytic Study of the Child,* 1:53–74. New York: International Universities Press.

—— (1946), Anaclitic depression. An inquiry into the genesis of psychiatric conditions in childhood, II. *The Psychoanalytic Study of the Child,* 2:313–342. New York: International Universities Press.

—— (1959), *A Genetic Field Theory of Ego Formation.* New York: International Universities Press.

—— (1965), *The First Year of Life.* New York: International Universities Press.

Sroufe, L. A. (1979), Socioemotional development: In: *Handbook of Infant Development,* ed. J. D. Osofsky. New York: John Wiley.

—— Fleeson, J. (1985), Attachment and the construction of relationships. In: *The Nature and Development of Relationships,* ed. W. Hartup & Z. Rubin. Hillsdale, NJ: Erlbaum.

Sterba, R. F. (1934), The fate of the ego in analytic therapy. *Internat. J. Psycho-Anal.,* 15:117–126.

Stern, D. N. (1974), Mother and infant play: The dyadic interaction involving facial, vocal, and gaze behaviors. In: *The Effect of the Infant on Its Caregivers,* ed. M. Lewis & L. Rosenblum. New York: John Wiley, pp. 187–213.

—— (1977), *The First Relationship.* Cambridge, MA: Harvard University Press.

—— (1983), The early development of schemas of self, other, and "self with other." In: *Reflections on Self Psychology,* ed. J. Lichtenberg & S. Kaplan. Hillsdale, NJ: Analytic Press, pp. 49–84.

—— (1985), *The Interpersonal World of the Infant: A View from Psychoanalysis and Developmental Psychology.* New York: Basic Books.

Stolorow, R., & Atwood, G. (1979), *Faces in a Cloud: Subjectivity in Personality Theory.* New York: Jason Aronson.

Strachey, J. (1934), The nature of the therapeutic action of psychoanalysis. *Internat. J. Psycho-Anal.,* 15:127–159.

Strupp, H. H., & Binder, J. L. (1984), *Psychotherapy in a New Key.* New York: Basic Books.

Sue, D. W. (1981), *Counseling the Culturally Different: Theory and Practice.* New York: Wiley-Interscience.

Thomas, A., & Chess, S. (1980), *The Dynamics of Psychological Development.* New York: Brunner/Mazel.

Tolpin, M. (1971), On the beginnings of a cohesive self. *The Psychoanalytic Study of the Child,* 26:316–351. Chicago: Quadrangle.

Tomkins, S. S. (1962–1963), *Affect, Imagery, Consciousness,* 2 vols. New York: Springer.

——— (1980), Affect as amplification: Some modifications in theory. In: *Emotions: Theory and Research and Experience,* ed. R. Plutchik & H. Kellerman. New York: Academic Press, pp. 141–164.

Tower, L. (1956), Countertransference. *J. Amer. Psychoanal. Assn.,* 4:224–255.

Tronick, E. Z., & Gianino, A. (1986), The transmission of maternal disturbance of the infant. In: *Maternal Depression and Infant Disturbance,* Vol. 34, ed. E. Z. Tronick & T. Field. San Francisco: Jossey-Bass, pp. 31–47.

Truax, C. B., & Carkhuff, R. R. (1967), *Toward Effective Counseling and Psychotherapy: Teaching and Practice.* Chicago: Aldine.

Uzgiris, I., & Hunt, J. (1975), *Assessment in Infancy.* Urbana, IL: University of Illinois Press.

Vygotsky, L. S. (1978), *Mind in Society.* Cambridge, MA: Harvard University Press.

——— (1986), *Thought and Language.* Cambridge, MA: MIT Press.

Wachtel, P. (1980), Transference, schema, and assimilation: The relevance of Piaget to the psychoanalytic theory of transference. *The Annual of Psychoanalysis,* 8:59–76. New York: International Universities Press.

Waelder, R. (1936), The principle of multiple function: Observations on overdetermination. *Psychoanal. Quart.,* 5:45–62.

Werner, H. (1948), *The Comparative Psychology of Mental Development.* New York: International Universities Press.

White, R. W. (1959), Motivation reconsidered: The concept of competence. *Psycholog. Rev.,* 66:297–333.

REFERENCES

———— (1963), Ego and Reality in Psychoanalytic Theory: A Proposal Regarding Independent Ego Energies. *Psychological Issues,* Monograph No. 11. New York: International Universities Press.

Winnicott, D. W. (1953), Transitional objects and transitional phenomena: A study of the first not-me possession. *Internat. J. Psycho-Anal.,* 34:89–97.

———— (1958), The capacity to be alone. In: *The Maturational Processes and the Facilitating Environment.* New York: International Universities Press, pp. 29–36.

———— (1960), The theory of the parent-infant relationship. In: *The Maturational Processes and the Facilitating Environment.* New York: International Universities Press, pp. 37–55.

———— (1963), Communicating and not communicating leading to a study of certain opposites. In: *The Maturational Processes and the Facilitating Environment.* New York: International Universities Press, pp. 179–192.

———— (1965), *The Maturational Processes and the Facilitating Environment.* New York: International Universities Press.

———— (1971), *Playing and Reality.* New York: Basic Books.

Wolf, E. S. (1988), *Treating the Self: Elements of Clinical Self Psychology.* New York: Guilford Press.

Yahalom, I. (1993), A psychoanalytic exploration of the creative and detrimental components into the compulsion-to-repeat. Paper presented at the Southern California Psychoanalytic Institute, Fall.

Zeigarnik, B. (1927), On finished and unfinished tasks. In: *A Source Book of Gestalt Psychology,* ed. W. D. Ellis. New York: Hartcourt, Brace & World, 1938, pp. 300–314.

Zero to Three/National Center for Clinical Infant Programs (1994), *Diagnostic Classification of Mental Health and Developmental Disorders of Infancy and Early Childhood.* Arlington, VA: Zero to Three/National Center for Clinical Infant Programs Publications Department.

Zetzel, E. R. (1970), *The Capacity for Emotional Growth.* New York: International Universities Press.

Zigler, E. (1989), Addressing the nation's childcare crisis: The school of the twenty-first century. *Amer. J. Orthopsychiatry*, 59:484–491.

———— Trickett, P. K. (1978), IQ, social competence, and evaluation of early childhood intervention programs. *Amer. Psychol.*, 33:789–799.

Name Index

Abraham, K., 56
Abrams, S., 55
Adelson, E., 215
Ainsworth, M. D. S., 27, 52, 147
Altschul, S., 102
Anthony, E. J., 79, 213
Appelbaum, A. H., 174
Arlow, J. A., 68
Ashby, R., 5, 32–33, 166
Atwood, G., 15
Auerbach, J. G., 213
Averill, J. R., 20, 63–64, 266

Balint, M., 115
Barber, J. P., 153n
Basch, M. F., 68, 90, 119, 172
Bates, E., 49
Beebe, B., 14, 27–28, 29, 33, 43, 55, 216
Bell, S., 27, 52, 147
Bennett, S., 52
Bergman, A., 4, 41, 48, 52, 54, 66, 119, 160
Bertalanffy, L. von, 5, 32, 122
Bibring, E., 111–112, 160
Binder, J. L., 153n
Bion, W. R., 52, 114–115, 118, 126, 137n, 173
Bollas, C., 15
Bowlby, J., 4, 43, 52, 119
Brazelton, T. B., 29, 33

Brenner, C., 68
Breuer, J., 109
Brooks-Gunn, J., 58, 59
Bruner, J., 162
Buber, M., 11–12, 139–140n
Burlingham, D., 213

Carkhuff, R. R., 153n
Carpenter, G., 52
Carr, A. C., 174
Cassirer, E., 41
Chandler, M. J., 14
Chasseguet-Smirgel, J., 61
Chess, S., 56, 80
Chessick, R. D., 78, 122, 128
Clark, G., 34, 175
Clark, R., 34, 175
Clarke-Stewart, K. A., 27
Cohler, B. J., 79, 213
Cohn, J., 27, 29–30, 31, 216
Condon, W., 131
Connell, J. P., 51
Cramer, B., 131, 216
Crits-Christoph, P., 153n

Dahl, E. K., 226
Dement, W. C., 52
Demos, V. E., 46, 90, 119, 136, 265
Dessaulles, A., 153n
Dobzhansky, T., 13
Dougherty, L., 46, 90, 265

Subject Index

Abandonment, 141
  analytic, 143–144
  fear of, 204
Abreaction, 111
Abstract thinking, 47
Accommodation, 14
Accountability, 6–7
Activity level, 56
Adaptation, 17, 21, 26
  accommodation and, 14
  in developmental functioning, 39–40, 45
Adaptive behavior, regulation of, 33
Adaptive equilibrium, 121
Affective disorders, 92
  parental, 225
Affect(s), 265t
  assessment of, 88–90
  developing coding system for, 179
  in developmental functioning, 47
  diagnostic implications of, 90
  expressed in psychoanalytic treatment, 90, 199
  reflecting and labeling of, 146
  reversal of, 150
  transformation of, in developmental functioning, 54
Agreement/cooperation, 38
  in characterologic functioning, 64
  in developmental functioning, 54

Aloneness, 33–34
American Psychiatric Association, *Diagnostic and Statistic Manual* of, 76–77
Analyst. *See also* Clinician
  authoritative position of, 111–112
  dishonesty of, 147–149
  speaking for infant, 219, 234
Analytic crisis, 142–144
  character armor and, 146–147
Anonymity, 140n
Antitherapeutic bids, 23
Apraxias, 92, 121, 163–164
Arrests, 78, 80–81, 92
  disorder parent-child relationships and, 212
Assimilation, 111
Assimilation-accommodation, 71
Asynchronous transaction, 36
Attention deficit hyperactivity disorder, 205–209
Attunement
  affect-laden, 116–117
  in interpersonal functioning, 28–29
  mismatched, 61–62
Autism, 222–223
Autonomous ego functions, 71
Autonomy, 37
Auxiliary ego, 162
Avoidance/disengagement, 64